Stay affloat

always,

Nessy

THIS BOOK BELONGS TO

_____
PLEASE RETURN WITH CARE*

QUESTIONABLY LEGITIMATE LIBRARY CARD NO. _____
LOOKS COOL ANYWAY

NEW YORK BOOKMARKS	PAGE NO.
FOUND A TREASURE ON A VISIT TO…	
ATE LIKE A KING AT…	
GUILTY PLEASURE ALERT:	
THAT PECULIAR PLACE:	
GOOD TIMES AT…	

*IF LOST OR OVERDUE, PLEASE KINDLY CONTACT _____

DON'T BE A TOURIST IN NEW YORK

==

THE MESSY NESSY CHIC GUIDE

A BOOK BY VANESSA GRALL

with writers and explorers

Luke J Spencer, MaryFrances Knapp and Scott Walker

Staple Street Bridge, pg47

A TIME TRAVELLER'S
MAP OF NEW YORK

When opening the cover of this book, you may have expected to find a well-worn phrase like "New York, the city so nice, they named it twice," written in a glittering typeface across the first page. And while there are dozens of widely published guidebooks on the shelf that will start with lines like that, you've just picked up the underdog, and we're about to take on the almighty city of New York. You better believe we're doing it differently.

This book doesn't promise to make you a New Yorker – the city itself will take care of that. In the words of the great American novelist, Tom Wolfe, "One belongs to New York instantly, one belongs to it as much in five minutes as in five years."

This book invites you to travel in a way that tourists rarely do, whether you're a lifelong New Yorker looking for an excuse to leave your apartment or a first time visitor searching for a companion that won't drag you around like a sightseer. This book can wake up your inner explorer; tap into your curiosity and help you to discover all five boroughs like a roaming detective; a seeker of stories and collector of local secrets.

Perhaps we've met before, across the ocean where I was your Parisian confidante in *Don't be a Tourist in Paris*. Or maybe you've fallen down one of the rabbit holes on MessyNessyChic.com, where for the past ten years, I've been sharing stories about the unusual, the unknown and the unsung. This story may have begun in Paris, but as of this moment, it's a tale of two cities. Along the way, I've met writers, explorers, outsiders, and of course, New Yorkers, who've become a part of this ongoing journey. Together, we've created Don't be a Tourist in New York, a true compendium of unique ideas and off-beat addresses that we felt this city has been missing for a long time.

Guidebooks are often organized by borough, or by the times of day, or categorized by activities that tourists are expected to do. But as you'll start to realize, we don't travel by the rules. These chapters are created around a person's mood and the cards that life has dealt us on any given day. Because when you wake up in New York City, a new adventure awaits...

Nessy
Founder, Editor and Janitor of Messy Nessy Chic

What's in this Book

Before You Start

The borough of Brooklyn on its own would be the 4th largest city in the United States; Queens would also rank the 4th most populous nationally. That is to say that New York City and its five boroughs are extensive and there's much more to this city than Manhattan. At the end of each recommendation in this book, you'll find an address, including the neighborhood, telephone number, opening hours and websites or social media handles for more information. Sometimes we've even provided the GPS coordinates.

Don't make exhaustive itineraries for yourself or plan every minute of the day using this book. Think of each address as a clue, pointing you in the direction of an area that's worth exploring further. Once you're there, you can always check the handy "What's Near Me?" index.

Do yourself a favor and get a metro card as soon as you can from any station booth. Learning to ride the subway is both an experience in itself and a rite of passage. Failing to carry cash in this city is always a mistake.

That vintage map of New York from the Library of Congress on the previous page is lovely to look at while finding your bearings, but it probably wouldn't cut it for pinpointing specific locations. You have a smartphone, right? If you're coming from abroad, GPS for Google and Apple Maps doesn't use data, so you can find your way around even when you're not connected to Wi-Fi. But whatever you do, don't get in the way of New Yorkers on a busy thoroughfare. If you must stand still in the flow of pedestrian traffic to use your phone, move as far to the side as possible.

New York thrives on change without warning. Calling the telephone numbers beforehand or checking the websites provided is always a good idea. If you discover a change in one of our recommendations or want to suggest something, you can slip us a note at *contact@messynessychic.com* or via Instagram *@messynessychic*.

Whether you keep this book on the coffee table or close to you at all times, don't be afraid to dog-ear your favorite parts, circle stuff and personalize it like your own scrapbook. These pages are yours now.

Sunset over New York City. Manfred Curry. Verlag F. Bruckmann, München,
1932

01
Big City Dreamer

Small-towners, first-time visitors and long-time dreamers: welcome to the big city. It's been a long journey and the streets of New York can be unforgiving to those who don't yet know exactly where they're going. The weary traveller needs a warm and welcoming drink, so let's find your beacon in the night and dive head first into some of New York's finest establishments for gifted wanderers, urban gysies and poets alike...

Dive into New York

Dive bars and welcoming drinking dens

Midnight Cowboy

Ask any New Yorker how they feel about a visit to Times Square and most likely you'll be met with an audible and inward groan. Packed with millions of selfie stick brandishing visitors every year, a trip to Times Square is, to the native, as appealing as a rush hour subway car. But there is one oasis, a veritable safe haven on a side street, so small that most people pass by without knowing it's there: the last great dive bar of Times Square, **Jimmy's Corner**. Before the sweeping Giuliani clean up of the late 1990s, Times Square was a gritty and dangerous place, where garish neon signs advertised sex shops, peep shows, grindhouses and seedy saloons. It was the stomping ground of the street hustlers unforgettably portrayed by Dustin Hoffman and John Voight in *Midnight Cowboy* in 1969. Don your best 70's leather jacket and step through a doorway on West 44th Street that leads to the heart of old Times Square. Every inch of the place is covered with boxing memorabilia, for Jimmy's Corner is owned by the legendary Jimmy Glenn, the long-time boxing trainer and cutman to some of the greatest fighters of the metropolis, including none other than Muhammed Ali. At Jimmy's Corner, the Christmas lights are on all year round and regulars are served their usual without saying a word. Enjoy the cheapest drinks for miles around (beers are $3), play some oldies on the jukebox and jump in anytime on the conversation around the bar. If Jimmy himself is around to share some tales, even better. The bell that rings for last orders is the old corner bell from Madison Square Garden, which sits on the left-hand side of one of the most special bars in New York.

(140 W 44th St, Manhattan, New York, NY, 10036; +1 212-221-9510; open every day until 4am)

Happy Hour at the Sunset Tiki Dive

Somewhere between the dive bar from *Top Gun* and Walt Disney's "Enchanted Tiki Room" is **The Rusty Knot**. You could be on a Navy base in Guam, but you've just docked at New York City's West Village and stumbled upon a nostalgic watering hole that feels like home. Overlooking the Hudson River through its retro wooden blinds, this bar is packed with enviable mid-century kitsch furniture. Take a seat on one of the leather and bamboo armchairs and stretch your legs out facing the sunset at happy hour (Mon, Wed, Thurs Fri 4pm-7pm) with a devastatingly strong drink in one hand and the city's highest-rated pretzel dogs in the other.
(425 West St, West Village, NY10014; +1 212-645-5668; Mon-Fri 4pm-4am, Sat & Sun 2pm-4am; Facebook.com/rustyknotnyc)

Just a waitress with a dream

Before the star was born, Stefani Joanne Angelina Germanotta, aka Lady Gaga, was an after-school waitress at a diner on the Upper West Side, cutting her teeth as a musician in small venues to catch a break. Some of her earliest gigs were for the regulars at **Welcome to the Johnson's**, a grunge-tastic dive bar on the Lower East Side. She was dating the bartender on and off for years and probably used the graffiti-covered toilets as an impromptu dressing room more than once. Real dive bars are a rarity now in Manhattan but this place keeps it real, its prices reflecting a time when you could still get by on the island as a struggling artist. The place is lit like a Christmas tree all year round (a recurring theme for most true dives), there's a jukebox to accompany your pool game and a couch that looks like it's been there since the 70s, but despite the grimy decor, it's always good vibes in here. Gaga still mentions this spot in interviews as the best bar in New York and has been known to drop by unannounced when she's in town.
(123 Rivington St, New York, NY10002; Mon-Fri 3pm-4am, Sat & Sun 1pm-4am; facebook.com/pages/Welcome-to-The-Johnsons)

Bowling in the Midwest with views of Manhattan

Look for a vintage Coca Cola sign swinging in the wind, the Empire State building and the Manhattan skyline glowing across the river in the distance. The bright lights of the big city are beckoning, but they can wait. We're ducking into **The Gutter**: a dive bar and bowling alley straight out of the sleepy Midwest that's somehow found its way here to Brooklyn. The vintage bowling emporium was literally plucked from a defunct alley in small-town America and re-installed in Williamsburg, plank by plank. Get a kick out of counting your strikes on the *oldest*-school scoring machines you've seen since 7th grade. The bar itself looks about ready for a line-dancing competition with cozy wooden booths, faux-Tiffany Budweiser lamps and walls covered in Americana kitsch. Games are $7 per person and there's a 2 for 1 bowling happy hour Sunday–Wednesday from 11pm to 2am.

(200 N 14th Street, Brooklyn, NY 11249, +1 718-387-3585; open everyday until 4am, from Mon-Thurs 4pm-4am, Fri 2pm-4am, Sat & Sun 12am-4am; Thegutterbrooklyn.com)

The Bar you wish you Lived Upstairs from

Everything at the **Capri Social Club** is old, slightly worn and simple. Just think, until the seventies women could only sit in the back room of this neighborhood establishment. Now owned by Irene, a young-at-heart Polish lass in her late 60s, this spacious dive bar has stood the test of time, adapting to changes in the area's demographic. From the hip locals that crowd around the backroom jukebox at weekends to the midweek regulars watching the local news on the TV by the bar, it's still a local's local. The no-frills cinematic aesthetic has made it a location for numerous films and TV shows. During the week it can be a pleasantly quiet place to indulge in your New York nostalgia, but if you're looking for a livelier gathering, head over at the weekend for the $3 PBRs and the very cheap (and dangerous) jello shots.

(156 Calyer St, Brooklyn, NY, 11222; Sun-Thur 6pm-12am, Fri-Sat 5pm-4am)

Shots and Shuffleboard

Nancy Whiskey Pub is the only bar in all of New York with a bank shuffleboard. Informal play goes on all week, with tournaments at the weekend – beginners welcome. Serving up cheap drinks with a warm smile since 1967, this bustling corner dive, with pressed tin ceilings, and a first-rate jukebox, is a most loveable holdout to the widespread gentrification that's taken over much of Tribeca.

(1 Lispenard Street, New York, NY, 10013; +1 212-226-9943; Mon-Sat 11am-4am, Sun 12pm-4am; Nancywhiskeypub.com)

Anywhere but Starbucks

Coffee Shops and inspiring workspaces

The Last of the Beatnik Coffee Houses

A lot has changed in New York since the Beatnik era – except **Caffe Reggio**. In fact, this Greenwich Village time capsule has hardly changed a thing since opening day in 1927 when its Italian founder, Domenico Parisi, introduced America to the cappuccino. His rare espresso machine still towers in a corner next to a 16th-century painting from the school of Caravaggio, a 500-year-old Medici family bench and various antiques from his Italian homeland. When Beatnik coffee houses flourished on Macdougal Street, you could find Jack Kerouac or Allen Ginsberg here when they weren't drinking over at the White Horse Tavern. You can picture them chain-smoking and furiously scribbling down their thoughts in one of Reggio's dimly-lit corners, the last holdout of a lost generation. No wonder this place is a dream location for movie scouts looking for unchanged New York. You'll see its moody interiors perfectly captured in that Coen brothers movie about a struggling folk singer in 1960s New York, *Inside Llewyn Davis*. While other archetypal Greenwich hangouts of the era have either closed or become tourist traps, Reggio somehow still has that authentic and magical nostalgia. If you have some writing to do, grab a seat by the window, order a cappuccino, a slice of cheesecake and wait for the inspiration to kick in.

(119 Macdougal St, Greenwich Village, NY 10012; +1 212-475-9557; open Sun-Thurs 9am-3am, Fri-Sat 9am-4am; Instagram: @caffe_reggio)

Caffe Reggio

Doing Good at the Library Café

If you need a place to park yourself with your laptop, wouldn't you prefer to be surrounded by mahogany shelves and spiral staircases? Make yourself at home at the beautiful **Housing Works Bookstore Cafe** in Soho where books, caffeine, and activism combine. Since 1990, the non-profit has been helping AIDS victims and the homeless, providing lifesaving services for over 30,000 New Yorkers. All of the books are donated, the staff are volunteers and 100% of profits go to helping those in need. Make yourself cozy at a table on the wraparound balcony with a birdseye view of the library. Snacks at the café are very fairly priced, and knowing that all the proceeds go to charity might just increase your productivity levels by 120%.

(126 Crosby St, Lower Manhattan, New York, NY 10012; +1 212-334-3324; Mon-Thurs 10am-9pm, Fri-Sun 10am-6pm; Housingworks.org/locations/bookstore-cafe)

Molasses Bookstore

A Literary Clubhouse

Have you wondered what Brooklyn was like when the very first writers and artists of New York's beat generation came over the bridge from Greenwich Village? Before we called them "hipsters", (back when Jack Kerouac was only starting to use the term at the dawn of its popular coinage) and before the gentrified coffee shops and craft beer bars moved in on almost every corner – what was it really like for the OG hipsters of Brooklyn? Located on an ungentrified and reassuringly scruffier side of Bushwick, **Molasses Books** paints that picture: the last of the original hipster homesteaders (before the stereotypes were born). Behind the coffee counter is a friendly girl in overalls, who likes painting and learning French in her spare time. There's a slow but steady stream of characters walking in and out of the bookshop – one guy looking like a young Ginsberg dropping off a box of books, or another guy who's lived on this street since the 1950s, and comes in every morning for a coffee and a chat with the girl in overalls while she polishes glassware. The books are organized by genres like "sexuality/gender" or "Religion/ Occult/ Nu Age". This is a bookshop where you can find anything from gender studies to UFO theories and also pick up a well-read vintage copy of *Jurassic Park*. A sign says "laptops must be put away by 8 pm" to set the mood for intimate events like the live jazz nights, the Molasses drawing club, book readings and even karaoke. It's all chalked up on the board. Molasses even has its own independent publishing arm, focusing on both contemporary writers as well as out of print or public domain works. Spend some time here getting to know the space and people and see if it doesn't become your second home in Bushwick. Bonus: they serve wine and beer at a reasonable price until midnight. *(770 Hart St, Brooklyn, NY 11237; open every day, 10am-12am; Instagram: @MolassesBooks)*

For more inspiring workspaces, see Bibliophile's Paradise on pg 143. Coffee addicts see McNulty's Tea & Coffee Co pg 182.

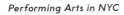

A Star is Born

Performing Arts in NYC

From the bright lights of Broadway to the tiniest theatres in the Village, there's no shortage of talent in New York City. If you're an aspiring actor, dancer, comedian, playwright, performer – perhaps we can also point you towards the right place at the right time...

Broadway Idol

Grab that pal who missed their chance on Broadway, buy them a shot, and throw them on stage at **The Cabaret Showdown.** What can only be described as a hybrid game show of musical theatre improv, karaoke and Jeopardy, this

The Cabaret Showdown
at the Kraine Theater

monthly competition takes place at a 99-seat theatre hidden away on the first
floor of a red-brick townhouse in the East Village. Each round, contestants
are given a mystery song to perform after choosing from themes listed on the
Game Board. The winner's prize? Your very own, hour-long show at the Kraine
Theater – home to some of New York's best Off-Off Broadway artists and
theatre groups, as well as the notable fringe theatre festival, FRIGID. "Second
only to a walk-on part in *Hamilton*, this is the kind of exposure any vocalist
would love to add to their portfolio", said New York events site *Opplaud.com*.
Get some pre-game show Dutch courage at the upstairs **KGB Bar (see pg 332)**,
a Soviet-era hideout lost in time. *(Cabaret Showdown: every second Sunday of
the month at Horse Trade, 85 E 4ᵗʰ St, East Village, NY 10003; +1 212 777-6088; visit
Cabaretshowdown.com/about for details)*

Broadway's Secret Afterparty

New York is full of talented professional actors but where do they hang out? You'll
be in good company at **Bar Centrale**, one of those word-of-mouth spots, housed
in a Victorian brownstone that looks like someone's private home. Climb the stairs
and pass through the heavy oak doors to find Broadway's stars decompressing
with a post-show cocktail. A spot at the bar or in the booths are both highly
coveted at this parlor-floor boîte, so you'll want to make a reservation at least a
week in advance. Choose your attire wisely to fit with the smooth jazz and elegant,
intimate ambiance if you want to stand any chance of chatting with the stars.
*(324 W 46th St, Hell's Kitchen, New York, NY 10036; +1 212-581-3130; open everyday,
5pm-midnight, until 11pm Sun & Mon; Barcentralenyc.com)*

Stage Door Access

From Broadway chorus casting calls to local commercials to student films, start with the "casting bible," **Backstage** *(Backstage.com)*, a New York City industry staple that's been launching the careers of actors and performers since 1960. When you're not working, keep your head in the game with summer or evening classes offered at reputable studios like the **Maggie Flannigan Studio** *(Maggieflaniganstudio.com)* and the non-profit off-Broadway **Atlantic Acting School** *(Atlanticactingschool.org)*.

Talent Scouts in the Audience

Like the dive bars, many of the authentic music venues of Manhattan have moved on, but there are still a handful of solid places to find up-and-comer gigs in the Lower East Side. One of the best is **Mercury Lounge**, a 250 capacity holdout where The Strokes got their break in 2000. Known for hand-picking impressive new talent for the stage, Mercury Lounge packs its calendar with some seriously cool indie bands and talented songwriters waiting to be discovered by fans and industry heavyweights alike. In this new age of digital distribution however, it's no longer a priority to get in front of the music executives who have less and less to do with shaping the future of musical tastes. Put on a great show, try to get some buzz going on social media and establish your own fan base. Talent scouts will be there anyway. There are often two separate shows a night at Mercury, with one to three support acts usually preceding the headliner. If you want to land a gig, send your stuff to submissions@mercuryloungenyc.com. Shows generally begin 30 minutes after doors open.
(217 E Houston St, Lower East Side, New York, NY 10002; check the website for show opening hours; Mercuryeastpresents.com/mercurylounge)

The New East Village

So where did the up-and-coming music scene of the Lower East Side and Greenwich village go? Across the river to Brooklyn. Just a subway ride away, what we'll call the "New East Village" is centered around the areas of Ridgewood, Bushwick and East Williamsburg. Notable venues include **Trans-pecos**, an experimental music venue by night and community space by day, that's hosted concerts for the likes of Dev Hynes aka Blood Orange. **Alphaville**, is a dark dive with a hidden venue behind a door in the back that features self-starter bands and folk-rock music. **Sunnyvale** is a thriftily decorated and spacious venue, offering an eclectic line-up of acts as well as artist showcases, movie screenings, and karaoke events – and cheap drinks. Use the website contact information to inquire about talent bookings and check social media to catch a show.
(Trans-pecos, 915 Wyckoff Ave, Ridgewood, NY 11385; TheTranspecos.com; Alphaville, 140 Wilson Ave, Brooklyn, NY 11237; Alphavillebk.com; Sunnyvale, 1031 Grand St, Brooklyn, NY 11211; Sunnyvalebk.com)

The Recording Studio built by Jimi Hendrix

The year was 1968, and Jimi Hendrix was at the top of his career. Jimi and his manager Michael Jeffery struck a deal to buy up a shuttered nightclub in Greenwich Village where Jimi had frequently graced the stage for late-night jam sessions. They transformed the space into the ultimate bohemian hit factory, and **Electric Lady Studios** was born. It was one of the first artist-owned studios in existence, but for history's greatest guitarist it would be the last time he ever recorded in a studio. Within ten weeks of finding his new musical home, Jimi was on a plane to England where he would take a fatal overdose of sleeping pills and never wake up. After Hendrix's untimely death, Electric Ladyland continued to do what it set out to do, and has seen many of the greats walk through its doors on their way to stardom: Stevie Wonder, David Bowie, AC/DC, Led Zeppelin, the Clash, Adele, Guns & Roses – the list goes on. If you're looking to get into music, drop your CV/ mix-tape off here, and while you're at it, pick up one of the retro t-shirts from the online merch store. We figure that if you walk into an audition or an industry interview wearing an Electric Ladyland t-shirt, you'll probably get their attention. Fake it 'til you make it, right?
(52 W. 8th Street, Greenwich Village, New York, NY 10011; Studio reservations; Electricladystudios.com/merch)

Bob Dylan's Basement Bar

On a freezing winter night in 1961, a scrawny teenager stepped off the subway and came to Greenwich Village's **Cafe Wha?** to play a few Woody Guthrie songs. He'd hitchhiked all the way from the West Coast to find the dank little café at the heart of the city's bohemian scene – and it's a good thing he did, or we might've never known Bob Dylan. Founded in 1959, Cafe Wha became a right of passage for talents like Dylan, Jimi Hendrix, Bruce Springsteen and others hoping to find their break. These days, it's a little less, well, "underground," but still remains hallowed ground for any music lover. They have an insanely good house band that will blow you away any night of the week. From rock'n'roll to reggae, their talented singers and musicians cover it all – just make sure to reserve your seats online beforehand.
(115 Macdougal St, Greenwich Village, NY 10012; +1 212-254-3706; open Tues-Sun 8pm-3am; Cafewha.com)

A Theatre with Soul

In the early 1960s, an African-American pioneer of avant garde-theatre, Ellen Stewart, welcomed struggling playwrights and directors whenever she could; even housed and fed them in her Lower East Side basement. But Stewart herself was not given the same welcome by the neighborhood: the tenants of the all-white East Village building accused her of running a brothel and summoned authorities to investigate. The health inspector that showed up happened to be

CafeWha?

a veteran vaudevillian and helped Stewart get a license to open a coffee house that would moonlight as a theatre by night, seating just 25 people using orange crates as makeshift chairs. More than fifty years and several venues later, after a long and uphill battle to become accepted in the Off-Broadway community, today **La MaMa Experimental Theatre Club** has evolved into a world-renowned theatrical institution, paving the way for Off-Off-Broadway. It's helped blossom the stage careers of household names including Robert De Niro, Al Pacino, Morgan Freeman, Whoopi Goldberg, Harvey Keitel, Diane Lane, Bette Midler and more. Over four hundred diverse, challenging and experimental slate performances are staged at La MaMa each season under the artistic direction of Mia Yoo, who Stewart named as her successor before she passed away in 2011. There are all kinds of ways to get involved at this theatre club, from readings and meetups with curators to university programs (Lamama.org/get-involved). La MaMa also makes the first ten tickets of every performance available for only $10 each, making it possible for anyone to go to the theater for the price of a movie ticket. Now that is a theater with soul.

(66 E 4th St, East Village, New York, NY 10003; +1 212-254-6468; Lamama.org for ticket information)

Emerging Artist Masterclass

If you find yourself sitting in the audience of the beautiful Beaux-Arts theater at the **Brooklyn Academy of Arts**, looking up at the stage and thinking, *I want to do what they're doing*; then you might want to look into what this 150-year-old institution, better known as **BAM**, has to offer. A historic and highly respected center for progressive arts, including theater, dance, music, opera and film, master classes led by artists participating in BAM's mainstage programming are open to artists of all backgrounds and skill levels. There are multiple venues split over three closely-walkable sites, and classes generally run about two hours long, starting at $20 (Bam.org/master-classes). There's also a diverse range of workshops and showcases for grade school through high school level (find out more at Bam.org/education). Best-known for showcasing the work of emerging artists and innovative modern masters — who knows? Perhaps it could be you up there performing on the BAM stage, once graced by the likes of Isadora Duncan and Vanessa Redgrave. Get involved where you can.
(Main theatre: Peter Jay Sharp Building, 30 Lafayette Ave, Brooklyn, NY, 11217; Bam.org)

The Cherry Lane Theatre

A Stage for Picasso the Playwright

You don't want to be running late for a show at **Cherry Lane Theatre**. Get there early to soak up the charm of this historic little red-brick theatre, tucked away on a picturesque, tree-lined corner of Greenwich Village. Perfect for date night, the intimate venue was a launching pad for the avant-garde plays of T.S. Elliot, F. Scott Fitzgerald, Tennessee Williams, W. H. Auden, Samuel Beckett and even – Pablo Picasso. During the dark days of the Nazi occupation of Paris, the painter wrote a farcical play entitled, *Desire Caught by the Tail,* which had its first audience in a Parisian apartment after the liberation, with parts read by Simone de Beauvoir, Jean-Paul Sartre and Picasso himself. Albert Camus even directed it. The first place Picasso's little-known theatre piece would find critical success was at the Cherry Lane Theatre in Greenwich Village, New York. In the early 1960s, the theater hosted some musical performances too, providing a venue for a then-unknown Bob Dylan. In business since 1924, it's the city's oldest continuously running off-Broadway theater and a haven for counterculture productions as well as a beloved institution for mentoring and fostering talented young playwrights.
(38 Commerce St, Greenwich Village, New York, NY 10014; +1 866-811-4111; Cherrylanetheatre.org)

Writer's Workshop in a Bookstore

Writers looking for a safe place to share their short stories, scripts, poems or memoirs might consider signing up for one of the workshops offered at **Freebird Books**, a charming independent bookstore in Red Hook. For under $30 per session, the intimate workshops admit six writers at a time, guided by an instructor. Feedback from peers is part of the process, as well as copy-editing of your latest work and guidance on how and where to get published. Find out more about the Red Hook literary hub and its apocalyptic book club over on pg 105.
(123 Columbia St, Brooklyn, NY 11231; +1 718-643-8484; Sat & Sun, 11am-8pm; Freebirdbooks.com/tagged/workshops)

Bohemians & Beatniks Welcome

According to some historians, we can trace the birth of American poetry back to the publication of Walt Whitman's *Leaves of Grass* in 1855 by a print shop in Brooklyn. Continuing this legacy is the **Brooklyn Poets Yawp** with a "come one, come all" philosophy. Writers of all ages, levels and pedigrees flock to their monthly workshops and readings, so don't be shy. If you're a seasoned poet, just show up with 5 bucks and be ready to shine on the open mic. Events are held at the café and bar 61 Local in Cobble Hill, the second Monday of every month.
(61 Bergen St, Brooklyn, NY 11201; 7pm-9pm; check Brooklynpoets.org/events/yawp/ for details)

Training for Saturday Night Live

Amy Poehler, Donald Glover, Aziz Ansari, Nick Kroll — just some of the names that got their start at **The Upright Citizens Brigade**, a New York institution for comedy and home to the country's only improv and sketch comedy school. Their teachers and alumni include writers and performers for *Saturday Night Live, The Tonight Show with Jimmy Fallon, Broad City, Silicon Valley, The Daily Show, Drunk History* and more. Scope them out by attending one of their upcoming student shows in Hell's Kitchen or the East Village for less than $10. *(555 W 42nd Street, Hell's Kitchen New York, 10036 / 153 East 3rd St, East Village, New York; Visit Ucbtheatre.com for showtimes, Ucbtrainingcenter.com for course details)*

Remember my name, *Fame!*

Laguardia High School of Music Art & Performing arts is known as the real-life *Fame* high school. Notable alumni include Eartha Kitt, Al Pacino, Liza Minnelli, Jennifer Aniston, Adrien Brody and Timothee Chalamet. Their graduating class shows and concerts are open to the public if you're curious to discover the future stars of showbiz before the rest of the world. *(Laguardiahs.org for dates and tickets)*

Open mic at
Pete's Candy Shop

© Karen Foto

▶ ## Open Mic Nights of Note

Finding your first gig in the city

1   **Pete's Candy Store** has been running an open mic for 15 years in this
    former luncheonette and candy store in Williamsburg. Singer/ songwriters
    are encouraged to perform their own original material and play their own
    instruments. Sign up starts at 4.30pm. The cinematic stage looks like the back
    of a vintage train carriage, and for a bit of extra cash, you can get your set
    professionally video recorded.
    (709 Lorimer St, Brooklyn, NY 11211; +1 718-302-3770; Petescandystore.com)

2   **Postcrypt Coffeehouse** is hidden in the basement of the St. Paul's Chapel at
    Columbia University. It's hosted up and coming folk singers since the 1960s
    and is still run entirely by students. The tiny 35-capacity venue opens its doors
    every Friday and Saturday night during the academic year to showcase three
    emerging artists. But one Saturday a month, there's an open stage night. It's
    acoustic music only here, and sign-ups start at 8.15pm. Admission is always free
    and open to the public. Keep an eye on the Facebook page for updates. *(Alfred
    Lerner Hall, 2920 Broadway, Upper West Side; New York, NY 10027; Facebook.com/
    postcryptcoffeehouseofficial)*

3   **The Bitter End** was the first gig Lady Gaga ever played in New York CIty at the
    age of 15. Calling itself the city's oldest rock club, it has a long-standing tradition
    of showcasing new talent and hosts an *Afternoon Acoustic Open Mic* every
    Saturday from 1:00pm-6:00pm. Sign up is free, and there's no cover charge.
    Singers of all genres, from country to Hip Hop, get 2 songs each (backing tracks
    accepted), and comedians, actors and storytellers are welcome too, getting 8
    minutes each.
    *(147 Bleecker St, Greenwich Village, New York, NY 10012; +1 212-673-7030;
    Bitterend.com)*

4   At the **Village Underground**, make your open mic debut at the same joint
    that's hosted Mariah Carey, Chaka Khan, Stevie Wonder and Prince. Every
    Sunday night at 9:30pm, presented by Sony records A&R man Ron Grant, this
    prestigious spotlight will cost you $15.
    *(130 W 3rd St, Greenwich Village, New York, NY 10012; +1 212-777-7745;
    Thevillageunderground.com)*

Going for Broke
Surviving NYC on a budget

Dumplings and Karaoke
A proper hole-in-the-wall, **China North Dumpling** is the true connoisseur's choice, as well as a strong contender for the title of the city's cheapest dumpling joint. You can watch their mouth-wateringly good dumplings being made right behind the counter of this unapologetic no-frills canteen. Eat in or take away, but don't leave without ordering a life-changing sesame pancake for the road on the way to the karaoke bar around the corner. *(27 Essex St, Lower East Side, New York, NY 10002; open Mon-Sun, 9am-9pm; Cash only)*
Head down the block to Canal Street where a dingy, unmarked stairwell leads you to a Cantonese dive bar that just goes by the name **Up Stairs**. For down and out millenials looking for cheap & strong drinks and a karaoke bar where anything goes, this is the spot. Chinese businessmen and New York hipsters bond over *Top Gun* ballads, and it's an all-around good time if you don't take karaoke too seriously.
(59 Canal St, East Village New York, NY 10002; +1 646-559-0098; Sun-Thurs 6pm-3am, Fri & Sat 7pm-4am)

$7 Cocktails in a Fortune Teller's Lair
Happy Hour is every day at **Night of Joy** in the heart of Williamsburg from 5-8pm. The alluring corner bar is filled with bohemian antiques, boudoir seating, Persian rugs and surreal wall decor that make it feel a little like a clairvoyant's waiting room. Included in the happy hour are the house's signature cocktails and frozen Margaritas that come in flavors like peach, mango and pomegranate-blueberry. Take your drinks up to the roof terrace on a summer's night and dance under the string lights until late.
(667 Lorimer St, Brooklyn, NY 11211; +1 718-388-8693; open everyday 5pm-4am; Nightofjoybar.com)

$2 Beers in the East Village of Yesterday
Keep a lot of extra green in your pocket while sipping beer at the **Sly Fox Bar**, an old-school dive bar attached to the Ukrainian National Home complex. You'll get a peculiar but refreshing taste of an Eastern European watering hole that turns out $2 beers, $5 "carbombs", and wonderfully cranky bartenders – a dying breed in the East Village.
(140 2nd Ave, East Village, New York, NY 10003; +1 440-777-0961; Mon-Thurs 4pm-2am, Fri-Sat 4pm-4am)

The City's Best Burgers for Seven Bucks

Dreaming of a finger-licking burger as big as your face in the wee hours of the morning? Find it at **Corner Bistro** for $7. Head to their unpretentious Village location to refuel downtown, or to their equally low-key Long Island City spot. *(331 W 4th St, West Village, 10014, New York, NY; +1 212-242-9502 or 47-18 Vernon Blvd Long Island City, NY 11101, +1 718-606-6500; open Mon-Sun, 12am-4am)*

Night of Joy, p32

George Grantham Bain Collection (Library of Congress)

▶ ## Experiencing the New York Hot Dog: The Top 5

As iconic to the fabric of New York as the Empire State Building, no visit to the Metropolis is complete (or more affordable) without sampling a hot dog. So where do the weiner connoisseurs of New York get their fix?

1 **Gray's Papaya:** An authentic taste of old 1970s New York, from the slightly dingy neon to the "Recession Special", two hot dogs and a drink for $3.50, dating from the dark days when the city went bankrupt.
(2090 Broadway, Upper West Side, NY, 10023; +1 212-799-0243; Grayspapayanyc.com; open 24 hours a day, all year round)

2 **Nathan's Famous.** No one quite knows where the idea of serving frankfurters in long rolls first came from, but one story has them created by Charles Feltman down in Coney Island in the 1860s with his wheeled cart and portable stove, with a separate compartment to keep rolls fresh. For that old time experience, head down to the famous Coney Island Boardwalk, where Nathan's has been serving hot dogs since 1916.
(1310 Surf Avenue, Brooklyn, NY, 11224; +1 718-333-2202; Nathansfamous.com; generally open from morning until midnight, check website)

3 **Rudy's Bar & Grill.** This storied dive bar in Hell's Kitchen was one of the first to get a liquor license when prohibition ended in 1933. Dimly lit and often boisterous, each drink comes with a free hot dog. It's still just as popular with locals and late night drinkers as it was when Frank Sinatra used to bring Ava Gardner here.
(627 9th Avenue, Hell's Kitchen, New York, NY, 10036; +1 646-707-0890; Mon-Sat 8am-4am; Sun 12pm-4am; Rudysbarnyc.com)

4 **Crif Dogs.** A promising late night option in Williamsburg, Crif hot dogs aren't the cheapest in the city, but they're delicious in their own right (try the Chihuahua with avocado and sour cream). At the East Village location, venture into the phone booth in the corner of the restaurant, and if you are lucky, the door will swing open to reveal the small, secret cocktail bar, **Please Don't Tell**.
(555 Driggs Ave, Brooklyn, NY 11211/ 113 St Mark's Place, East Village, NY, 10009; Sun-Thurs 12pm-2am, Fri-Sat 12pm-4am; Crifdogs.com)

5 **Street Carts.** Easy to spot by their colorful umbrellas, often overlooked due to their ubiquitousness, but always more tasty than you remember. We had a particularly good one at SE corner of 71st and York. The pro order is with mustard and sauerkraut.

Macy's Ladies-Only Dormitory

The **Webster Apartments** are one of the few remaining women's only apartment buildings still operating in the 21st century. The building was founded in 1923 by the two senior partners of the nearby Macy's department store, Charles Webster and his brother Josiah. The apartments offered the company's unmarried shopgirls affordable living quarters, but also, a degree of protection for the impressionable young ladies hailing from small-town America. Charles Webster left virtually his entire estate to the Webster Apartments so that still today they offer heavily subsidized dormitory-style rooms for working women in the city. While the rates aren't as low as they were in 1923, eligible applicants must earn under a certain amount per month to qualify and many of the old rules still apply – gentleman callers are forbidden above the first floor unchaperoned. Just off the lobby are so-called 'beau parlors' where male guests can be entertained. Two daily meals are provided, and the building boasts a peaceful enclosed garden, roof terrace and an elegant Art Deco decor. The Webster Apartments are still thriving just as Charles and Josiah Webster intended.
(419 West 34th Street, New York, NY; +1 212-967-9000; Websterapartments.org)

Eclectically Furnish your Apartment on the Cheap

Junk shops and thrift stores these days tend to have a few things in common, including eccentric and grouchy owners at the helm, and a lot of well, junk, lying around with price tags that make your eyes roll, particularly in New York City. As a thrifter, these are obstacles you need to overcome as you dig for treasure and hunt for the bargains – like a rite of passage. Yes, **Mother of Junk** in Brooklyn has an aging owner with a reputation akin to the neighborhood boogeywoman who lives in the old haunted house at the end of the street. But think of your visit here as one of those childhood adventures; sneaking into that haunted house everybody warned you about; except this one is a big old depot on Driggs Avenue that looks like the inside of Stevie Nicks' brain. Fill your kitchen cupboards with an eclectic set of mismatched china, upcycle a vintage chest with huge potential and find quirky folk art to hang on that empty wall. If you want to haggle on a price tag, proceed with caution and a good sense of humor. You might even be disappointed if you *don't* cross paths with the infamous "Mother of Junk" who tends to work there in the evenings (the store is open everyday from 9am to 9pm). Because places like this certainly won't be around forever in the heart of gentrified Williamsburg.
(567 Driggs Ave, Brooklyn, NY 11211, +1 718-640-6299; open everyday 9am-9pm; Motherofjunk2.blogspot.com)

For larger household items like kitchen sinks, clawfoot bathtubs, wooden dressers, tables, reclaimed wood, appliances and much more, try **Big Reuse**, a

vast salvage warehouse in Brooklyn with an ecological mission. They also buy quality used furniture.
(One 12th St, Brooklyn, NY, 11215; Wed-Sun 10am-6pm; Bigreuse.org)

If you prefer to do without the dust and the questionable customer service, the **Dobbin St Vintage Co-op** has some very stylish vintage finds at Brooklyn-friendly prices. Somehow, they manage to make pink Italian leather couches from the 1980s look cooler than ever.
(37 Norman Ave, Brooklyn, NY 11222; +1 929-900-5441; open everyday 12am-7pm; Instagram: @Dobbinstcoop)

Over in Brooklyn's Park Slope, **Trailer Park** offers an elegant thrift shopping experience on a smaller scale. They've sifted through the junk for you without drastically hiking up the prices. From rustic kitchen tables to delicate antique settees, their theatrical display of high-quality pieces is reminiscent of the French flea market. The staff is helpful and the price tags are honest.
(77 Sterling Pl # A, Brooklyn, NY 11217; +1 718-623-2170; Tues-Sun 11am-6pm; Trailerparkslope.com)

Mother of Junk

Things to Do in NYC with $10 in Your Pocket

$10 & Under

CASH THIS COUPON

$7
Dine-in Cinema
Tickets
p57

VALUABLE OFFER

CASH THIS COUPON

$5
Monthly
Boxing class
p111

VALUABLE OFFER

CASH THIS COUPON

FREE
Sunday
Jazz Concerts
p83

VALUABLE OFFER

CASH THIS COUPON

FREE
Tango Ball
in Central Park
p62

VALUABLE OFFER

CASH THIS COUPON

$10
Theatre Tickets
in Greenwich Village
p27

VALUABLE OFFER

CASH THIS COUPON

$2.75
The best slice of
New York Pizza
p95

VALUABLE OFFER

CASH THIS COUPON

$3
Beers with the
best views of NYC
p59

VALUABLE OFFER

CASH THIS COUPON

FREE
Entry to a Museum
of Outsider Art
p104

VALUABLE OFFER

CASH THIS COUPON

$5
Downton Abbey
in the Bronx
p208

VALUABLE OFFER

CASH THIS COUPON

FREE
Classical Concerts
p150

VALUABLE OFFER

CASH THIS COUPON

$10
Vintage Fashion
bargains
p168

VALUABLE OFFER

CASH THIS COUPON

FREE
Tech Help for
Grandparents
p107

VALUABLE OFFER

CASH THIS COUPON

$10
to De-stress in a
Dreamlike Sanctuary
p85

VALUABLE OFFER

CASH THIS COUPON

FREE
Stargazing with
Telescopes
p62

VALUABLE OFFER

CASH THIS COUPON

$10
No-frills Brunch at
the Luncheonette
p96

VALUABLE OFFER

A Rags to Riches Tale: The Harlem Hip Hop Tailor

In the 1980s, he was selling custom-made clothing to Hip Hop's finest for thousands of dollars apiece, fashioned from rolls of fake Louis Vuitton, Gucci and Fendi prints out of his Harlem boutique. His name is **Dapper Dan**, and before the likes of Kanye West and Rihanna were doing it, this guy was the first to bring designer fashion into the context of street culture. Dubbed "Hip Hop's fashion godfather," Dapper Dan's client list included everyone from Harlem's hustlers to the likes of Run DMC, Mike Tyson, Salt and Pepa, LL Cool J and Bobby Brown, who would spend hours at his store on 125th street that welcomed clients day and night for 8 years. "Dap", born Daniel Day, was originally a furrier but was looking for a way to keep his sales strong through summer. He recognized there was a demand in the market for tailoring designer prints in a way that the high-fashion brands were not.

In the beginning, he bought real designer bags right from the stores, cut them up and outfitted them back together to create custom streetwear with the high-fashion logos. It would take luxury fashion years to catch up and recognize the value of streetwear and underground urban culture. Without access to the fabrics, Dan started a clandestine DIY operation out of an apartment in Harlem, screen-printing designer fabrics from machines using highly toxic chemicals. In 1988, two of Dapper Dan's clients, boxers Mike Tyson and Mitch Green, crossed paths at his Harlem boutique in the early hours of the morning. The encounter resulted in an almighty scuffle that hit headlines, thrusting Dan's operation into the spotlight. As a result of the exposure, Louis Vuitton, Gucci and Fendi all sued him.

In the nineties, he laid low; his fashions disappeared from the MTV videos, and his business went dormant. But with the arrival of a new generation, Dapper Dan began to find his way back via the internet where yours truly stumbled upon vintage photographs of his unique logo-tastic designs. In 2013, an article published on *MessyNessyChic.com* sharing Dapper Dan's story, was met with widespread circulation online. "Over the years, that article has made a big impact" his son and business partner, Jelani Day tells us today. In a twist of fate, it all came full circle in 2017 when the iconic house of Gucci sent a near-exact replica of a 1980s Dapper Dan coat down the runway. In the blink of an eye, the internet was up in arms about the use of Dan's design, many calling out the dangers of cultural appropriation and the lack of diversity in the fashion industry. But Gucci responded in the best possible way, announcing a long term official collaboration with Dapper Dan. Finally, he would have all the designer fabrics a tailor could dream of inside a beautifully-restored Harlem brownstone dripping in red velvet and Italian furnishings. Gucci supplied endless rolls of the most luxurious fabrics from Italy and once again, the household names were knocking at his door. While the new space certainly represented how far he'd come from his old clandestine workshops, the appointment-only atelier was also designed to pay homage to his African-American roots and achievements at the intersection of fashion and culture.

"You know people always said, 'Oh, this guy he was doing knock-offs. But Dan never saw it that way," says Harlem-raised Robert Carter, who came from the Gucci menswear team to work with the atelier. "He was never copying these big designers, he was making things that were completely unique that they hadn't even thought of. They were 'knock-*ups*' as he said." Despite his success and worldwide media interest, the tailor has chosen to remain in Harlem, walking the same streets to work everyday, frequenting the same neighbourhood haunts. And as the fashion industry begins to take steps towards a more inclusive future, Mr. Day has become a leading voice and activist for a new generation of black visionaries. From underground tailor to American high-fashion designer, as Dap's legacy continues to evolve and flourish in Harlem, his story has come to embody a new kind of American dream in a fascinating rags to riches tale. "To see that happening for a black man who stayed in Harlem? That's powerful", says Carter. And it only goes to prove– this city is tailor-made for the underdog. *(By appointment only: Dapperdanofharlem.com)*

"I had trouble sewing my life together, so God made me a tailor. Then, a dream of being a designer was born. I didn't let anything nor anybody rip that dream away from me. Now, from the corners of Harlem to the runways of Europe, by way of Africa, I'm living that dream."

– Dapper Dan

02

New York, Like it is in the Movies
(and on Instagram)

You've got big expectations for New York. It should be exactly as you imagined it: romantic, eccentric, gritty, iconic– you want to walk down the street and feel like you're in a goddamn movie. The good news is, we're on the same page (literally and figuratively). This is the chapter for the most charming and imaginative date spots, cinematic streets and dramatic diversions. If you want to see New York like it is in the movies, it's time to start thinking like a location scout, or at least like a professional instagrammer.

An Instagrammer's Field Guide to New York

#DBTNYC

Even if you've sworn off social media forever, or, at least until the end of the week, you never know when a list of camera-ready locations might come in handy...

Most Picturesque Streets

Vinegar Hill: Make a break for the sleepy streets of Brooklyn's 400-yr-old cobblestone village in the city. Perched on a hill by the old Navy Yard, you'll find 19th-century homes and timeworn shopfronts, vintage cars, and sun-bathing cats. Stop in at the charming Vinegar Hill House restaurant (see pg 189), with its wily plants and grandma-centric decor; one could easily hole up here for an entire Sunday afternoon. Zigzag your way through a 3-4 block radius via Hudson St, Plymouth St, Water St. and a handful of others that show the wear of Dutch and Irish immigrants who settled the area. Get there via the Line F at the York Street subway stop.

(Vinegar Hill House: 72 Hudson Avenue, Brooklyn, NY 11201. + 1 718-522-1018; Mon-Fri 6pm-11pm. Weekend Brunch is served Sat-Sun 10:30am-3:30pm)

Vinegar Hill

Pomander Walk: Humphrey Bogart used to live in this quaint haven of Tudor-style cottages and his green bodyguard shed is still visible at the top of the stairs. Find it discreetly tucked away behind an inconspicuous metal gate at 265 W 94th Street. Hint: Those "studying architecture" usually get a pass from residents coming and going.
(Entrance at 265 W 94th St, Upper West Side, New York, NY 10025)

MacDougal Alley: All of the brick houses in this Greenwich Village cul-de-sac were once carriage houses or had working stables, and its proximity to the bohemian main drag made it a haven for artists like Jackson Pollock (who lived at number 11) and Gertrude Vanderbilt, whose decision to set up a sculpture studio at number 19, forever colored her as the black sheep of the family. This mews requires a key for entry, but if you can't settle for a photo from the fence, try our usual trick of waiting around for a friendly resident.
(Across from 175 MacDougal Street, through the small iron gate; Greenwich Village, NY 10011)

Patchin Place: A quiet cul-de-sac that's home to the last working 19th-century gaslight lamp post in the city, though the light is now electric. Other than that, aesthetically this street remains a time capsule of the 1840s when the houses were first built. Writer E. E Cummings once lived at number 4, but today it's nickname is "therapy row" being home to numerous psychotherapist offices.
(Greenwich Village, 10011, NY)

Troutman Street Murals: Always camera-ready for an impromptu urban fashion shoot in Bushwick, the walls of Troutman Street are a veritable open-air museum of street art, curated by the Bushwick Collective which was started by a local guy who wanted to clean up his neighbourhood by beating the relentless graffiti taggers at their own game. Start at the crossing with Wyckoff Avenue.
(Brooklyn, NY 11237)

Sylvan Terrace: One of those parts of New York where residents seem to be living in a secret world of their own, time traveling inside their clapboard houses back to the late 19th century. These high-stooped row homes, 20 exactly, were commissioned in 1882 as housing for servants from the nearby Morris-Jumel Mansion (see pg 135). Restored in the 1970s, the residential community of wooden homes has been known to attract Hollywood film scouts – perhaps you might recognize it from Boardwalk Empire.
(Sylvan Terrace, Washington Heights)

Sylvan Terrace

Staple Street Bridge: A cast iron pedestrian skybridge over a century old connects the two sides of this obscure alley in Tribeca (pictured on pg 5). Built in 1907 for the New York City Hospital House of Relief which had expanded to the building across the street, today it's a Tribeca dream mansion that's been on and off the luxury real estate market for years, listed for $35 million as recently as 2018. You can google photos of the interior quite easily, but the real prize is the satisfaction of snapping that unique architectural oddity from the street. *(9 Jay St, Tribeca, NY 10013)*

Webster Place: A "Little San Francisco" hides on a small street in Park Slope, Brooklyn. Find an unexpected collection of six beautifully maintained Queen Anne-style homes with columned porches and pastel accents. *(Brooklyn, 11215, NY)*

 Find more instagrammable streets in Brooklyn Heights on pg 284, 290-291.

Insta-ready Shopfronts

Birdbath Bakery (aka. Vesuvio Bakery): The iconic green storefront at 160 Prince Street has been there since 1920, run by an Italian family of bakers. Anthony Dapolito delivered bread by bicycle for his parents as a child and became known as the unofficial "Mayor of Greenwich Village," serving the community into his old age. After his death in 2003, the shop had a worrying period of uncertainty before the current tenants moved in and decided to keep the historic design intact and serve delicious cookies and savory Italian bread. *(160 Prince St, Greenwich Village, NY 10012; +1 646-556-7720; open everyday)*

Birdbath Bakery

Above: Brooklyn Farmacy
Right: Urban Backyard

Urban Backyard: From the picture-perfect front patio area to the gorgeous tiled flooring, you won't be able to resist the photo opportunities at this tiniest of coffee shops. Order a Lavendar Latte and a couple of their oh-so-Instagrammable miniature cactus cupcakes.
(180 Mulberry St, NOLITA; +1 646-692-9957; open everyday Mon-Sat 7am-7pm, Sun 8am-7pm; Urbanbackyardnyc.com; Instagram:@urbanbackyardnyc)

Brooklyn Farmacy: This 1920s apothecary turned nostalgic soda fountain is as charming inside as it is outside. Perch on the pink bench with an ice cream and make sure to get all those lovely vintage fonts in the frame. (Go inside on pg 92)

Hildebrandt's Ice Cream and Soda Fountain: She may be a little ways out past Queens on the road to Long Island, but boy is this grand old dame worth it. That beautiful pistachio green facade and those dreamy neon fonts – *swoon!* Going "since 1927 ... because one person tells another" says the menu, which offers homemade ice creams, drinks served in the old fashioned soda fountain glasses and according to American food critic, George Motz, one of top 100 Hamburgers in the country. Hildebrandt's is begging to be discovered by film scouts. *(84 Hillside Avenue, Williston Park, NY 11596; +1 516-741-0608; Tues-Sat 11am-8.30pm, til 11pm on weekends)*

Circo's Pastry Shop: This is a corner where time has stood still since 1946 when the Bushwick baker first opened. You get the feeling Edward Hopper's *Nighthawks* might be sitting across the street from the gorgeous neon signs of this time capsule Mom & Pop shop. Help them stay in business for another 50 years and go in to sample the cannoli. *(312 Knickerbocker Ave, Brooklyn, NY 11237; +1 718-381-2292; circospastryshop.com)*

French Garment Cleaners (now Bird): Find a rare Streamline Moderne façade of what was formerly "French Garment Cleaners", now Brooklyn fashion boutique Bird. The preserved chrome storefront has some very special signage topped off with a glittering Eiffel Tower. *(85 Lafayette Avenue, Brooklyn, NY 11217; +1 718-858-8667; Open every day from early afternoon to evening)*

Pssst! Let's trade secrets online using the "Don't be a Tourist in New York" hashtag #DBTNYC. See you on the Instagram trail @MessyNessyChic

Circo's Pastry Shop

Date Night

Restaurants   worthy of a "When Harry Met Sally" sequel...

Classic Casanova ❤❤

Spaghetti under the Stars

Palma might just be New York's most beautiful restaurant. Picture your dream summer evening somewhere in Italy; you stumble upon a family-run garden restaurant in the rolling hills of Umbria. It's rustic and decorated with fresh flowers, white stucco walls and twinkle lights under the atrium. And don't get us started on the smell of fresh homemade Italian food that curls around you like a grandmama's embrace as you make your way to the table. Even in the midst of winter, you can take your companion on a summertime date in Italy (ask for a table in Palma's covered back garden), but if you're really serious, enquire about the cooking holidays they offer in Puglia. You must try their crispy Arancini risotto bites to start, and don't panic if your date is going gluten-free – the kitchen makes gluten-free fettuccine and ravioli too. A lunch date under the atrium's natural sunlight goes down just as well here, and there's a private carriage house for intimate dinner parties (see pg 174) to keep in mind.
(28 Cornelia St, Greenwich Village, NY 10014; +1 212-691-2223; open Mon-Fri, closed for lunch on Monday; Palmanyc.com)

Palma

Cocktails on the Orient Express

Turn date night into an Agatha Christie adaptation at a cocktail bar designed to look like a vintage railway carriage. All aboard the **Orient Express** of the West Village, where you can imagine finding Poirot in the dining car, seated at one of the Parisian-style bistro tables ready to solve a mysterious murder before midnight (he recommends the zucchini pancakes with your Pernod Absinthe by the way). Clink your glasses under the overhead luggage racks as you pretend to speed your way through Paris, Vienna, Bucharest and Constantinople.
(325 West 11th Street, Manhattan, New York, NY, 10014; +1 212-691-8845; Sun-Wed 5pm-1am, Thurs 5pm-2am, Fri-Sat 5pm-3am; Orientexpressnyc.com)

A Luxurious Library of Bottles

Walking inside the **Brandy Library** is like stepping into a sumptuous bibliophile's haven complete with plush chairs, dark wood and old fashioned ladders that glide silently along the shelves on well-oiled wheels. But instead of rows of venerable tomes, imagine bookcases filled with every bottle a connoisseur of liqueurs could dream of. Sequestered away from the street, with subdued, elegant lighting, the drinks menu is as thick as an encyclopedia, and every bit as knowledgeable. Once you've ordered, the 'librarians' will locate your choice from the book shelves. The ideal place to seduce over a single malt.
(25 North Moore Street, New York, NY, 10013; +1 212-226-5545; Sun-Wed 5pm-1am, Thurs 4pm-2am, Fri-Sat 4pm-4am; Brandylibrary.com)

A Date with Sinatra

They just don't make 'em like **Volare** anymore, but the good old times never left this West Village Italian *ristorante*, and the extended Mediterranean family you never knew you had is waiting here with open arms and homemade cannoli. No menus needed, like any true Italian restaurant, tell Sal or Falco what you like and they'll make it from scratch. They also pour a drink the way a drink should be poured, so sit back and settle in at this sub-street-level dining room ready for a Martin Scorsese scene with its history-covered, wood-paneled walls, white tablecloths and old world charm. That could indeed be the ghost of Sinatra sitting over in the corner, slapping the backs of his rat pack buddies as they tuck into their *lasagna pasticciata* and *pollo alla sorrentina*.
(147 West 4th Street A, West Village, NY 10012; +1 212 777-2849; Open from noon to near midnight Mon-Fri, only evenings on Sat, and closed on Sun)

Haunted Romance

With its weathered walls, mottled antique mirrors and gold framed daguerreotypes of forgotten faces, there's something ghost-like about **Hotel Delmano**. Inside this cinematic Brooklyn address bearing no signage from the outside, time seems to have stopped one fateful night in 1920-something, maybe earlier. From the elegantly curved marble bar, order the "Devil's Garden," a cocktail so good it'll put you further under the spell of this mysterious saloon The intimate, paneled back rooms have all the eerie sensuality of a 19th-century Parisian salon, and true to Paris, you can order charcuterie boards, but we'd suggest the daily oysters as an aphrodisiac. You'll be wishing you really could get a room at the Hotel Delmano, which alas, is not an actual hotel. On a summer night, this twinkling corner bar in Williamsburg is a magnet for beautiful Brooklynites draped around the outdoor patio. Choose your date night wisely at a place such as this – weekends promise a longer wait for those sinfully good cocktails, whereas weeknights do the ambiance of Hotel Delmano justice.
(82 Berry St, Brooklyn, NY 11211; Open early evening to 2pm daily, and 3pm weekends)

Oysters and Absinthe with Napoleon

On a hot summer's eve, **Maison Premiere** has the air of a 19th-century courting hotspot. Globe lights beckon from the lush garden hiding out back, while the dining room nods to French colonial decor. The old world ceiling fans hypnotically spin over a horseshoe-shaped bar that serves exquisite absinthe cocktails from a fountain topped with a miniature Napoleon. If that doesn't set the mood, the finest oysters in Brooklyn are on the menu, as well as New Orleans-inspired gumbo and fresh lobster rolls. Make a reservation, and with some luck, they'll give you a table in the garden.
(298 Bedford Avenue, Brooklyn, NY, 11249; +1 347-335-0446; open everyday for lunch, Fri & Sat dinner, bar open 'til late Thurs-Sat; Maisonpremiere.com)

Hotel Delmano

Maison Premiere

Courtesy of Syndicated Bar Theatre Kitchen

Cool & Casual ♥

A Late-Night, "take-shelter-from-the-rain" kinda date

It's been sitting under a bridge in Brooklyn for some 20-odd years making it the perfect place to dash into just as the heavens open with a raincoat over your head, exactly like they do in the movies. They call it, **Diner**, because that's exactly what it is: a 1920s Pullman carriage converted into a beautiful, cozy diner whose curved, low roof and attention to detail are entirely satisfying. We like it for the tablecloth menu (servers literally sit down next to you and scribble the daily offerings onto your table), and love it for their unexpected and rustic European-style cuisine.
(85 Broadway, Brooklyn, NY 11249; Open every day until late for dinner + brunch Fri–Sun)

Dinner at the Movies

Find dinner, drinks and Art Deco movie magic under one roof at **Syndicated Bar Theatre Kitchen**. There are two parts to this Brooklyn set up. You can opt for the beautiful walk-in bar & kitchen; a hip and spacious hangout projecting cool movies all night on the converted warehouse walls. Or you can go for the stylish retro 60-seat cinema in the back where food & drinks can be ordered from the utensil-free menu throughout the film from the comfort of your seats. The expertly-curated programming "varies from repertory cult classics to new indies" – so that means anything with Tilda Swinton and the best out of Sundance, but also, your favorite guilty pleasures from high school and all the best midnight movies you might have missed. Not feeling a full movie? Grab some pulled-pork sliders or a chickpea burger, and cocktails at the marble countertop bar out front. The constant stream of films projected above the bar can make good conversation starters. Keep an eye on the cinema's calendar and Instagram account for Wes Anderson trivia nights or the chance to see *Twin Peaks* on the big screen. And if you're an aspiring filmmaker, Syndicated also accepts submissions for short films to complement their regular programming, as well as offering its space to show feature-length movies for your friends, family, cast and crew between regular screenings (apply online). Don't forget to book cinema tickets through the website before (only $7), as this intimate little cinema tends to fill up fast.
(40 Bogart St, Brooklyn, NY 11206; +1 718-386-3399; Open late afternoon 'til midnight, and 2am on weekends; Syndicatedbk.com; Instagram: @SyndicatedBK)

Bring Your Own Booze to the Secret Thai Spot

The doorway to **Kuma Inn** is easily missed and once you find it, don't be put off by the dreary stairwell of this former tenement building. Lead your date up two flights of stairs, bottles of wine in hand, to a cozy restaurant offering its finders a taste of Filipino, Thai and Southeast Asian comfort food. Unique fusion recipes are served on small plates for under $10 each, so you can swing for a few dishes and share. The firm favorites here are the sautéed Chinese sausage and the fried rice crêpes. The restaurant doesn't serve alcohol so don't forget to bring your wine to this local "BYOB" spot on the Lower East Side. If you're up for something a little crazier after dinner, you might consider poking your head into the **Mehanata Bulgarian Bar** downstairs (see pg 156). *(113 Ludlow St, New York, NY 10002; +1 212-353-8866; Sun-Wed 6pm-11pm & Thurs-Sat 6pm-12am)*

A Sunken Tavern in Manhattan

You could miss **The Smile** in the blink of an eye, ever so discreetly tucked away below street level in a 1880s townhouse. Ideal for a cozy winter rendez-vous in Downtown Manhattan, you'll be in the company of a stylish in-the-know crowd, but still able to have an intimate conversation with the music at just the right volume and menu options for every preference. The secret is out during the weekend brunch rush, but on weekdays you can have this cozy den more or less to yourself and a few other locals. *(26 Bond St, NoHo, NY 10012; +1 646-329-5836; Mon-Fri 8am-11pm, Sat 9am-11pm, Sun 9am-10pm)*

Creative ❤ ❤

Going, going, gone

Inject a little unexpected excitement and culture into date night by crashing an auction at the iconic house of **Christie's**. In business since 1766, Christie's has sold everything from Da Vinci's *Salvator Mundi* (for just over $450 million) to Audrey Hepburn's LBD from *Breakfast at Tiffany's*. But you don't have to be a millionaire to get up close and personal with a masterpiece. Open to the public all year round, it's essentially a free museum, where upcoming auction lots are on view in Rockefeller Center in the days leading up to the sales; so you can wander around pretending which fine art pieces and priceless jewels you'll be bidding on. If you want to get your hands on a bidding paddle, you'll need to sign up for a financial clearance check beforehand, but you can also just sit in on most of the auctions without being registered. Check the website for upcoming auction listings and information on how to bid. *(20 Rockefeller Plaza, New York, NY, 10020; +1 212-636-2000; viewing Mon-Fri 9.30am-5pm; Christies.com)*

Coffee & Cards Against Humanity

Break the ice on a Tinder or a blind date at **The Uncommons**, Manhattan's
only board game café. Test their sense of humor with a round of *Cards Against
Humanity* or stick to the classics with a nostalgic game of *Scrabble*. They serve
craft beers and snacks, and it stays open until midnight on weekdays or until 1
am on Saturday and Sunday. Let the dads and their kids take over when school's
out, but after dark, this Greenwich Village hangout is the perfect safety net for
the awkward perils of online dating.
*(230 Thompson St, New York, NY 10012; Greenwich Village; +1 646-543-9215;
Mon-Thurs 8.30am-12pm, Fri & Sat 8.30am-1pm, Sun 8.30am-11pm;
Uncommonsnyc.com)*

Unexpected Romance on the Staten Island Ferry

Would you believe that one of the most underrated bars in New York City is
the **Staten Island Ferry Snack Bar**? Located on the second floor of the iconic
commuter and tourist boats, we realize this may seem like an ironic choice
coming from a book with a title like ours, which is exactly why we're suggesting
it. Never take yourself too seriously, especially on a date! Climb aboard the
iconic ferry (for free) buy a couple of Coors Lights from the bar, take them to the
back of the boat and watch the city go by. The views are hard to beat. At $3.50 a
beer, this also makes it one of the cheapest dates in the city. Plus, you'll sail right
past the Statue of Liberty with a front row seat. Fun fact about Lady Liberty to
impress your date: that star-shaped base she stands on was originally a military
fort, built to defend the United States against the British.

You can stick to a simple back-and-forth trip or disembark at St. George Ferry
Terminal to explore Staten Island. Win points with *him* by suggesting a ball
game with the *other* Yankees (see pg 225), just a seven-minute stroll along the
water. Win points with *her* by proposing a visit to the little Victorian farmhouse
of 19th-century feminist photographer, Alice Austen (pg 135), a short bus ride
south along the water. The ferry runs 24 hours a day, seven days a week every 15
or 20 minutes (try to avoid rush hour).

Back on Manhattan soil, wander over to the historic Pier A harbor house
across Battery Park to warm up with an old fashioned at **Black Tail**. Time travel
to Hemingway's Finca Vigía with the Havana-sourced antiques in the lobby,
Chesterfield couches, tropical plants, vintage ceiling fans and of course, cigars
on offer. The stunning stained glass roof above the main bar is the cherry on the
cake. On Tuesdays, Thursdays and Sundays there's live Cuban jazz and food is
served from 5pm until late – the perfect way to end a perfect date.
*(2nd floor, Pier A Harbor House, 22 Battery Place, Battery Park, NY 10004;
+1 212-785-0153; Open seven days everyday 5pm-2pm; Blacktailnyc.com)*

© Alyssa / GravityWinsAgain

Sunset views from the Staten Island Ferry, pg 59

9½ Weeks in Training

Don't ya just hate those couples that can effortlessly "throw together" chic last-minute dinner parties for their friends? And you might have heard that couples who cook together allegedly have happier (and sexier) relationships. Become one of those couples you love to hate at **The Brooklyn Kitchen**. In their exposed-brick loft, they offer a range of cooking courses with date-appropriate themes like "sausage making" (think of the endless puns), "risotto & gnocchi technique", and of course, the "date night" class, which is essentially an elegant hands-on dinner party where you'll create a family-style meal while making new couple friends and drinking wine. If all goes well, by the time you get home, you'll be ready to recreate that steamy kitchen scene from *9½ Weeks* – or just watch the movie in your PJs while eating leftovers together, which is basically the same thing, right?

(100 Frost St, Brooklyn, NY 11211; +1 718-389-2982; Visit thebrooklynkitchen.com for the class calendar)

Chasing Waterfalls Between Skyscrapers

So there's a gorgeous, cascading 25-foot waterfall in Midtown Manhattan, hiding between the skyscrapers. Share the secret with your new love interest and pull up a chair amidst the lush oasis of **Greenacre Park** for the most tranquil of coffee dates in the heart of the city. There's a little takeout café and tables with a front row seat to the waterfall that drowns out all the noise of the other (concrete) jungle. *(217 E 51st St, Midtown New York, NY 10022; open daily 8am-6pm, until 8pm in the summer months)*

A Tropical Wonderland in the Bronx

Come rain or shine, take your date for a tropical turn inside a 19th-century Victorian greenhouse. Inspired by Kew Gardens in England, **The Enid A. Haupt Conservatory** is named after the woman who saved it from an extreme state of disrepair in the 1970s. Today, it's the crown jewel of the New York Botanical Gardens in the Bronx. Heat things up (literally) with a stroll in tropical temperatures year round and stop for a smooch on a bench surrounded by exotic flora and the sound of trickling water. Go one step further, and check the NY Botanical Gardens calendar online. There's always something going on, from beer tastings and live blues on the conservatory lawn, to the fantastic annual miniature train show inside the greenhouse. Under the twinkling glow of the glass roof, an elaborate model train whizzes around a New York City jungle, stopping at hundreds of city landmarks crafted out of bark, leaves, pine cones and other natural materials. There are adult-only "Bar Car Nights", for an after-dark viewing of the train show with a cocktail in hand while being serenaded by roving a cappella groups (see pg 234 for more details). Local couples might also like the idea of signing up to one of NYBG's weekend and after-work classes. Botanical illustration or mushroom horticulture anyone?
(2900 Southern Blvd, Bronx, NY 10458; open Tues-Sun 10am-6pm + out of hours events; Check Nybg.org for more details)

© Lori L. Stalteri

Miniature model of the Enid A. Haupt Conservatory at the Holiday Train Show

Crazy in Love ❤ ❤ ❤

Proposal Perfect

With its manicured plant beds, enchanting statues, wisteria and tulips in
the spring, Central Park's **Conservatory Garden** ticks all the right boxes for
romantic gestures and tear-jerking proposals. Divided into three distinct garden
styles; French, Italian and English; pick the perfect moment as you wander
the alleys of pink and white crab apple trees or linger by the water lily pool
surrounding a memorial sculpture for the author of *The Secret Garden*. (*402 5th
Avenue, Upper East Side; open everyday from 8am until 5pm in winter/ as late as
8pm in high summer, Centralparknyc.org*)

Stargazing with Telescopes on the High Line

Are your stars aligned? Picture this: you and your date, heads together, geeking
out as you both peer into a telescope lens, looking up at the big dipper from
Manhattan's park in the sky. The High Line, an elevated railroad that was
abandoned in the 1980s and then transformed into a linear urban park, is one of
the more unusual places to see the stars up close on a Tuesday evening in New
York City. High powered telescopes are provided by the Amateur Astronomers
Association of New York, who are on hand to guide you through the celestial
skies over Manhattan. **Stargazing on the High Line** is free, and takes place
every Tuesday between April 10th and October 30th, beginning at dusk. The
astronomers club can be found on the High Line, near Little West 12th Street
south of the Standard Hotel, which crosses over the High Line near 13th Street.
One Tuesday each month during the summer, they also do solar observing
using telescopes equipped with special filters for viewing the sun.
(*Check hours and dates at aaa.org*)

Midsummer Night's Manhattan

On the west side of Central Park, a stone-throw away from Belvedere Castle,
the highly coveted **Shakespeare in the Park** sets up every summer with
productions often starring household names from Al Pacino to Meryl Streep.
Tickets are free but queues start at dawn, so if your significant other manages to
snatch tickets, they must *really* like you!
(*Delacorte Theatre, 81 Central Park West, New York, NY 10023, USA, entrance at
W 81st Street or East 79th; Publictheater.org/Free-Shakespeare-in-the-Park*)

A Summertime Tango in Central Park

As long as the weather is good, tango enthusiasts (never-before-danced to
advanced) gather to dance with friends, a lover or that perfect stranger under
the late summer sun. **Central Park Tango** has been a free, warm weather
tradition since the 1990s, that welcomes novices, pros and those who just want

to park out on a bench and be hypnotized by flawless *ocho* (the most important basic sequence of Argentine tango). It all happens under the gaze of the Shakespeare Statue, the event's meeting point, unless it's raining, in which case, the event is held nearby at the Dairy Visitor Center.

(Central Park, Center Drive, Upper East Side, NY 10019; Every Sat. from the end of May to the first Sat. in September from 6pm-9:30pm; Visit facebook.com/groups/ centralparktango/ for more info)

▷ Location Scouting with Wes Anderson

Finding whimsical aesthetics in New York.

Grand Brooklyn Wonderland

There is nowhere else in the city like **Grand Prospect Hall**. A fabulously kitsch, American take on Versailles, this four-story wonderland is the last outpost of Victorian grandeur in New York. Gene Hackman and Gwyneth Paltrow dined here on ice cream together in *The Royal Tenenbaums*, and Al Capone himself is said to have acquired his infamous scar in the old gentleman's clubroom. Legendary local duo, Mr. & Mrs. Halkias bought this sleeping beauty banquet hall in 1971, saved her from impending ruin, and have been running the show ever since with their family and an eccentric staff, all worthy of their own Wes Anderson character.

Grand Prospect Hall

The space was originally built as a kind of masonic temple, and you can still find clues to its past in the architectural oddities. During the height of the Gilded Age, its sprawling indoor and outdoor spaces were a "temple of music and amusement," a social, cultural and political mecca for Brooklyn. The men arrived in top hats, and the women stepped out of carriages in the latest fashions from Paris. They came for the opera, the masquerade balls, high-class vaudeville and motion pictures screened in the Venetian gardens. The venue also boasted the first "French birdcage" elevator (which is still there in all its gilded glory). From the massive ballroom that dazzles with crystal chandeliers to bowling alley frozen in time, there's no end to the wonders of the Grand Prospect Hall. Visit their **Brooklyn Bavarian Biergarten**, open Wednesday to Sunday, and keep in mind they usually host a big party on New Year's Eve (check their Facebook events). The entire venue can also be hired out for extravagant shindigs, film & photo shoots.

(265 Prospect Ave, Brooklyn, NY 11215; +1 718-788-0777; the beer garden is open seasonally Wed-Sun, 4pm -11pm,12pm-1am on Saturday; Grandprospect.com)

The Accidental Wes Anderson Hotel

Checking in to the **Jane Hotel** feels very much like checking into Anderson's own *Grand Budapest Hotel*. The staff is dressed in burgundy bell boy uniforms, the concierge stands in front of an antique key rack and the Victorian lobby is a step back in time. Situated near the Hudson River, just minutes from the heart of the West Village, the hotel was initially intended for sailors and famously used to house the survivors of the ill-fated RMS *Titanic* upon their arrival on American soil. The $100 per night standard cabin rooms still resemble the compact living quarters of a ship, designed for a sailor's needs at 25 cents per night circa 1908. You'll need to be organized, but yours truly can personally attest to spending 3 nights in a cozy 50-square-foot, Wes Anderson-inspired cabin without complaint. Bunk bed rooms are available too, and bathrobes and slippers are provided for making your way down to the clean communal bathrooms at the end of the hall. Upgrade to the spacious Captain's cabin with an ensuite bathroom for an entirely more luxurious experience; you might even land RuPaul's old room at the top of the octagonal tower. The drag performer lived here in the 1980s when the hotel had a less-than-stellar reputation as a flophouse for the down and out. It was heading for demolition when developers behind the Bowery Hotel fixed up the Georgian-style landmark in the late 2000s. Today, hip young things flock to its bohemian ballroom on weekends or the rooftop bar and nightclub in the summer, so if you're staying overnight, ask the bellboy to allocate you a room away from the festivities. For the smart traveler on a budget, there is no better deal in Manhattan for a charming and historic boutique hotel.

(113 Jane St, West Village, New York, NY 10014; +1 212-924-6700; Thejanenyc.com)

The Last Manhattan Lighthouse

It's an improbable sight – **The Little Red Lighthouse**, our cover image, sitting a little lonely in these modern times, under the George Washington Bridge. The conical cast iron red tower was first lit in 1921, and made famous by a 1942 children's book about a Manhattan lighthouse that's feeling inadequate under the imposing new bridge built overhead. Equipped with its own navigational lights, the wise steel bridge reassures the little red lighthouse: "I call to the airplanes...I flash to the ships of the air. But you are still the master of the river. Quick, let your light shine again. Each to his own place, little brother!" (*The Little Red Lighthouse and the Great Gray Bridge*, by Hildegarde Swift). Ironically, the Coast Guard did eventually decommission the lighthouse in 1948, and if it weren't for the protests and outcry from fans of the children's story, Manhattan would have lost its quirkiest little landmark, which now belongs to the New York City Department of Parks and Recreation. On the first weekend of every month between April and September, you can catch a guided visit inside the lighthouse (1pm-3:30pm). Don't forget your binoculars to spy the Manhattan skyline...and maybe Steve Zissou sailing by.

(Fort Washington Park, 178th Street and the Hudson River, Upper Manhattan, NY 10032; +1 212 628-2345; Visit the HistoricHouseTrust.org for more information)

The Little Red Lighthouse

A Little Lady with a Giant Prop House

This is embarrassing to admit now, but when we first saw Suri Bieler pop
her head out from behind a doorway as we called out "anybody here?" in the
entryway of a 95,000-square-foot warehouse in Queens, we assumed she might
be an office assistant; maybe a weekend volunteer. Because there was no way
we were prepared for this achingly sweet, 4-foot-something little lady to be
the founder and owner of **Eclectic Encore Props**. It's the largest prop rental
company on the East Coast, with nearly two million props in its inventory, many
as big as a fully grown elephant. Vast rooms over three floors of the former
Pepsi Cola factory look like theatrical sets of their own; a vintage schoolroom,
Tiki lounge, haunted cemetery, Santa's workshop and a mad professor's
laboratory. Hundreds of props move in and out of here everyday, on their way to
or returning from local film and television sets. Over the years, the prop house
has decorated the sets of *Sex & the City, Boardwalk Empire, Gangs of New York, The
Wolf of Wall Street, Ghostbusters, Taxi Driver* – if it's filming in New York, Suri is
probably renting to them. If you can get over the logistical enigma of managing
a prop house the size of an airport terminal (the complete inventory is now
online too), then try to wrap your head around how Suri Bieler started the
entire thing with just $175 in 1979. A bank loan enabled her to purchase her first
warehouse space in Manhattan before acquiring a century-old prop house ten
years later. In 2012, rising rents meant that Suri had to relocate her collection
(by that time over a million props, packed into an army of trucks with less than

Eclectic Encore Props

20 employees) across the river to Long Island City. It makes your moving day feel like a walk in the park and Bieler suspects it won't be long before they'll have to do it again. If you're a props coordinator or planning a themed party, you can browse her eclectic wonderland during business hours, or sign up for an exclusive visit with the New York Adventure Club (*Nyadventureclub.com*), guided by Suri Bieler herself, the unassuming queen of Queens.
(47-51 33rd St, Long Island City, NY 11101; +1 212-645-8880; Mon-Fri 9am-5pm; Eclecticprops.com)

A Date with Richie Tenenbaum

A tennis-court-turned-concert-venue so charming, it even caught Wes Anderson's eye, this is where Richie Tenenbaum has his career-defining meltdown in *The Royal Tenenbaums*. In the 1960s, **Forest Hills Stadium** hosted the likes of The Beatles, The Rolling Stones, and Bob Dylan. If you're in the mood to catch a show in the city, it's worth a trip to Queens for a concert experience that feels intimate despite its size. There's not a bad seat in the house. The pastel color palette and Futura fonts throughout the venue ooze Wes Anderson vibes and Richie Tenenbaum's tennis sneakers might even still be there, tacked up on the stadium walls next to a plaque in his honor.
(1 Tennis Pl, Forest Hills, NY 11375; +1 888-929-7849; Foresthillsstadium.com).

Motel Moonrise Kingdom

If you're looking for an American motel just like you saw it in the movies, take a weekend trip out to Long Island and book yourself a room at the **Silver Sands Motel**, situated right on the beach at Pipes Cove. These 1960s-era seashore lodgings haven't changed a lick, and with good reason. The folks at Silver Sands have figured out they're better off not changing their real-life *"Twin Peaks"* rooms or that fabulous old neon sign above the check-in office. The motel is regularly booked for fashion and film shoots and for Wes Anderson fans, it'll feel like a weekend back in time at summer camp.
(1400 Silvermere Rd, Greenport, NY 11944; +1 631-477-0011; Silversands-motel.com)

Manhattan, 1888,
by Jacob Riis

Gangs of New York

Haunts of the Underworld

From the Five Points gangs that ruled 19th century Manhattan to the American mafia that emerged in impoverished Italian ghettos of East Harlem and Brooklyn, let's meet the city's darker alter ego and take a turn through "Gotham City", a nickname that can be traced all the way back to 1807 when Washington Irving first used it his satirical periodical *Salmagundi*...

Spaghetti Marinara with the Mob

It's not a true mobster movie if the family doesn't sit down for that all-important dining scene featuring an Italian feast to make your mouth water. At 119 years-old, **Rao's** is New York's toughest table. There's very little chance you'll get one unless you "own" one, inherit one, or know someone that has. Who are the lucky few? A curious mix of wiseguys, politicians, insiders and even rock stars who stick to weekly, biweekly, monthly or quarterly reservations, and can offer those spots to friends at their discretion or even auction them off if they can't make it to dinner at Rao's. Owner and sometimes actor, Frank Pellegrino Senior, will only open his reservation book to newcomers on very rare occasions. There are four main tables, six booths and one table for two, which sometimes offers a loophole for walk-ins. Well-dressed ladies and gentlemen have a better chance of being invited in for a drink at the bar, where they might end up sitting next to Frank himself, who spends most nights at the restaurant if he isn't moonlighting as a Hollywood mobster (you may recognise him as the Italian-American racketeer, Johnny Dio in *Goodfellas*). If you get to talking and hang around long enough, the charismatic Italian or one of his relatives might just offer you that table for two, at which point you should count your lucky stars. Order the house favourites: mozzarella in carrozza, the meatballs, lemon chicken and the famous pasta with cabbage.
(455 E 114th St, Harlem, NY 10029; +1 212-722-6709; Mon-Fri dinner only)

When you can't get into Rao's, you can usually find a lunchtime table waiting for you at **Emilio's Ballato** – if you can get past Emilio that is; the wise-talking boss who talks like Tony Soprano and occupies the table by the door, making nervous newcomers feel like they've just interrupted a mob meeting. Emilio moved to Little Italy from south of Naples at the age of 9. Black-and-white antique photographs of his family in the old country hang alongside autographed celebrity portraits on the weathered walls. We could be dining in an old restaurant in Sicily, where the ghost of Vito Corleone is lurking in the secret back room, reserved for Emilio's VIP guests. Everything that comes out of the kitchen tastes like it's been sent straight from Italy, but they have a veal cutlet parm you can't refuse and one of the best selections of Italian wine in the

city. Come dinnertime there's a little more competition for tables, and the boss doesn't take reservations – unless you're part of the "family".
(55 E Houston St, Nolita, NY 10012; +1 212-274-8881; open everyday 12am-11pm until midnight Fri & Sat)

 Also see: the Sicilian Mom & Pop shop Fernando's Foccaceria on pg 329.

An Original Speakeasy turned Gangster Museum

Howard Otway had no idea what secrets were waiting to be uncovered when he took over the small East Village theater at St. Marks Place. Under the stage, he found a maze of tunnels, two safes containing two million dollars in expired gold certificates, and the remnants of a bomb hard-wired into the walls, set to detonate in the case of a police raid. As it turned out, this old theater had once been a clandestine speakeasy during Prohibition, making it the ideal location to open a **Museum of the American Gangster.** Filled with historical artifacts of organized crime, you'll find bullets from the St. Valentine's Day Massacre, the death mask of John Dillinger, the bullet that killed Pretty Boy Floyd and original art from Goodfella Henry Hill. But the real treasure is the building itself. Down in the basement, where bootlegger and gangster Walter Scheib once ran a speakeasy, you can still see telephones that were connected to a lookout spot across the street to give warning of Federal raids – the bomb sealed into the wall was to be the last resort. The theatre is still up and running in what was once the dance hall; look up at the ceiling and you can see the original chandelier. Behind the stage is a now a bricked-up secret passage that once led to the back of a butcher shop on First Avenue which was the speakeasy's original entrance. Today, the butcher is a Persian restaurant, but look up at the windows, and you can see a tell-tale sag in the building where the tunnels have compromised the foundations. End your visit by stopping by the William Barnacle Tavern adjoined to the theatre, offering one of the best collections of absinthe in the city. Raise a glass of the green fairy in remembrance of those who once drank here in secret.
(80 St. Marks Place, New York, NY, 10003; +1 212-228-5736; Mon-Sun 1pm-6pm, guided tours Mon only at 1pm, 2.30pm, 4pm and 5.30pm; Museumoftheamericangangster.org)

Getting Boozy with the Bowery Boys

Step behind the facade of a working 19th century-style deli into a theatrical den worthy of Bill the Butcher and his Bowery Boys. The rustic, antiquated decor of **Sons of Essex** pays tribute to the earliest days of the Lower East Side when the city's most nefarious gang of dandies ruled the streets in their stovepipe hats. You can reign over your own rounded leather booth at this joint, where the weekend's high energy, whisky-soaked mood is not recommended for anyone looking for a quiet conversation. Beloved by the downtown party crowd since 2011, you can expect "Hen and Waffles" on the menu, lobster rolls, Truffle Mac & Cheese, chocolate desserts with bacon bits and bottomless Mimosas. Throw in some 90s Hip Hop music, and you've got yourself a modern-day Bowery Boys party. *(133 Essex St, Lower East Side, NY 10002; +1 212-674-7100; Tues-Thurs 5pm-12am, Fri 4pm-12am, Sat 11am-4am, Sun 11am-8pm; Sonsofessex.com)*

For a hot whiskey punch with the Bowery Boys' sworn enemies, head to **The Dead Rabbit**, named in honor of the Irish American street gang of the same name, which operated in the old Five Points slums during the 1850s. In the heart of today's financial district, there are three floors to discover decked out like the set of *Gangs of New York*. Find the city lads letting off steam after work here the Irish way. *(30 Water St, Financial District, NY 10004; +1 646-422-7906; everyday 11am-4pm; Deadrabbitnyc.com)*

New York's Oldest Dim Sum Den and the Dark Secrets of Chinatown
Secreted away in the heart of Manhattan's Chinatown is a small, peculiar street with a sharp, angled bend. They call it Doyers Street, but in old New York parlance, it had a much more chilling name: "Bloody Angle". Once one of the most dangerous streets in the city, it was built upon a warren of subterranean tunnels and escape routes used by the local gangs, and crowded with tenements, opium dens and gambling houses. Home to the Hip Sing Tong,

"Chinatown"
Doyers Street, 1900-1910

who waged vicious gang warfare with the rival On Leongs, according to law-enforcement officials at the time, more people met a violent death at Bloody Angle than at any intersection in America. The Hip Sings are still around today and were the target of a major drug raid in 2012. You can find the sign for The Hip Sing Association, Inc. around the corner on Pell Street, operating out of number 15, sandwiched between what used to be an opium den and the home of their gang's principal hitman.

For those who love their soup dumplings and roasted-pork buns laced with a taste of historical lawlessness, today the Bloody Angle is home to Manhattan's oldest dim sum restaurant. The venerable **Nom Wah Tea Parlor**, nestled in the corner of Bloody Angle since 1920, has been a silent witness to all that's happened in this cramped part of Chinatown. Having kept its nearly century-old patina, ancient tin tiles decorate the ceiling and vintage red vinyl booths line the wall. Behind the Art Deco countertop is the old cash register and a seventy year-old stove. But the food itself has a modern twist and everything is made fresh to order. Don't miss the shrimp shumai but be careful not to over order either. Stop in at odd hours early in the week to avoid a wait.
(13 Doyers St, Chinatown, New York, NY 10013; +1 212-392-6800; open daily 10:30am-10pm, until 11pm Thurs-Sat; Nomwah.com)

Doyers Street has seen its recent fair share of gentrification in recent times; a few doors down from the Nom Wah Tea Parlor is **Chinese Tuxedo**, a contemporary upscale restaurant situated inside a former theater where the so-called "Chinese Theater Massacre" took place. In 1905, the Hip Sings opened fire on the audience, wiping out an entire rival gang. Next door inside a former opium den is the swish **Apotheke cocktail bar** disguised as a bygone pharmacy.
(9 Doyers St #1, Chinatown, NY 10013; Mon-Sat 6.30pm-2am, Sun 8pm-2pm; Apothekenyc.com)

My Cousin Vinny in the City

If you can recite the best bits of Joe Pesci's closing argument from *My Cousin Vinny*, taped most of *Law & Order* or you're just curious about the real-life drama that unfolds in an American courtroom, you should probably consider adding the **New York City Criminal Court** to your bucket list. We'll file this one under "dark tourism". As you pass through the metal detectors at the South Entrance Hall and the officers ask why you're there, now is probably one of the few times it's okay to let them know you're "just a tourist". They'll happily point you in the direction of a courtroom in session. Discreetly take a seat on the benches, not too far forward, and get your bearings as the judge plows through arraignments for recent arrests covering all kinds of crimes, from petty theft to murder. You'll find that it both is and isn't "just like you saw it in the movies."

For one, the lawyers don't deliver their lines as clearly as they do in the movies, and if you haven't studied law, decoding the legal language can be a strain. But the criminal drama is there, it's very real and it's a humbling look at what's really going in the city. The daytime docket runs from 9am-5pm, and night court goes from 5pm-1am, when proceedings get a little more unusual. A misbehaving celebrity might even make a late-night cameo — notable defendants that have passed through here include everyone from David Bowie for a weed bust in the seventies to French politician Dominique Strauss-Kahn and bad boy actor Shia LeBoeuf. Visitors are free to walk in and out of proceedings as they please, a freedom you'll leave feeling mighty grateful for. On your way out, keep in mind the area surrounding the courthouse sits more or less directly on top of what was once the hellish crime-infested streets of the notorious Five Points slums (recall scenes from *Gangs of New York*). Much of it was wiped off the map when the state and federal governments took over, but there are still some original buildings from the neighborhood around Columbus Park and in Chinatown, including some of the city's oldest tenement buildings (see pg 321).
(100 Centre St, , NY 10013, +1 646-386-4500; Mon-Sun 9am-1pm; Criminallawsny. com/manhattan-criminal-court)

New York City
Criminal Court

How to Ride in the back of a Police Car without being Arrested

One of the most surreal ways to tour the streets of New York City? Tag along with those whose job it is to keep them safe. The **Ride-Along Program** is a little-known part of the NYPD's worthwhile Community Affairs Bureau that provides an opportunity to actually ride in a working police car on patrol, as the officers go about their daily work. Pick a borough, time of day, sign a waiver, don a bulletproof vest, and experience a brief taste of what the NYPD have to encounter every day. From monitoring street activities to responding to radio alerts, it is a truly unique experience into the gritty side of the city. Apply at your own risk, in advance at this address www1.nyc.gov/site/nypd/bureaus/administrative/programs.page. The Ride-Along takes place either at 7am or 3pm and last two to four hours depending on whether you get any unexpected 911 calls at the last minute. Photographs and recording devices are strictly forbidden.

Superheroes of New York

Where your favorite childhood movies come to life...

Who you gonna call?

Immortalized as the iconic HQ from the 1984 film *Ghostbusters*, the Tribeca firehouse at the corner of North Moore and Varick is still an actual working fire station. Home to Hook & Ladder Company 8, the **"Ghostbusters" firehouse** was one of the first *Beaux-Arts* fire stations in the city and dates back to 1903. While they may not "cross the streams," the friendly firemen do proudly sport the iconic Ghostbusters logo on their uniforms. If the doors are open, you can inquire about buying your own patch with the celebrity ghost.
(14 North Moore Street, New York, NY, 10013; +1 718-999-2000)

The Real-Life Indiana Jones Clubhouse

"First to the North Pole," "First to the summit of Mt. Everest," "First to the Deepest Point in the Ocean" and "First to the Surface of the Moon." There's only one place in the world that can list accomplishments like these on a brass plaque in the lobby – and that's **The Explorer's Club**. Founded in 1904, its enterprising and courageous members have carried the hallowed club flags to the far corners of the earth, and even beyond it, in the case of Neil Armstrong. And lest we forget, to visit the Explorer's Club is to walk in the footsteps of the real Indiana Jones – who was just as cool as you think.

While there's been a lot of speculation as to who could've inspired George Lucas' beloved Indiana Jones, no one fits the bill quite like Roy Chapman Andrews. The dinosaur egg hunter, lost civilization chaser, fedora hat-wearing American was always the kind of man who made his own luck. He got his foot in the door by working as a janitor at the American Museum of Natural History while pursuing a masters in Mammalogy. One of his earliest assignments was to retrieve the skeleton of a dead whale from Long Island Beach. That complete skeleton is still on display at the Museum of Natural History's department of Mammalogy.

Andrews spent the next decade circling the globe and skirting death in a fedora with the same cheeky wit as Dr. Jones. He fell off cliffs, was almost eaten by wild dogs and nearly drowned in a typhoon, but it was in Mongolia that our

The Explorers Club

cowboy-paleontologist made the discovery of a lifetime: an entire preserved nest of dinosaur eggs. The world had never seen dinosaur eggs before 1925. When Chapman returned to New York City with those eggs, he became a hero.

His legacy lives on at the Explorer's Club in New York City, where the worn, red flag he took to the Gobi Desert is framed upon the wall. Members like Chapman who prove themselves in the pursuit of exploration (and live to tell the tale) return to the friendly confines of their clubhouse armed with mementoes and artifacts to add to the walls, adding to its treasures. The first floor has a coffee table made out of a hatch cover from the the only research vessel that survived Pearl Harbor, and somewhere upstairs is the sleigh used by former club president Robert Peary in pursuit of the North Pole. The club's iconic 'trophy room', displays the tusk of a wooly mammoth.

Still flourishing today, the members of the Explorers Club meet regularly to swap tales, plan trips and sponsor expeditions. While membership is exclusive to individuals who have contributed to scientific exploration, the club holds regular events that are open to anyone with a spirit of adventure. On Monday nights, there's usually a wine & cheese reception and student tickets are just $5. Mingle with like-minded travellers before a film screening or spend an evening discovering the world of a renowned cave diver. You can also join the

"Friends of The Explorers Club," and students from the age of 16 to 30 can apply to become members for $60 annually with no initiation fee. Most importantly, the club awards student grants for fieldwork, ranging from $500 to $5,000. The Explorer's Club is no doubt proud of its history but it's also looking toward the future to foster a new generation of explorers. And no matter the age, you can always recognize the glint in the eye that comes from a love of exploring.
(46 East 70th Street, New York, NY, 10021; +1 212-628-8383; More information about events, memberships & grants at Explorers.org)

Roy Chapman Andrews, aka "The Real Indiana Jones"

Clark Kent's Office

Walk with Clark Kent, Lois Lane and Jimmy Olsen through the Art Deco lobby and former home of ***The Daily News***. You'll instantly recognize the enormous vintage globe which has been spinning on its axis since 1930, set into the floor under a domed black glass sky, weighing 4,000 lbs – it's one of the city's hidden treasures. The impressive space was of course used as the fictional location of the *Daily Planet* in the *Superman* films, and you'll notice photographs of Christopher Reeve hanging on the wall, as well as some gorgeous Art Deco clocks giving the time in cities around the world from Panama to Paris.
(220 East 42nd Street, New York, NY, 10017; +1 212-949-1100)

► ## The Last Diners of Old Manhattan

An icon of American culture

Today, in Manhattan, there are just five stand-alone diners remaining – which practically makes them an endangered species – but also, about as quintessentially New York as the Chrysler building. Their story begins across the Hudson River in New Jersey, where the production business was once booming, making prefabricated, streamlined, stainless steel diners that resembled railroad cars in style, size and shape. In fact, it's no creative coincidence that the American diner closely resembles a train car. They looked like trains because that's how they were delivered to America's growing fast-food cities; pre-built and ready-to-go; easily loadable on and off the tracks. Many diners were even upcycled from actual retired railroad cars. After all, it was during the golden age of rail travel, in those elegant dining cars of the 1920s, where the standard for modern dining on-the-go was set. While new and trendy dining concepts seem to be popping up every minute in this city, don't forget about the humble American diner from a bygone era.

1 **The Square Diner** has been serving up delicious comfort food to Tribeca residents since 1922, and it shows. Enter this authentic railroad car and step back in time. You'll find snug booths, wood paneled walls, chrome fittings and the kind of staff you just don't come by anymore. The menu is huge, as a diner menu should be, so take your time choosing over a glass of freshly made lemonade. Old photographs show that the original stainless steel railroad car is unchanged except for the added roof outside, which has left this cozy diner looking appropriately like a hybrid between a train carriage and a country cottage. *(33, Leonard Street, Tribeca, NY 10013; +1 212-925-7188; Mon-Fri 6am-9pm; Sat & Sun 7:30am-4pm; squarediner.com)*

2 **The Empire Diner** is perhaps Manhattan's most iconic stand-alone diner, designed and built in the sleek Art Moderne style of the 1940s by the Fodero Dining Car Company of New Jersey. Despite being featured in Woody Allen's Manhattan and on the cover of Tom Waits' album *Asylum Years*, the cinematic diner has had a turbulent life. The original space from the 1940s was abandoned for many years before being refurbished in the 1970s to cater to Chelsea's thriving art scene (the previous owners had a piano in there). Today, the Empire is back on track with an excellent American omelet, must-try buttermilk biscuits and a modern twist to the decor while still staying true to its streamliner roots. *(210 10th Ave, Chelsea, NY 10011; +1 212-335-2277; open everyday 8am-11pm until midnight Fri & Sat; Instagram: @Empire_Diner)*

3   Dwarfed by skyscrapers, hidden amidst the modern glass and steel office buildings, the **Pearl Diner** is one of those anomalies in New York, where real estate is measured in millions. Located in the heart of the Financial District, this small, stand-alone diner has somehow survived and continues to serve wholesome diner food in cozy, familiar surroundings.
(212 Pearl St, Financial District, NY 10038; +1 212-344-6620; Mon-Fri 7am-9pm, Sat & Sun 8am-2.45pm)

4   The no-frills **Hector's Cafe and Diner** is one of the last old-fashioned places to eat in a neighborhood that has lost almost all of its working class roots. Hector's once catered to the workers of the old meatpacking plants and slaughterhouses of the 1960s. Today, the meatpacking industry has mostly been replaced by the glitz of high-end boutiques and hotels like The Standard. But tucked away underneath the High Line, this 24-hour diner has thankfully survived the onslaught of tourists and power brunchers. Nothing on the menu is over fifteen bucks. *(44 Little W 12th St, Chelsea, NY 10014; open 24 hours Wed-Sat, Mon & Tues 2am-8pm)*

5   The understated **Star on 18** is also a far cry from the gleaming, stainless steel of the classic diners, but step inside, and you will find that homey, cozy ambiance you're looking for with traditional booths, counter stools and homemade muffins. Neither number 4 or 5 on this list will likely ever make it into any other guidebooks, so here's hoping we can help them stick around.
(128 10th Ave, Chelsea, NY 10011; +1 212-366-0994; everyday 6am-10pm, until 6pm on Sun)

New York City 1935

03
Lonely Hearts Club, New York

"New York is an ugly city, a dirty city.
Its climate is a scandal,
its politics are used to frighten children,
its traffic is madness,
its competition is murderous.
But there is one thing about it — once you have
lived in New York and it has become your home,
no place else is good enough."

– John Steinbeck

Lose the New York Blues

When the city's given you a few hard knocks...

Her Tiny Apartment is New York's Most Secret Jazz Club

For the past 25 years, Marjorie Eliot has been hosting free jazz concerts out of her apartment every Sunday for strangers. Harlem's beloved jazz queen of Sugar Hill is single-handedly upholding the musical legacy of a neighborhood that nurtured legends like Duke Ellington and Billie Holiday during the Harlem Renaissance. The buzzer at #555 Edgecombe Ave, apartment 3-F starts ringing at exactly 3:30pm every Sunday with patrons already lined up in their Sunday-best to impress the lady of the hour. Eliot, a frail, soft-spoken lady who's always wearing a colorful kaftan dress, embraces every single visitor. Her apartment features warm red lighting, mismatched cushions on fold-out chairs, offering the kind of intimacy that no jazz bar could provide. Despite the DIY set-up, **Jazz at Marjorie Eliot's** was officially declared a New York institution by the New York Center for Urban Folk Culture in 2015 and the woman herself is now officially a jazz legend. Awards, photo memorabilia and concert fliers decorate the walls of her pre-war apartment. Eliot began her Sunday jazz jams 25 years ago as a means of coping with the loss of her son. She starts off on the piano and invites various musicians to play, sing or even recount poems with her. Concerts are free, although donations are appreciated. Out-of-towners often come to New York just to hear Eliot play and her audience is diverse and international. Entering her world is somewhat disorienting, transporting us a century back when jazz evenings in private apartments were a regular scene of the Harlem Renaissance. In the 1920s, a social phenomenon known as the "Harlem rent party" played a major role in the development of jazz and blues music. The clandestine parties were organized by tenants to raise money in order to pay extortionate New York City rent prices by hosting jazz soirées in their own apartments. Eliot's secret jazz club is the kind of urban myth that hails from those times. *(555 Edgecombe Avenue at 160th Street, "The Triple Nickel", Studio 3F, New York, NY 10032; +1 212-781-6595 phone; Sundays 3:30pm - 6pm)*

Pinball and Cocktails on Laundry Day

In an overcrowded city, having your own washing machine and dryer is a rare luxury. Neighborhood laundromats are a common sight, and doing the laundry is typically the bane of many a New Yorker's week. That is unless you head to the **Sunshine Laundromat & Pinball** in Greenpoint. Slip past the lady folding freshly cleaned whites and find the secret door leading to a bar in the back that's also home to possibly the largest collection of pinball machines in the city, some vintage classics, others newer, all in pristine working order. What better way to get through your weekly laundry chores than with a beer and some pinball? Tip: Bring change, games are 75 cents a go to become a pinball wizard. *(860 Manhattan Avenue, Brooklyn, NY, 11222; +1 718-475-2055; sunshinelaundromat.com)*

The friendliest little bar in NYC

At any given night at **Pocket Bar** in Hell's Kitchen, don't be surprised if you
end up belting out Tina Turner hits and feel-good classics alongside strangers-
turned-drinking buddies at this cozy neighborhood joint. Drinks like the
"Sharnado Sangria" come served with little rubber shark bath toys and a
bag of popcorn. They also have wine on tap. Let the friendliest bartenders
in Manhattan be your host for the night and don't be shy to strike up a
conversation with your neighbors. Come back for Monday's bingo night.
*(455 W 48th St, Hell's Kitchen, NY 10019; +1 646-682-9062; Sun-Wed 4pm-12am,
Fri-Sat 4pm-1am; Instagram: @pocketbarnyc)*

Happy Hour at the Church of Musical Theatre

The plaque outside **Marie's Crisis** quotes the revolutionary writer Thomas Paine,
"*all mankind are my brethren*", and nowhere does that feel more the case than at
a late night session around the piano in this wonderful Greenwich Village dive.
Under the twinkle lights of the cozy basement bar, the crowd becomes your
family for the night and lets you leave your troubles out there above ground.
Popular with the LGBT community for several decades, every night and every
piano player is different, but the drinks are always cheap and spirits are always
high. The bar is rich in history and first opened in the 1850s as a brothel, lasting
through Prohibition as a boy bar. There's plenty of good memories to be made
here if it's not bursting with them already, so gather round and get ready to belt
out your favorite Broadway show tunes to your heart's content. In an age of
internet loneliness, nothing quite beats the blues like a good old fashioned sing
along with a group of strangers. *(59 Grove Street, New York, NY, 10014; +1 212-243-
9323; Mariescrisis.us; open everyday 4.30pm-3am)*

Marie's Crisis

Cheaper than Therapy

Where to de-stress from city life

Secret Electric Dreams

Forget those unanswered emails, that impending deadline, the bills you forgot to pay, the mother you forgot to call; let the worries of everyday life wash over you at what might just be one of the rarest spaces left in modern-day New York City. The **Dream House** is the fantasy of an artist couple who saturated a third-floor apartment in TriBeCa with nothing but ambient, neon magenta light and a near indescribable, relaxing "humming" sound that's perfect for an afternoon of space-age mediation. Stay for ten minutes, or ten hours lying on its floor with a pillow, for a donation of $10. Somewhere in between a secret sleep café and a hippie art space, this visual installation has been running since the experimental art scene days of the 1960s, moving around to various locations, including highly prestigious ones like the Solomon R. Guggenheim Museum and Dia in Chelsea, before settling here in the 1990s, above its creators Manhattan loft. American avant-garde composer, La Monte Young and his wife, light artist, Marian Zazeela, designed the concept to immerse its city-dwelling guests in a much-needed relaxing environment, but the term "Dream House" has since come to define any kind of continuously-running work of art. It's a concept that seems near-impossible in a city where rent prices are as high as the skyscrapers, but somehow, The Dream House is still there. Just ring the doorbell of the unmarked black door and head upstairs, ready to leave your stress behind on the streets of TriBeCa. For a neon fix that's more like a kick of caffeine, head to one of the Dream House's favorite collaborators down the street, **Let There Be Neon**. Founded in 1972, it's one of the country's leading neon sign ateliers, and its team has worked with everyone from Keith Haring to John Lennon and Yoko Ono. *(The Dream House, 275 Church St, Tribeca, NY 10013; +1 917-972-3674; Fri 9pm-11pm; Melafoundation.org & Let There Be Neon, 38 White St, Tribeca, NY 10013; +1 212-226-4883; Mon-Fri 9am-5pm, closed weekends; Instagram: @Lettherebeneon)*

Cartoons & Cereal at the Cinema

Remember Saturday morning cartoons in your PJ's gorging on cereal? Brooklyn's **Nitehawk Cinema** and *Secret Formula* events (secretformulany. com) host monthly "Spoons, Toons and Booze" matinees: 2 hours of non-stop cartoons from the 1940s through to the early 2000's plus an all-you-can-eat sugar cereal bar with all the marshmallowy, fruity, chocolaty cereal you crave (soy milk available for the dairy-free adult in you) and shots of Baileys to spike your cereal. This is priceless therapy to erase bad childhood memories with only the good ones, so make sure to book your seat in advance. If you miss the morning cartoons, Nitehawk Cinema is open every night of the week, taking the novelty of dinner-and-a-movie one step further. You can quite literally snack on everything from a Dr. Pepper braised rib sandwich to a Kale salad while sipping frozen Margaritas through the film. In fact, the Nitehawk is single-handedly responsible for overturning the Prohibition-era New York State liquor law that made serving alcohol in motion picture theaters illegal. Choose between the OG Williamsburg location or the recently renovated landmark theater in Park Slope with a nostalgic cinema marquee. *(Nitehawk Williamsburg: 136 Metropolitan Ave, Brooklyn, NY 11249; +1 718-782-8370/ 188 Prospect Park West, Brooklyn, NY 11215; +1 718-782-8370; Nitehawkcinema.com)*

It's a Ruff Life

Is there anything more therapeutic than a cuddle from a Corgi wearing a cardigan and a propeller hat? We can't all keep a furry friend in the city to lower our stress levels, but fortunately, the **New York Corgi Meetup** group is happy to share theirs with you for an afternoon. The NY corgi scene gets together every last Sunday of the month (weather permitting), typically drawing a crowd of up to 50 of the Queen's favorite canine. Corgi parents and non-committed enthusiasts of the short-legged breed alike are welcome to attend the outdoor meet & greets held in various parks around Manhattan and Brooklyn. Warning: side effects may include involuntary use of baby voices and excessive urges to provide tummy rubs *(Find meetups via Meetup.com/New-York-Corgi-Meetup or Facebook.com/NewYorkCorgis).* Over in Bushwick, you can get your five-minute therapy fix by taking your coffee break in front of the pedestrian window of **Brooklyn Bow Wow**, giving you a look into the playful goings on at Brooklyn's finest doggy daycare, training and dog walking business. *(1581 Dekalb Ave, Brooklyn, NY 11237; +1 929-234-6236; everyday 7am-11pm; Brooklynbowwow.com)*

Create your own Colors in a Pigment Shop

Wassily Kandinsky once said, "Color provokes a psychic vibration. Color hides a power still unknown but real, which acts on every part of the human body." He would have liked **Kremer Pigments**, a painter's treasure that New York is lucky to have. The front of house is a library of color where you can gaze to your heart's content at the shelves packed with transparent sacks of powdered pigments. If you're at all intrigued at how these powders become paints, join a crash course and discover how to make oil-based and water-based paints, discuss recipes and basic methods, which are not all that different from cooking. Beginners (and beginner questions) are welcome to all classes, which take place at the back of the shop on Saturdays from 11 am and last approximately 2 hours. Seating is limited to 20 per class and cost $15 on a first come first serve basis. You'll find making your own paint can be addictive, especially when you're working with rare earths, minerals and forgotten historic pigments of the old masters.
(247 W 29th St C, Chelsea, NY 10001; +1 212-219-2394; Mon-Sat 11am-6.30pm; Shop.kremerpigments.com/en)

The friendliest New Yorkers

Kremer Pigments

▶ ## Feeding a Broken Heart (or a Hangover)

Hungry in NYC

From the New Yorker diet staples to outrageous foodie feasts, we can't guarantee this list will cure a broken heart, but there's strong evidence it could help cure a hangover...

Gospel Brunch in Harlem

Waffles & fried chicken from the "Queen of Soul Food," with a side of gospel at **Sylvia's**. Going since 1962 in the heart of Harlem on Malcolm X Blvd, the family-run restaurant serves authentic and delicious soul food every day of the week, but on Sundays, there are live gospel singers to accompany your brunch. We won't let you order anything else but the waffles & fried chicken (and don't forget the syrup). It all comes with grits or home fries and biscuits; a feast for under $20. (*328 Malcolm X Blvd, Harlem, NY 10027; +1 212-996-0660; open everyday 8am-10.30pm, Sun 11am-8pm*)

The Cuban Cure

Nurse a hangover at **Cafe Habana**, a Cuban-inspired kitchen that opened 20 years ago in a landmark American diner in vibrant Nolita. Generous portions of tacos, grilled corn, sweet plantain and of course, Cuban sandwiches, are served by hip and sassy waitresses that could almost be "Jenny from the block" 20 years ago on her day shift. They've got a guava Margarita that will turn that hungover frown right upside down and perk you up again for some boutique shopping around Nolita, (turn to the shopping guide on pg 165). In the summer, pay a visit to their Brooklyn playground in the sun, the Habana Outpost, see pg 163.
(*17 Prince St, Nolita, NY 10012; +1 212-625-2001; Wed-Sat 9am-12am, Sun-Tues 9am-10pm; Cafehabana.com*)

Grilled street corn
at Cafe Habana

A Rookie's Guide to New York's Most Important Bagels

From its humble origins in the old Jewish communities of Eastern Europe, the bagel has become the quintessential New York breakfast. You'll find them in every corner bakery and deli, but where can you find a bagel to remember?

1 **Russ & Daughters:** Family owned since 1914 and one of Manhattan's most cherished institutions, their wide range of smoked salmon is sliced so thin according to *New Yorker* writer, Calvin Trillin, it's "thin enough to read a newspaper through." Take a ticket, prepare to wait a little, and order a toasted onion bagel with scallion cream cheese and the traditional salt-cured belly lox. *(179 East Houston Street, New York, NY, 10002; +1 212-475-4880; Mon-Wed 8am-6pm, Thurs 8am-7pm, Fri-Sun 8am-6pm; Russanddaughters.com)*

2 **Barney Greengrass:** one of the highest-ranking Jewish delis in the city and another charming time capsule of old New York, the bustling 100-year-old deli is for perfect solo diners and quick lunches, powered by a boisterous team of local boys. Famous for its fresh salmon, sturgeon, lox, and about every other smoked fish you can pair with a bagel. Cash only. *(541 Amsterdam Ave. Upper West Side, NY 10024; +1 212-724-4707; Tues-Sun 8am-6pm)*

4 **The Bagel Store:** If you want to get a little creative (and seriously Instagrammable) with your bagels, this Williamsburg shop is responsible for everything from the rainbow bagel craze to the cragel (croissant-bagel hybrid), and boasts cream cheese flavours like chipotle, cannoli or pumpkin pie cream cheese. *(754 Metropolitan Ave, Brooklyn, NY 11211; +1 718-782-5856; everyday 7am-6pm; Thebagelstoreonline.com)*

5 **Brooklyn Heights Deli:** This old general store has been around so long the owners think it's haunted, and it gets our vote as New York's most underrated historic deli. It just so happens that they serve a world-class bagel too. Go all out with a toasted poppy seed bagel with butter, warm roast beef, Pepper Jack cheese and hot sauce. Located on the corner of a leafy street in Brooklyn Heights, this is one of the few delis we've found with outdoor tables, so plant yourself on the patio and watch the neighbourhood go by. *(292 Henry St, Brooklyn, NY 11201; +1 718-643-1361; Mon-Fri 7am-9pm, Sat & Sun until 7pm)*

Myers of Keswick

Homesick Brits

Ask any homesick English ex-pat: nothing is quite as comforting as a portion of good old fish & chips. But where to find that taste of home in New York? **A Salt & Battery** on Greenwich Avenue is a proper chippy, with traditional British fryers behind the counter and proper brown vinegar on the tables. *(112 Greenwich Avenue, New York, NY, 10011; +1 212-691-2713; Asaltandbattery.com).*

Just next door, you can cozy up in an old-fashioned English tea room straight out of the Cotswolds (see pg 194), and a five-minute stroll 'round the corner, find a family-run grocery shop selling British household staples – from that familiar bottle of Fairy washing up liquid to Hobnob biscuits. For the 250,000 or so British expats that call the tri-state area their home, **Myers of Keswick** (pronounced Kessic, after a small town in England's Lake District) has been curing the homesick since 1985. Much like the old Tuck Shops that British school kids could stop into on the way home for a bar of Cadbury's chocolate and prawn cocktail crisps, all it's missing is an iconic red telephone box outside. Enjoy the novelty candies but don't leave Greenwich Village's "Little Britain" without one of the Myers' famous homemade pies.

(634 Hudson St, New York, NY, 10014; +1 212-691-4194; open everyday 10pm-7pm, Sun 12pm-5pm; Myersofkeswick.com)

Yellow Cab Driver's Comfort Food

After a disastrous date in the big city, burn away the aftertaste of disappointment with the comfort of a friendly no-frills Indian takeaway at **Punjabi Grocery and Deli**. The prices are unbeatable for Manhattan and the food is fast (and microwaved) – which would make you think it's going to be awful but actually, it's delightful. Dig into a samosa chole with everything on it or a delicious veggie curry served with chapati or potato pancakes. This is an all-night lifesaver, a favourite with locals in-the-know and particularly, with yellow cab drivers looking for an authentic Indian meal in the early hours of their shift. Perhaps one of them might be kind enough to drive you home when you're done with that curry. *(114 E 1st St, Manhattan, New York, NY 10009; +1 212-533-3356; open 24 hours every day).*

American Chinese Food Done Right

You'd better try and rally a few friends to join you in sampling every dish on the menu at **King's County Imperial** if it's even possible; from the Dan Dan noodles to the chicken & cinnamon dumpling – it's all seriously delicious. Almost everything here can be made vegetarian/vegan, and you'll wonder where their delicious "Mock Eel" has been hiding all your life. Enjoy your feast under a red-lit, low-slung ceiling worthy of an old film noir movie or in the back garden on a summer's day. *(20 Skillman Ave, Brooklyn, NY 11211; +1 718-610-2000; Open daily from early evening until near-midnight)*

Brunch on a Stick

Get your brunch on a stick at the **Smorgasburg Street Market**, the largest weekly open-air food market in America. Look out for the Brunch Street stand (@BrunchStreet) which offers bacon-stuffed pancakes on skewers topped with syrup. Also try the fried eggs skewers topped with cheddar sauce, avocado puree and tortilla chips or truffle sauce and parmesan. Don't believe you can fit all that on a skewer? You have to see it to believe it. *(Every weekend in various Brooklyn locations depending on the season, Smorgasburg.com)*

Pho Good

Meet your partner in crime at **Bep Ga** to piece together the events of last night over a soothing bowl of Pho soup surrounded by instagrammable pastels and comforting aromas. Parisian graffiti artist André Saraiva is the designer behind this pretty in pink hole-in-the-wall and the chef is French-Vietnamese Mr. Xuan, who mastered his grandmother's chicken pho and rice-based recipes, just as she would have made them back in Saigon. *(70 Forsyth St; Lower East Side, NY 10002; +1 917-261-4716; open Mon-Fri for lunch and dinner, Sat for lunch)*

Gimme somethin' Sweet

1   If someone you know just got dumped, the best thing you can offer them is one
     of **Steve's Authentic Key Lime Pies**. It's out in Red Hook (one of our favorite
     neighborhoods on pg 201), but you won't care how far you have to travel once
     you discover the fresh-squeezed, fresh-baked pie, which really is the best you'll
     ever try. Trust a guy (Steve) who started a business more than two decades ago
     selling one thing and one thing only.
     *(185 Van Dyke St, Brooklyn, NY; +1 718-858-5333; Mon-Thurs 12pm-6pm,
     Fri until 7pm, Sat 11am-7pm, Sun 11am-6pm; Keylime.com)*

2   Open the menu at **Brooklyn Farmacy & Soda Fountain** and you'll be grinning
     from ear to ear. Comfort yourself the old-fashioned way, with a visit to a
     traditional American soda fountain, housed inside a former 1920s apothecary.
     This is the place to indulge in century-old delights like an authentic Brooklyn
     Egg Cream or countertop sundaes with fun names like "Breakfast in Bed,"
     "Elvis" and "Peanut Buttercup". At this undeniably instagrammable Cobble
     Hill treasure, the abundance of nostalgic decor (mostly original and salvaged
     from the old apothecary that operated here before) will take you right back
     to the simple pleasures of the good old days when soda fountains were the
     cornerstone of every neighborhood.
     *(513 Henry Street, Brooklyn, NY, 11231; +1 718-522-6260; Mon-Thurs 11am-10pm,
     Fri 11am-11pm, weekends from 10am; Brooklynfarmacyandsodafountain.com)*

3   Find your personal artisanal chocolate library at **The Meadow**. You'll feel as if
     you've stepped into a charming village apothecary, but one whose walls have
     swapped tonics for floor-to-ceiling chocolates, artisanal salts and bitters.
     Consider it your new medicine cabinet. *(523 Hudson St, The West Village, NY
     10014; +1 212-645-4633; Mon-Thurs 11am-9pm, Fri-Sat 11am-10pm, Sun 'til 8pm;
     themeadow.com)*

4   Rediscover layer-cakes from the 1950s at the **Ring Ding Bar**: Is this what a
     rainbow tastes like? Maybe. Pure nostalgia for the baby boomer generation.
     *(179 Duane St, TriBeCa, NY 10013; +1 212 274-8447; Open daily from 8am-7pm;
     ringdingbar.com)*

Brooklyn Farmacy & Soda Fountain

Scott Weiner
at Luigi's Pizza's

© Randy Duchaine

Scott Weiner

© Michael Berman

Advice from a Pizza Philosopher

Scott Wiener eats 15 slices of pizza a week. He knows exactly where, and when, because each one is recorded in a spreadsheet with precision. It's all a part of his ongoing quest to understand more about our to pizza: how we bake it, eat it, share it, or lose our heartbreak in it. Eating pizza in NY, he says, is an experience that can be both completely singular and shared; a culinary staple with endless possibilities. Wiener is kind of an optimistic pizza philosopher, and he's convinced you can't really be heartbroken, or at least, lonely, in New York for very long...

Where do you go when New York gets you down?
A slice shop. The interaction with people behind the counter is there – it's kind of like a bar – but it's not depressing like bars can sometimes be. It's always a mix of people, some there for the first time, who I always get into a conversation with.

Three pizza spots for NYC novices?
1   There's historic New York pizza: **Totonno's** down at Coney Island, founded in 1924, a real Brooklyn pizza with a coal-fired oven. It's always busy but almost everyone forgets about the wait once they've had a piece of the pie.
(1524 Neptune Ave, Brooklyn, NY 11224; +1 718-372-8606; Thurs–Sun 12pm–7.30pm; Totonnosconeyisland.com).

2   The classic slice shop: **Joe's** is a Greenwich Village institution, a classic slice shop open until 4am most nights. Take your slice and enjoy it while people watching at the nearby Washington Square Park.
(7 Carmine St, New York, NY 10014; +1 212-366-1182; everyday 10am–4am, until 5am on weekends; Joespizzanyc.com).

3   The "now" spots which take the rules and ignore them: **Paulie Gee's** in Greenpoint is an excellent choice for a date spot serving fluffy, doughy thin crust pizzas straight out of a wood-fired oven. It's rustic, romantic and candlelit, and the wine is worth ordering a second pie for. *(60 Greenpoint Ave. Brooklyn, NY 11222; +1 347-987-3747; Open daily from early evening 'til 11pm but 10pm Sun).*

Do you remember any slices of pizza in the same way you remember a lover?
Absolutely. The first time going to **Grimaldi's** changed my life and taught me
that pizza is an elevated food. It's a legendary full pie-only joint by the Brooklyn
Bridge. I'll also never forget my first time eating pizza at **Di Fara Pizza**, a no-
frills slice shop going since 1964 in Brooklyn.
(Grimaldi's, 1 Front St, Brooklyn, NY 11201, +1 718-858-4300; everyday 11.30am-
10.30pm, til 11.30pm Fri & Sat; Grimaldis-pizza.com / Di Fara Pizza,
1424 Avenue J, Brooklyn, NY 11230; +1 718-258-1367; Mon-Sat 12pm-8pm; Sun open
from 1pm; Difarany.com)

Favorite places to be alone in New York City?
Pier 40. It's just a pier next to a parking lot, but with great views of New Jersey
for the sunset, and no one ever goes out there except for this one eccentric guy
named Gus. Yeah, I see Gus every once in a while.

*Discover more about New York pizza with **Scott's Pizza Tours** (from $55 a head,*
experiences typically last 2h30m; Scottspizzatours.com)

▶ Party of One

There are over 8 million people living in this city, but sometimes, you're simply
better off alone...

The Beer Whisperer
Amidst the old tenements and dive bars of the East Village is **Burp Castle**, a
peculiar little monastery-themed watering hole with a whisper-only policy that
makes it the perfect spot to pull up a stool and finish that book with a fine pint
of ale. Soft Gregorian chanting on the stereo, a remarkable medieval-style mural
that fills the whole candle-lit bar, the occasional hush and friendly wink from
the bartender when conversation levels get too high – Burp Castle provides the
peace and quiet (and Belgian Trappist beer) you can't get at home.
(41 E 7th St, East Village, NY, 10003; Mon-Fri 5pm-12am, Sat & Sun 4pm-2am;
Burpcastlenyc.wordpress.com)

Solo at the Luncheonette Counter
For those allergic to the word brunch, especially when used as a verb, there's
the good ol' **La Bonbonniere**: an old-school no-frills luncheonette where you
can grab a stool at the formica counter, order your cheap black coffee that's
been reheating since 6 am and a warm chicken soup or a challah French toast

alongside the city's construction workers. Your buillshit-free breakfast is cash only. *(28 8th Ave, Greenwich Village, NY 10014; +1 212-741-9266; Hours vary, but open Mon-Fri for an early breakfast til 1pm, until 4pm on Sat, 'til 8pm Friday & Sunday)*

A rare find in luncheonette comfort food is the vegetarian factory of happiness and borscht, **B&H Dairy**, delivering kosher staples and infectious positivity even on a rainy day for over 60 years. Every order comes with a side of sweet-soft challah dripping in butter. We love a good sulk on a barstool, and no one indulges us in that department better than B&H. *(127 2nd Ave, St. Marks Pl., East Village, NY 10003; +1 212-505-8065; Open every day from 7am to about Midnight)*

Don't settle for just any Italian deli

Take a seat by the window at **Regina's Grocery**; a place that feels like your Nana's old kitchen; watching the passersby from behind a vintage lace curtain while you wait for one of the most delicious Italian sandwiches of the Lower East Side. At this old school joint decorated with the Grandinetti family photos on the wall, there are two favorites: "Uncle Jimmy" (Prosciutto, Fresh Mozzarella, Hot Sopressata, Smoked Ham, Arugula, Regina's Hot Pepper Spread, Balsamic & Roasted Reds on Striato Bread) and "Uncle John" (Prosciutto, Provolone, Mortadella, Hot Sopressata, Smoked Ham, Lettuce, Red Wine Vinegar & Roasted

Above: Burp Castle

© Katherine Pelaka

Right: Courtesy of Regina's Grocery

Reds on Semolina Bread). Both are made with nothing but love. *(27 Orchard St, Lower East Side, NY 10002; everyday 12pm-6pm, til 5pm on Sunday; Instagram: @ ReginasGrocery)*

Bathing in Red Wine

Housed in an old Tribeca textile factory from 1883 – and possibly the only place in New York where you can unwind in a 17th-century Venetian well filled with red wine – soothe your soul in the Greco-Roman atmosphere of the **Aire Ancient Baths**. Dip in and out of six candle-lit thermal baths with intense massaging jets and finish up in the eucalyptus-infused steam room, all the while, being treated like royalty in a peaceful, über luxurious setting of exposed brick and serious mood lighting. The red wine bath is for very special occasions (and would make a pretty special gift at $450), but the thermal experiences start at $96, and you can throw in a massage for an extra $50 – the price you pay for a heavenly sanctuary in the middle of the concrete jungle. *(88 Franklin Street, New York, NY, 10013; +1 646-878-6174; Beaire.com/en/aire-ancient-baths-new-york for booking details).*

 For a spa day on a smaller budget, try the Russian & Turkish baths on pg 98

An Afternoon at the Pictures

1   **From New York to Paris with Carrie Bradshaw:** In the words of Carrie Bradshaw, "the most amazing thing about living in a city like New York is that any night of the week you can go to Paris." The Paris she means is Manhattan's last single-screen theatre in existence, **Paris Theatre Cinema**, whose 1948 ribbon-cutting was performed by Marlene Dietrich, and whose selection includes European art house films, celebrated documentaries and period classics. This is the perfect cinema for going it alone with a large serving of their excellent house popcorn all to yourself. Its yellow neon lettering on the old school marquee is a heart-warming sight for any *Sex & the City* fan, and the perfect follow up to a shopping spree à la Carrie Bradshaw chez Bergdorf Goodman next door. *(4 W 58th St, New York, NY 1001; Citycinemas.com/paris/showtimes-and-tickets/now-playing)*

2   **Film Lover's Forums:** New York offers some excellent independent cinemas in lieu of parking yourself at one of the soulless blockbuster chains on a rainy Sunday afternoon. **Spectacle Theater** in Williamsburg calls itself a "microcinema" with a 30-seat capacity, entirely run by volunteers who love film – forgotten film in particular. The collective curates and projects obscure and offbeat treasures by "mining the depths of VHS and the darkest corners

of the internet." There's a bi-monthly kung-fu matinee on Sundays, harking back to a time when New Yorkers could still smoke in theatres and watch badly-dubbed Bruce Lee at one of the many infamous Times Square theaters. Tickets are cheap enough ($5) that you could stay for the next screening of an overlooked 90s flick or a contemporary indie film premiere with an up-and-coming director. If you fancy yourself as a bit of a movie curator, you might be interested in joining the collective by sending an email to the volunteer address on the website *(124 S 3rd St, Brooklyn, NY 11249; Check website for showtimes; Spectacletheater.com).*

Over in Greenwich Village, the **Film Forum** has been around since the 70's when it began as an alternative screening space for independent films with just a couple of folding chairs and a single projector. Nowadays, you can catch new American indie and foreign art films, and even quirkier choices, from a mid-week screening of *My Cousin Vinny* to the first full-color American 3D movie circa 1940. Admission to most films is $15, open 365 days a year. *(209 W Houston St, New York, NY 10014; check website for showtimes; Filmforum.org)*

3   **Wes Anderson's Favorite Cinema:** While Netflix is keeping everyone at home in their pajamas, **The Metrograph** is the kind of cinema you can dress up for to match your suave surroundings. The elegant picture house shows digital and 35mm print films in its two intimate theaters with old-fashioned cinema seats. The knowledgeable team hosts regular Q&A events with the directors, actors and writers of the works themselves. There's a bar and eatery called The Commissary, inspired by Hollywood's on-set studio restaurants from Hollywood's golden age, and a small bookstore selling arthouse film books to browse. At $15 a ticket, the prices are a little higher at the Metrograph than at some of our other independent cinemas (see pg 85) but it's not hard to believe that this is the place Wes Anderson himself likes to catch a film. *(7 Ludlow St, Lower East Side, +1 212-660-0312; NY 10002; check for showtimes; Metrograph.com)*

 Find more of New York's excellent independent cinemas on pg 57 and 85.

▶ ## League of Marvellous and Magical Misfits

Where to find kindred spirits that don't quite fit in society's square box

A Secret World of After Hours Magic

In a nondescript office building, hidden away up six flights of stairs, with no signpost at street level to give you a clue, is the oldest operating magic shop in the city. Since 1925, **Tannen's Magic** has catered to the somewhat peculiar and unique needs of professional and budding amateur magicians alike. A pair of Houdini's handcuffs, from when he was thrown manacled into the East River, hang on the shop's walls. But after closing time, the secretive ambiance of this magic shop is taken a step further. The lights are dimmed and faint sounds of New Orleans jazz accompany flutes of champagne as **Magic After Hours** begins, hosted by one of the city's premier professional magicians, Noah Levine. "I came here when I was a kid," says Levine, whose grandmother first brought him to the hidden magic shop, "Lots of magicians are lone guns, so having a community is amazing...It's really important to be around other people in the same boat as you."

When you discover Tannen's, you're following in the footsteps of magicians such as David Copperfield and David Blaine, both of who came here as young, aspiring conjurors. Today, this legendary fixture of the New York magic scene provides a unique backdrop for Noah's intimate magic show every Tuesday and Wednesday night at 8 pm. "Old magic is very strong," says Levine, "because it has stood the test of time. The real challenge is to find a way to work with the classic material and bring it to the present day." Whether you know everything about magic or nothing, all are welcome – before and after dark.
(45 W 34th St #608, New York, NY 10001; Midtown; Book tickets for Magic After Hours via MagicAfterhours.com)

The Addams Family Bar, Williamsburg

Duff's is where heavy metal dreams come true, but it's also just a really good bar. Crawl inside this joint (or one of its coffins) for a taste of pre-hipster Williamsburg with $1 beers, an electrocution throne, metal memorabilia covering the walls and endless oddities to peruse. Despite appearances, this is one of the friendliest and most welcoming bars in New York, where you can talk to anyone and be at ease with whatever flag you're flying. The music isn't so loud that you have to shout and you don't even have to be a die-hard metal fan to dig this place either – they'll play old school and soft rock too, and they aren't afraid of a good old-fashioned Elvis tune.
(168 Marcy Ave, Brooklyn, NY 11211; +1 718-599-2092; open daily 6pm-4am)

Stonewall Inn

Drag Queen Bingo and the LGBT Heroes

Banish the Monday blues with a visit to the **Stonewall Inn** for a few rounds
of Drag Queen Bingo with Kenny Dash beginning at 9pm or catch one of the
fabulous weekly drag shows from 10pm on Tuesdays. This is the bar where
Gay Pride began, where the Stonewall Riots broke out in the early hours of
June 28th, 1969 during a routine police raid that erupted into a full-fledged
rebellion. Just inside the door, they've framed the sign left by police that night
as a reminder of the struggle and injustice. "This is a raided premises", says the
old sign which frequently hung outside the doors of lesbian and gay bar across
the Village during police shut-downs. Patrons were lined-up, interrogated,
insulted, frisked and arrested if they weren't wearing at least three pieces of
clothing appropriate for their sex (which was checked by female police officers
in the bathroom).

Stonewall Inn

THIS IS A
**RAIDED
PREMISES**
POLICE DEP'T
CITY OF NEW YORK
HOWARD R LEARY POLICE COMMISSIONER

© Kathy Drasky

After tolerating decades of abuse, humiliation and oppression, the LGBT uprising that took place was comparable to a scene from the civil rights movement of the 1950s, and saw gays, lesbians and trans women in the hundreds, fighting back against the law on the streets of Greenwich Village. The riots paved the way for the first gay pride parades in New York and Stonewall Inn became the first place to be landmarked by the city for its role it played during the gay rights movement. *(53 Christopher Street, New York, NY, 10014; +1 212-488-2705; Thestonewallinnnyc.com)*

Don't forget the city's oldest gay bar (not to mention one of the oldest bars in Manhattan) **Julius'**, which paved the way for serious policy changes in legitimizing LGBT bars at its 1966 "Sip-In." Inspired by civil rights sit-in in the south, it was one of the earliest public actions for LGBT rights which saw gay patrons declare their sexuality before ordering a drink to challenge discriminatory serving laws. Any bars that refused service were called out publicly in the media. On any given night at Julius', you could find Tennessee Williams or Truman Capote ordering a cocktail, and it was the birthplace of Mattachine, one of the country's oldest LGBT organizations that continues to gather there to this day, every Thursday from 9 pm. There's also a long-standing tradition of serving old timers a complimentary juicy burger, but otherwise, you can order them for a steal at $6. PS. Saturday night is dance night.
(159 W 10th St, West Village, NY 10014; +1 212 243-1928; Open from 11am-4am Tues–Sun, Mon 12pm-3am.)

Not for the Easily Offended

The neon pink "F*ck Off" sign sets the tone for **Boobie Trap**, New York's sassiest dive bar, whose ambiance of humorous kitsch packs a loveable punch. Tattooed ladies serve cheap and strong "fancy-ass dranks", but if you're unsatisfied by a $5 beer & shot deal, or easily offended by the adult coloring books and topless imagery around the bar, think twice about blasting your thoughts on Yelp – you could end up with your photo on their wall as "Shitty Yelper of the Month," right above the fake ID hall of fame. Brimming with surreal bric-a-brac from floor-to-ceiling, a sign behind the counter says "*You don't have to be crazy to work here, we'll train you.*" Above the bottles, another sign reads, "*Man Bun Special: One full booze bottle in return for one man bun removal*", which explains those ponytails nailed to the top shelf (somewhere in Bushwick this morning, a hipster sobered up with a new haircut). But the fun doesn't stop there. All your favorite board games from childhood are out for customers to enjoy. Who knew "Connect 4" or "Hungry Hippos" could be so much more fun after a couple of margaritas? The bathrooms are pretty trippy too (check out that chandelier made of dolls) and we were certainly amused by the "Pee Pee Panic" doorbell outside the cubicles and the "Hey Puke Face" box of hair ties by the sink. Pro tip: If you get those late-night hunger pangs, you can order from their sister restaurant, Pizza Party, across the street (open until 4 am, vegan options included) and they'll bring your food to you at Boobie Trap. Drop in for the Drag Queen Bingo night on Tuesdays, the Drink & Draw afternoons on Thursdays and fly your freak flag every day of the week at this dive bar, well worth venturing a little deeper into "new Bushwick" for. *(308 Bleecker St, Brooklyn, NY 11237; +1 347-240-9105; Open daily from noon to 4am, closes at midnight on Sundays; Instagram: @boobietrapbushwick)*

Brooklyn Beauty Shop for Mermaids & Unicorns

When you wanna "wash that man right out of your hair" and transform yourself with rainbow-colored tresses **Tomahawk Salon** is your place. Accommodating all kinds of mermaidesque makeovers, the warm and welcoming crew of stylists are extremely knowledgeable when it comes to color (and color correction). Head stylist Kristin Jackson even makes handmade hair swatches to help you choose a new look before taking the leap. Need an icy pink 80s mullet? An electric neon bob? You're in good hands for the most adventurous and multidimensional hairdos, but even if you're looking for a no-frills haircut to start a fresh, Tomahawk Salon is just the kind of uplifting and quirky place your inner-mermaid should get it done.
(17 Thames St, Brooklyn, NY 11206; Call or text for an appointment on +1 646 399-6873; Open daily from midday to evening, closed Tuesdays; Instagram: #TomahawkSalon)

Museum of Outsiders

Their abilities don't come from any artistic establishment, they didn't have any formal training and they see beauty in things that most of the world doesn't. They have been labeled by the art world as "outsider artists," "folk artists" or "naïve artists". **The American Folk Art Museum** is a free museum, devoted to the appreciation of those individuals and their creative expression of unconventional ideas, extreme mental states and elaborate fantasy worlds. The museum holds the largest collection of archival materials from Henry Darger, one of the greatest self-taught artists of the 20th century, whose work was discovered posthumously when his landlords were cleaning out his home upon his death in 1973. No one knew that hidden behind the door of his single-room apartment in Chicago, the penniless and reclusive janitor was living a secret life, creating densely typed volumes of fantasy manuscript, possibly the longest novel ever written at more than 15,000 pages, accompanied by several hundred striking drawings and paintings, many over 10 feet long.

Hiding in plain sight on busy Lincoln Square, the museum is an oasis of calm where you can immerse yourself in the curious creations of those who exist on the fringes of society. The exhibits never disappoint, and there's a wonderfully quirky gift shop for browsing too. *(2 Lincoln Square, Upper West Side, NY 10023; +1 212-595-9533; Tues-Thurs & Sat 11.30am-7pm, Fri 12-7.30pm, Sun 12am-6pm)*

Where to Start a Conversation

It's an easy task to get a New Yorker talking but a harder one to make the conversation last...

Revolutionary Social Club

Curious to know what it means to attend a 'Propaganda Party' or a 'Feminist Wikipedia Edit-athon'? **Interference Archive** is an open-door, volunteer-based organization in Brooklyn with a true grassroots spirit; wallpapered with the kind of revolutionary imagery you'd expect to have seen at universities in the Paris of May 1968. Join a social justice book club, catch a film screening, take a workshop to become a pro-researcher (knowledge is power) and mingle with kindred spirits. If you feel strongly about something, join the movement. *(314 7th Street, Brooklyn, NY 11215; Thurs 1-9pm, Fri-Sun 12-5pm. Call ahead for groups of 5 or more; interferencearchive.org)*

A Shortlist of NYC Book Clubs

1   **Romance Book Club at Word Bookstore**: Meeting every first Saturday of the month at 2:45 pm "to read about smart women finding respect and love without compromise, to explore the intricacies of the female fantasy, and to consume many bottles of wine!"
(126 Franklin St, Brooklyn, NY 11222; +1 718-383-0096;
Wordbookstores.com/romance-book-group)

2   **Post-Apocalyptic Book Club at Freebird Books**: By the water's edge in Red Hook (see pg 201), there's a charming used bookstore with a wooden storefront that could have been plucked from a ghost town out West. Since 2008, their monthly weekend book club has focused on post-apocalyptic and dystopian novels. From Mary Shelley to Stephen King, the club seeks to understand why the sub-genre is so oddly appealing.
(123 Columbia St, Brooklyn, NY 11231; +1 718-643-8484; Sat & Sun, 11am-8pm;
Freebirdbooks.com/tagged/bookclub)

3   **The Literary Swag Book Club (usually at the Brooklyn Circus)**: Hosted by Yahdon Israel, founder of the "Literary Swag Movement", this is a refreshingly diverse monthly book club for hip young things looking for community and honest conversations about really good books that matter.
(Yahdonisrael.com/book-club)

4   **Feminist Book Club at Bluestockings**: In the #MeToo era of feminism, at a bookstore inspired by the Bluestockings Society, a revolutionary 18th-century women's educational movement (which also started out as a women's literary discussion group), this book club is a safe space, inclusive of all genders, political persuasions and familiarities. You'll also find this volunteer-run bookstore hosts events like "Ukulele for Social Change" and "Queer Socialist Meet-Ups." *(172 Allen St, Lower East Side, NY 10002; +1 212-777-6028;*
Bluestockings.com/events/calendar)

5   **NYC History Book Club at McNally Jackson:** If you're passionate about urban history, which New York City is certainly not short of, you'll find like-minded folks on the first Wednesday of the month at the McNally Jackson bookstore in Williamsburg. Their Prince Street location also has an international literature book club.
(76 N 4th St, Brooklyn, NY 11249; +1 718-387-0115; Mcnallyjackson.com/book-clubs)

6   **The French Literature Book Club at Albertine:** Bond with other Francophiles over a glass of wine while exploring the best of classic and contemporary French literature. Speakers of French and English are both welcome. Free and open for students and Albertine members.
(972 5th Ave, Upper East Side, NY 10075; +1 212-650-0070; Albertine.com/albertine-book-club)

7   **Book Parties at the Bonnie Slotnick Bookstore:** Bonnie's bookstore is hiding away in the basement of a red brick townhouse in the East Village, and while there's technically no book club here, there are frequent parties for new cookbook releases, where the author and chef offers recipe tastings. You can buy a signed copy, browse the shop's amazing collection and mingle with other food lovers over canapes.
(28 E 2nd St, New York, NY 10003; +1 212-989-8962; Check the Facebook page for events, linked on Bonnieslotnickcookbooks.com)

Albertine Bookstore

In Conversation with ...

Join household-name celebrities, journalists, politicians, artists – you name it – in conversation at the nonprofit community center, **92nd Street Y**. Founded in 1874 on the Upper East Side, the programming ranges from on-stage talks and film screenings to community dances and family education. We particularly appreciate the free "Tech Support for Grandparents" classes every Wednesday followed by an open session of Israeli folk dancing. Have a browse of their website to discover just how much this community center offers before heading on down.
(1395 Lexington Ave, Upper East Side, NY 10128; www.92y.org)

Like the Secret Garden. If it Composted.

Pro-active New Yorkers are fully within their right to use online resources such as *LivingLotsNyc.org* to seek, locate, unlock and improve the city's neglected spaces. A good example of this is **Know Waste Lands**. Peer over the chain-link fence on Myrtle Ave and into a lush community garden in the middle of industrial Bushwick founded on composting, camaraderie, and growing as many sunflowers and mushrooms as possible in this former vacant dump. You can usually find locals maintaining it on Sundays and welcoming curious newcomers interested in helping to transform vacant lots into beautiful and impactful community spaces. It's time to take back the concrete jungle!
(1309 Dekalb Ave, Brooklyn, NY 11221; +1 917-678-5395; Facebook.com/knowasteland)

Back to the Golden Age of Billiards

We tend to forget that billiards was once one of the most popular pastimes in America, and during its golden age in the mid-19th century, US cities were home to several hundred pool halls to keep up with demand. **Amsterdam Billiards** is a legendary testament to that forgotten age. Walking past this neon-lit hall, you can't help but stop and notice that impressive display of billiards tables through the windows amidst the rich oak paneling and velvet armchairs. This is no seedy pool hall. Drink servers come to you, and the 25 full-sized tables are kept in good condition. If you fancy yourself becoming a bit of a pool shark, this is the place to start, and maybe even join a league. As one of the first pool rooms in the country to offer pool leagues, they cater to beginners, intermediate and advanced players.
(110 E 11th St, New York, NY 10003; Sun-Thurs 11am-3am, Fri-Sat 11am-4am; Amsterdambilliards.com)

Let's Talk about History Repeating itself

It's important to have a place to argue without being argumentative and disagree without being disagreeable. **The Brooklyn Historical Society** hosts several weekly evening talks, roundtables, screenings and workshops that revolve around a range topics from exploring Islamophobia post-9/11 to a hard look at the broken misdemeanor system, women's issues and more; they'll go anywhere history might be repeating itself. Find the program's events calendar online to reserve your seat (Brooklynhistory.org). During the day, camp out in the Hogwarts-like library on the second floor (see pg 143).

Freshen up like a Real New Yawker

Descend some slightly grungy stairs to a basement shop underneath Astor Place to discover a New York institution since 1947. **Astor Place Hairstylists** is like the United Nations of grooming, with barbers and aestheticians hailing from all corners of the world; Italy, Russia, Morocco, the Dominican Republic – name a country and it's probably represented here. You might walk in on a salsa dance party at one end of the shop and encounter a celebrity getting their monthly trim in another, but you'll never have to wait in line at Astor Place. For decades, this sprawling, 70 chair barbershop has been the cheapest, chattiest and most efficient place to get your haircut in the city. The room is filled with the constant chatter of every language under the sun and the haircuts are as expertly done as they are quick – you can be in and out in 15 minutes. Regulars usually ask for their preferred barber, otherwise just approach the main desk and you'll be sent to whoever is up next. Andy Warhol first led his factory of cool kids here in the 70s, and David Bowie later became a regular too. The countless signed publicity photos are a roll call of New York pop culture. Just know that whichever barber you get assigned may end up being your friend for the next twenty years.
(2 Astor Place, New York, NY, 10003; +1 212-475-9854; Mon 8am-7:30pm, Tues-Fri 8am-9pm, Sat 8am-7pm, Sun 9am-6pm. Haircuts currently start at $18 and up. Pay at the main kiosk by the entrance and don't forget to go back and tip your barber, Astorplacehairnyc.com)

Playing the Game of Life in New York's Chess District

There's nowhere in the world where chess is played the way it is in New York. Historically, Washington Square Park was the mecca of chess and outdoor play in the city, going back decades, when players like Bobby Fischer (considered by many as the world's greatest chess player) made Greenwich Village an iconic location for the game. Whatever you think about chess being a long, quiet and structured game, forget about it. In New York, it's a fast-paced street game where a lot of money changes hands. Hustlers trash talk each other as spectators huddle round to watch them play at lightning speed during five-minute or one-minute games of Blitz chess. Having migrated seven blocks north from Washington Square Park to Union Square where they can find more unsuspecting tourists to challenge, some hustlers are known to make up to $400 a day. If you know better than to jump into a trap, just down the street from where it all started in Greenwich Village, you can find the **Chess Forum**, one of the last old-fashioned gaming parlors in the city. A cozy neighborhood gem with a friendly community of players, don't feel intimidated to just pick up a game with a stranger or brush up on your Queen's Gambit with a regular. It's $5 an hour to play ($1 for senior citizens). Chess and backgammon lessons are also offered. Located across the street from the Uncommons board game café (see pg 59), kids play for free here and the forum also hosts free lessons on Saturdays from 2pm-4pm. Their motto? Smart people, not smartphones! *(219 Thompson Street, New York, NY, 10012; +1 212-475-2369; open 7 days a week, from 11am-midnight, or much later if the games continue; Chessforum.com)*

© *courtesy of the Chess Forum*

▶

All Dressed Up and Nowhere to Go

Where elegance is always welcome...

Bar Murals of New York

Amidst the countless bars to be found in the city, there are some that still hark
back to the days when the people dressed as well as the cocktails were made.
One of the first things you'll notice about the **Monkey Bar** is that it still has a
hat check. The next thing you'll notice is that every available wall surface is
painted with monkeys. Located inside the Hotel Elysée in midtown Manhattan,
bar legend has it that the unusual decor was inspired by Tallulah Bankhead,
who lived for a while in the hotel with a pet monkey and a pet lion cub named
Winston Churchill. Not much has changed in the Monkey Bar since the days
when Ava Gardner, Isadora Duncan and Babe Ruth used to drink here. To add
to the bar's legendary status, Tennessee Williams actually died in the hotel
upstairs. More clubroom than bar room, the Monkey Bar also leads onto a
sumptuous Art Deco dining room decorated with an astonishingly vast wrap-
around mural painted by New York artist Ed Sorel. The mural features over
sixty legendary figures from the Jazz Age, many of whom were patrons of the
whimsical Monkey Bar.
(60 E 54th St, Manhattan, New York, NY; +1 212-753-1066;
open until 1am Mon-Sat; Elyseehotel.com)

From the grand old hotels of Fifth Avenue to the sprawling denizens of the
East Village, bars decorated with large scale and remarkable hand-painted
murals are dotted around the Metropolis, providing a charming backdrop, often
whimsical and cartoonish in character. But our favorite can be found inside the
iconic Carlyle Hotel on the Upper East Side at **Bemelmans Bar**. Every corner,
lampshade and wall space of the bar is hand painted by Ludwig Bemelman,
creator of the much loved *Madeline* children's books. The mural depicts Central
Park filled with ice skating elephants, picnicking rabbits and courting squirrels,
and took Bemelman just over a year to complete. Rather than being paid, he
asked that his family could live in the hotel for the time it took him to finish
the job. It's the only privately-commissioned work by the artist that's open to
the public. Bemelman's bar also has a nightly live three-piece jazz ensemble
centered around a grand piano. If it feels like being in a Woody Allen film, it
almost is: he plays here with his jazz band most Monday nights. Here, a touch
of old Manhattan elegance endures, but it comes at a price; there's $15 cover
charge to sit at the bar or $25 for a table from 9pm. Go for after-work early
evening cocktails and avoid the charge.
(35 E 76th St, Manhattan, New York, NY 10021; +1 212-744-1600;
open every day from 12pm; Rosewoodhotels.com)

Take yourself to the Ballet

From the classical Russian companies to flamenco troupes to a ground-breaking multi-ethnic ballet company out of Harlem, treat yourself to the opulence of the **New York City Center** theater, where tickets start at $35. The stunning Moorish Revival building dates back to 1923, originally built for a Masonic society founded in Tampa, Florida, known as the "Ancient Arabic Order of the Nobles of the Mystic Shrine." The building's cornerstone (spot it at West 56th Street) was laid by New York's Grand Master of Masons. The interiors are covered in exquisite terra cotta tilework and Moorish-style murals – beware of getting a stiff neck from gazing up at it all night. One of the first dance companies to perform regularly here was the Ballet Russe of Monte Carlo in the 1940s, and the theater was home to both the New York City Opera and Ballet until the mid-1960s. Montgomery Clift, Orson Welles, Helen Hayes, Charlton Heston and Marcel Marceau have all graced the stage of this venerable performing arts center located just around the corner from its more famous neighbor, Carnegie Hall. Having overcome numerous threats of demolition in the past century, the recently-renovated landmark also became notable for the revival of Broadway musicals such as *Show Boat*, *South Pacific* and *Oklahoma!* Whatever you have a ticket for, the magnificent theater is an attraction in its own right, and well worth getting dolled up for.
(131 W 55th St, Midtown, NY 10019; +1 212-581-1212; Nycitycenter.org)

Detox Day

Healthy living

Ya know... once in a while.

Boxing Class in an old Dive Bar

It used to be a no-frills club in Williamsburg called "The Trash Bar" and it definitely still looks like a dive with the neon lights and beat up lockers, but it's all part of the underground atmosphere of New York's coolest boxing gym, **Overthrow**. While it's a great place for newbies too, you'll be pleasantly surprised by how authentic the training is. This is not just a cardio class with a boxing theme. Varying classes involve basic technique, heavy bag work, footwork, shadow boxing as well as ring work for learning what it feels like to move and box like a real fighter. Sessions last 45 minutes with high-intensity music, and gloves are included. Book single classes for $34, 10 classes for $280 or split a private training session with a friend to get your confidence up for $60. The first Monday of every month, the studio offers a donation-based class (from $5) with proceeds benefiting Planned Parenthood. Become a gym member to hit the bag anytime you like.
(256 Grand St, Brooklyn, NY 11211; +1 718-233-3480; open every day, Overthrownyc.com)

The Best Avocado Toast & Kale Salads in the City

Despite its moniker, **The Butcher's Daughter** is in fact, a meat-free "vegetable slaughterhouse" with an airy, feminine take on an old-world butcher shop. A stool seat at this plant-based restaurant and juice bar is also one of New York's most coveted people-watching spots in Nolita. *(19 Kenmare St, Lower Manhattan; NY 10012; +1 212-219-3434; open everyday 8am-10pm; Thebutchersdaughter.com)*

Working out like a Victorian Dandy

Sal Anthony's Movement Salon is not your average gym. It's been an alleged hideaway for German WWII spies and a post-war jazz club; a university pub and an immigrant meeting hall. This establishment is owned by the restaurateur Anthony Macagnone, who began training in Martial Arts to unwind from the stress of his Italian eatery. Since 1999, his "Salon" has been serving up his meticulously curated blend of Pilates and Gyrotonic machine exercises, Yoga and spa treatments in an antique setting. With its stunning skylight, this 19th-century building is probably one of the more surreal places in the city to take a class. *(190 3rd Ave, Union Square, NY 10003; +1 212-420-7242; Open from about 7am-9pm daily)*

The best 'fake' burgers in the city

Forget best vegan burger, this is going to be one of the best burgers you've ever tasted. At **Superiority Burger** order the house burger or the "Megamouth" with frizzled onions and don't miss the burnt broccoli salad. *(430 E. 9TH St., East Village, NY 10009; +1 212-256-1192; Open daily from 11.30am-10pm)*

Recommended by Acupuncturists

Camouflaged amidst the wholesale shops, pharmacies and noodle bars of Chinatown is **Kamwo Meridian Herbs**, sworn by many to hold the ultimate cure for any ailment, but particularly stomach or gastro issues. The resident doctor will take your pulse, study your tongue and ask about your symptoms before prescribing a concoction of colorful and rare herbs from the rows of wooden compartments, weighed out on old-fashioned scales behind the counter. Take a consultation, bring your herbs home to boil and just see if you don't feel instantly better.
(211 Grand St, Chinatown, NY 10013; +1 212-966-6370; open everyday 1am-7pm; Kamwo.com)

The House of Collection, page 120

04
Cultural Flâneur

flâneur: French masculine noun [flah-NUR] — one who strolls, saunters, lounges around town, from the French verb flâner ("to stroll") — coined by poet Charles Baudelaire to describe "a person who walks the city in order to experience it".

New York too, is a city for the Baudelairian urban spectator. If it's inspiration you seek, there's no shortage of havens for the idle bohemian.

Collectors Addresses

Art, Antiques, Collectibles and Interior Design

City Relics for Sale, Saved from Demolition

Amazing places get demolished and modernized whether we like it or not. But have you ever wondered where some of their contents end up? In New York City, before the wrecking ball hits, a Harlem-based company called **The Demolition Depot** makes it their business to go in and salvage the irreplaceable pieces of a building's architectural heritage. They'll rescue everything from entire paneled rooms, fireplaces and staircases to antique door knobs and coat hooks. It's one of the most extensive architectural reclamation operations in the world, housing pieces of the Brooklyn Bridge, the Plaza Hotel, and you might even find something scavenged from a Vanderbilt estate. Whether you're interested in finding a vintage mirror for your bathroom, an old detective door for your office or an entire antique bar for your Prohibition-style drinking den, the Demolition Depot is the place to find such treasure. Start with the Harlem outpost, but consider making an appointment at their Connecticut facility, which is larger than one full city block and would take a full day to visit in its entirety.

(159 East 126th Street, Harlem, NYC; +1 212-860-1138; Mon-Sat, 10am-6pm; Demolitiondepot.com)

The Demolition Depot

Flea Markets of NYC

In just a little over a decade, **Brooklyn Flea** has become *the* go-to bazaar for New York's vintage lovers, set *en plein air* in Dumbo during the summer months; crawling down the streets under the impressive arches of the Manhattan Bridge; and under one roof in winter time at the Atlantic Center (with the added benefit of indoor restrooms). Don't miss vendors like Rascal Salvage Vintage for unusual and eclectic vintage additions to your closet and stop by Windsor Place Antiques and Spartan Antiques if you're looking for that perfect mid-century piece for the living room. The market is run by the same founders of the largest weekly open-air food market in America, **Smorgasburg** (pg 91) which means they've sprinkled tastes of their giant food bazaar into the flea market as well. With hundreds of vendors to meet and treasures to scour, you'll need your fuel. Have cash on hand to increase your chances of striking a good bargain. (*April-Oct at Dumbo: Archway under Manhattan Bridge, 58-80 Pearl St, Brooklyn, NY 11201; Sat-Sun 11am-5pm/ Nov-March at the Atlantic Center. 625 Atlantic Ave across from Barclays; Sat 11am-8pm, Sun 11am-5pm; Brooklynflea.com; Instagram: @bkflea*)

Meanwhile, over in Manhattan, the **Grand Bazaar** is the oldest and largest market currently operating in New York City. You'll find all sorts of vendors here selling antique cameras, Art Deco commodes, crates of tiny dolls hands, vintage kimonos, artisanal accessories and more. Look out for our favourite New York City diggers, Scott and Belle, selling incredible historical treasures they've excavated themselves straight from the ground in New York City (find their story on pg 260). This indoor and outdoor market, previously known as GreenFlea Market, started as a yard sale in 1982, organised by a group of parents trying to raise funds for their children's schools. Still today, it's the only market that donates 100% of its profits and it's open every Sunday throughout the year in the same location. (*100 West 77th St., Upper West Side, NY 10024; 10am-5.30pm; Grandbazaarnyc.org*)

Where to Shop for someone with Impeccable Taste

To achieve an elegant 19th-century Parisian flea market aesthetic at home (without actually flying to Paris), the **John Derian Company** should be your bohemian chic one-stop shop. The American decoupage artist has grown his little empire of curious home goods for over two decades with beautiful *objets d'art*, tableware, stationery, lighting, furniture and bedding. It's a dream for gift shopping, but you'll most certainly leave with something to add to your own cabinet of curiosities.

(6 E 2nd St, East Village, NY 10003 +1 212-677-3917 or 18 Christopher St, West Village, NY 10014; +1 212-677-8402; both open Tues-Sun 11am-7pm; Johnderian.com)

A Library of Buttons

Spot the giant gold button hanging above the street, which means you've arrived at the world's most charming button shop, **Tender Buttons**, the kind of place you might find Mary Poppins doing her morning errands. As rare as an umbrella shop these days, it's been on the East Side for over 50 years; the name borrowed from a work by Gertrude Stein. Sandwiched in between two competing shoe repair shops on the ground floor of an elegant brick townhouse, the shopfront is appropriately *as cute as a button*. In 1964, the late Diana Epstein purchased a large collection of antique buttons from an eccentric dealer she found and the business was born. Inside, the walls are covered in rare, precious and antique buttons from 18th-century French enamels to Art Nouveau silver to plastic kitsch from the 1940s. Behind each display of buttons is a drawer bursting with more buttons. Whether you're looking to transform an old coat, or searching for the finishing touch to a new jewelry project, Tender Buttons is a veritable jewel box of inspiration. *(143 E 62nd St, Upper East Side, NY 10065; +1 212-758-7004; Mon-Sat 10.30am-6pm; Tenderbuttons-nyc.com)*

Tender Buttons

A Liveable Cabinet of Curiosities

Paige Stevenson doesn't quite live in the same world as the rest of us. "People talk a lot about what it means to make art," she told us, "I just think, why not live it?" Hence Stevenson's aptly named apartment, **The House of Collection** (pictured on pg 114). In a city where space is the ultimate luxury, she's carved out 2,000 square feet for a living, breathing cabinet of curiosities that feels like Williamsburg's own Narnia. To make a home like this, it helps to have had an eccentric upbringing: Stevenson grew up in the 1970s, inside a tepee on a commune in California, then on a goat farm and later in a Victorian house in San Francisco which her father and stepmother shared with a troop of drag performers. In the mid-1980s, she left her nomadic life behind and settled in New York City to attend Columbia University, and never left. Her home feels like a portal into the past and present of her adventurous life, as well as a place where time stands still. There's the "Conservatory," (a dangerously cozy, pioneer-meets-Victorian-granny reading nook), a mermaid bathroom, as well as a kind of indoor jungle. And all of it is built out of antiques, mementos, and oddities. "I don't see it as a collection of objects," says Stevenson, "It's really a collection of people. Of stories."

(The House of Collection is available to rent for private events, shoots, and the like by emailing HouseofCollection@gmail.com or you can attend an organized home tour with the New York Adventure Club - Nyadventureclub.com)

Poster Paradise

Quite possibly the world's largest collection of vintage and rare posters is right here in New York. **Philip Williams Posters** (aka The Poster Musuem) has been around since 1973, and his collection stands at over an incredible half a million fabulous old artworks, many of which can be seen in his Tribeca store covering the walls and stacked enticingly on long tables. Part museum (where everything is for sale) and part marvelous place just to spend an afternoon exploring, it should be at the top of your list for finding that unique, beautiful piece of artwork for your apartment. Most date to the early 20th century, the golden age of poster art, featuring everything from travel to beverages to forgotten magicians, many of which you're likely to have never seen before.

(122 Chambers Street, New York, NY, 10007; +1 212-513-0313; Mon-Sat 10am-7pm, closed Sundays; Postermuseum.com)

Not just for the Distinguished Coin Connoisseur

Did you know Freddie Mercury is on the Zanzibar 500 rupee banknote? You needn't be a coin collector to be pleasantly surprised by the **American Numismatic Society**, the largest collection of coins, paper money and medals in the US. You use money everyday, but how much do you really know about it? *(75 Varick Street, 11th, Floor, New York, NY, 10013; +1 212-571-4470; Numismatics.org)*

The Largest Collection of Tiffany Glass is hiding in a Warehouse in Queens

Whose job is it to safeguard one of the most hated designs in decorative history? In the case of the Tiffany lamp, it fell to a New York City orthodontist and immigrant from Austria who happened to be furniture shopping in Greenwich Village in 1935 when his wife spotted a "strange, old-fashioned lamp." Dr. Egon Neustadt and his wife Hildegard didn't know it then, but by acquiring that first lamp, they were about to build the world's largest collection of Tiffany glass, the **Neustadt Collection**, which would become the only archive and existing association dedicated to the preservation, study and revival an under-appreciated all-American treasure.

You can seek out that archive, located on a quiet old industrial block in Long Island City, Queens. You might expect the collection to be under the care of an eccentric bohemian hoarder with 15 cats, but curator Lindsy R. Parrott is more like a cross between a glamorous Manhattan art gallerist and a passionate archeologist. She leads the bi-monthly visits to this little-known archive, which recently opened its doors to the public. Here is where you get to learn about all the forgotten and fascinating history of Tiffany glass that never occurred to you every time you walked into an antique junk shop and lusted over a dusty glass lamp; glowing with its warm, mysterious colors. The second guardian of the collection is Susan Tomlin, a quiet but brilliant woman, who is one of the few people in the world who knows how to perfectly restore and recreate an authentic Tiffany glass lamp. Because of course, not all "Tiffany" lamps are really Tiffany lamps.

Inspired by the Art Nouveau artisans he'd seen in Paris, Louis C. Tiffany, heir to the luxury jewelry and silver company, Tiffany & Company, developed his own soldering technique, which enabled a level of detail previously unseen in glassmaking. His signature lamps and mosaics became the marker of refined taste, wealth and the toast of Gilded Age high society. He won numerous design awards and critics made him one of the most celebrated artists of his time. There was a true artistry to the laborious process of combining the colors, textures, patterns, and opacities that made it uniquely Tiffany. He hired the finest artisans and chose what was then the rural setting of Corona, Queens to build a factory that would safeguard his secret glass formulas. It wasn't long before cheap imitations became big business. And what happens when you have too much of a good thing? It goes out of style, real quick.

By the 1930s, when Dr. Neustadt and his wife had their first encounter with a Tiffany lamp in a second-hand store, the decorative item had been consigned to oblivion like a 90's lava lamp. After nearly 40 years in business, Tiffany Studios shuttered in 1933 and closed its factory in Queens, located less than 2 miles from where the current archive lives today. The world had become so sick of seeing Tiffany lamps, they threw them in dumpsters and left them out on sidewalks. Vienna-born Egon Neustadt was the earliest collector of Tiffany

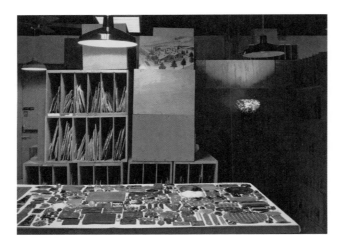

lamps after their decline, purchasing his first just one year after the company went bankrupt. Seeing ahead of the curve, he single-handedly initiated its eventual recognition as an iconic object of American design, classifying the different types of lamps and giving them serious collectible credibility. By the time of Dr. Neustadt's death in 1984, his Manhattan apartment was a veritable Aladdin's cave of Tiffany lamps and windows.

Today, the archive holds over a quarter of a million examples of Tiffany glass, from large uncut sheets that were salvaged straight from the old factory before its closure, to tiny shards unearthed in 2013 during the construction of a new school on the site of Tiffany's former studios (the glass was donated to the collection and the school was named The Tiffany School). It's impossible to know how many real examples exist in private collections around the world and only the keen eye of a specialist like Lindsy or Susan can tell a good fake from an original. Even if a lamp is marked 'Tiffany Studios', this is no guarantee of originality. The most valuable Tiffany lamp ever sold, "The Pink Lotus" went for $2.8 million at a Christie's auction in 1998. You never know where you might find a forgotten Tiffany treasure, so you'd better get yourself down to the Neustadt Collection in Queens and train your bargain-hunting eye.
(5-26 46th Avenue, Long Island City, NY 11101; +1 718-361-8489; Theneustadt.org/visit)

The Last Remnant of Radio Row

One of New York's great lost districts was known as Radio Row. It centered around Cortlandt Street downtown and was comprised of several blocks dedicated to the selling of radios and electronics. Often described as a 'tinkers paradise', Radio Row was demolished in 1966 to make room for the World Trade Center and is all but forgotten today. But up in the Bronx, one last remnant of the golden age of wireless can still be found. After Radio Row was torn down, **Leeds Radio**, originally opened in 1923, lived on for many years in Williamsburg, before recently decamping to the Bronx. Possibly the last place to track down elusive 1940s vacuum tubes, or original Bakelite tuning knobs to repair a beloved vintage radio, this place is an engineer's paradise. To give you an idea of what's there, the owner, Richard Matthews, also runs an Etsy shop stocking many hard-to-find parts (Etsy.com/shop/LeedsRadio). If you want to visit his collection in person, you'd do well to make an appointment first.

(175 Walnut Avenue, Bronx, NY, 10454; +1 718-963-1764; Leedsradio.com)

A Brooklyn Garage Hiding an Incredible Collection of Classic Cars

When you think of serious classic car collections, you might picture vast, well-lit storage facilities on fancy country estates. You don't expect something that resembles a mechanic shop hidden behind unmarked metal shutters in industrial Brooklyn. But that's what makes **Lenny's Garage** so special. For one, he doesn't even like driving – how powerful a car can be isn't what makes him tick. It's the design. Since 1967, Leonard Shiller acquired over 50 unique beauties that he maintains himself, from a 1947 International Soda Truck to a pink 1957 Cadillac convertible. His dusty 12,000 sq. foot garage space on the border of Park Slope and Gowanus rarely opens up to the public, but he's been known to give tours to local schools in Brooklyn and do special visits for neighborhood fundraising. If you happen to walk by, see Lenny opening up his shutters and introduce yourself in the right way, he's a nice enough guy that he might just let you take a look around. Lenny is also President of the Antique Automobile Association of Brooklyn Inc. (Clubs.hemmings.com/brooklyncarclub) which meets 10 times a year and sends out regular newsletters.

(Lenny's Garage, 304 Douglass St, Brooklyn, NY 11217)

Underrated Museums

How to avoid the crowds

They might have smaller advertising budgets than the major museums, but they've got just as much to share...

A Misfit Museum Like No Other

If ever there was a joint for NY's top-notch weirdos and their stuff to congregate, it'd be Williamsburg's **City Reliquary Museum**. Or, as Assistant Director Molly Cox calls it, "The Museum of Undeclared Monuments." For 15 years, the nonprofit has evolved a space for local oddball relics of all shapes and sizes, from a lightbulb that once lit the Statue of Liberty's torch, to a taxidermied alligator found in an Uptown sewer in 1935. "It's a *for-the-community, by-the-community* place," says Molly, "There's so much history packed into this space, and finding the story behind an otherwise ordinary object is half the fun." There's a small back room with rotating exhibits and a quirky backyard that occasionally hosts events. It may not be the Met, but the City Reliquary is the guardian of something a whole lot more personal when it comes to New York – and in that way, a whole lot more precious. Admission is $5-$7.
(370 Metropolitan Ave, Brooklyn, NY 11211; +1 718-782-4842; Thurs-Sun 12pm-6pm)

City Reliquary Museum

How Pianos Built a Forgotten Utopian Village in Queens

Almost entirely still handmade and assembled in New York after 160 years, Steinway pianos are known the world over. Lesser known is the fact that the company shaped the history of Queens when they created a utopian village out of the marshlands we now call Astoria. Walking into the **Steinway & Sons Factory**, where decade-old machines produce 1000 instruments a year, the first thing that hits you is the smell of sawdust; then you'll hear distant sounds of sanding, delicate hammering and wood-sawing. Still today, the secret techniques used to make a Steinway are passed down in the age-old tradition: from master craftsman to apprentice, generation after generation. Each stage of making the piano has the creator's name written on it. There's a story about an old Steinway that was brought to Astoria for renovation and taken apart, only for one of the craftsmen to see his grandfather's name etched on the inside of the piano.

Steinway Street Metro

© Lucius Kwok

Producing some of the world's finest pianos is just part of the Steinway story, and perhaps the greatest contribution the family made to the city of New York was the development of an entirely new part of Queens. In the 1870s, William Steinway, trudged through the marshlands in his waders in what is now Astoria, charting out a 400-acre site. It was here that Steinway's greatest vision was realized. Steinway Village wasn't a 'company town', but an idyllic, thoroughly modern and pleasant place for his employees to live and work. In designing the village, the Steinways sought to provide an escape from what they saw as an oppressive Manhattan. Walking around the neighborhood surrounding the factory today, many traces of this utopian village can still be found. Steinway Street runs through the district, where you can still see the rows of brick homes, designed as "country homes with city comforts." The Steinway

Reformed Church is still thriving today on 41st street, as are the schools, post office building and the Steinway Free library (now called the Queensboro Public Library), which started with books taken from William Steinway's own bookcases.

The piano company even built their own transportation system to take employees to and from work. The Steinway Trolley Line proved so successful and profitable that other neighborhoods wanted the company to build them their own trolley systems. Soon, much of Queens was connected together using the Steinway's trolley lines. William Steinway also funded the building of a tunnel underneath the East River that's still in use by the MTA subway today. Next time you ride the 7 train into Manhattan from Queens, remember that you are going through a tunnel built by the sale of pianos.

Lastly, the Steinways built their own pleasure beach and resort for employees, known as North Beach. It featured an amusement park lit by electric lights, including a Ferris wheel, a German beer hall and swimming pool along a Boardwalk that rivaled Coney Island. It was razed in 1929 to become an airfield, and all traces of the resort were buried for good a few years later underneath LaGuardia Airport.

Steinway Factory,
courtesy of Steinway & Sons

Many of the craftsmen at Steinway & Sons today have been there for decades and to discover their workshops is to step back in time to an era when the world's finest furniture was carved by hand. The Steinway Factory is open for visits, giving a rare opportunity to see the unique craftsmanship that goes into making one of their pianos and to discover the little-known history of a forgotten utopian village.

(Steinway & Sons, One Steinway Place, Astoria, Queens, NY 11105; +1 800-783-4692; steinway.com/about/factory-tour)

One Man's Trash...

Nelson Molina has been collecting since he was a child. Growing up in the projects of Harlem, he salvaged discarded toys and restored them for his siblings. His instinct for 'picking' became sharper when he took a job as a sanitation worker for the city and started rescuing objects that he saw value in. These rejected items would eventually grow into a collection of over 40,000 forgotten, abandoned and ignored objects that now comprise **The Treasures in the Trash Museum**. On the second floor of a garage in East Harlem, New York's unwanted treasure is categorized by size, material, and function, and you won't believe what some people will throw in the trash. Molina's co-workers in the Sanitation Department have helped the collection become what it is today, with enough paintings to fill another museum, more musical instruments than a recording studio could ever need, rows of typewriters, walls of toys, cameras, jewelry, taxidermy, you name it – this is not a museum of trash, it's a museum of *everything,* in bulk. Despite the name it's been given, the "museum" is not open to the public with regular hours. The collection is housed in a working sanitation building, and while the employees get to hang out there whenever they like, if you'd like to see this New York Aladdin's cave, you need to request access or find out when the next tour is happening by emailing tours@dsny.nyc.gov. *(By appointment only, MANEAST 11 Garage, East 99th St between 1st and 2nd Avenue, East Harlem, NY 10029)*

Digging for Treasure where the New York World's Fair Lives On

For the hopeless mid-century nostalgic, the **Queens Museum** and the surrounding park are a must. When compared to vintage postcards of shiny futuristic pavilions and crowds of happy tourists buzzing around the New York World's Fairs in 1939 and 1964, the site today may seem a little bleak, but stick with us. Modernist structures straight out of the Jetsons cartoons still tower over the grounds like dystopian ruins that once invited visitors to take a look at the "world of tomorrow" in the aftermath of the Great Depression. This is where television was introduced to the mass public, where Albert Einstein gave a speech about cosmic rays and Walt Disney exerted huge influence over the 1964 exposition. Originally built in 1939 for the second most expensive American world's fair of all time, the fairground covered 1200 acres of a former ash dump that F. Scott Fitzgerald once called "a valley of ashes" in *The Great Gatsby.* It was transformed into a veritable mini city from the future that could take two weeks to visit in its entirety. A total of 95 million people attended both world fairs, but that didn't save them from being financial disasters. Only a few buildings from the futuristic extravaganza were deemed worthy of keeping around after it was all over. In the 1970s, the New York pavilion was converted into a permanent museum (the Queens Museum) which now houses a collection of more than 10,000 items of World's Fair memorabilia, from vintage tourist souvenirs to original exhibition artifacts that were on display. The crown jewel is perhaps the 9,335 sq. ft. model of the entire city left over from the 1964 fair that has since been restored and updated. They even have binoculars set up so you can identify your favorite haunts amongst the 895,000 tiny buildings (and counting) and 100 bridges while little planes fly above your head to and from the local airports. An unexpected treat for Tiffany glass lovers awaits too, with a large portion of the Neustadt collection on display (the full archive is hiding in a warehouse in Long Island City (see pg 121). Head outside into the park and you can't miss the empty and decaying New York State Pavilion built in '64, once equipped with elevators that whisked visitors into the sky. In the 1997 film *Men in Black*, the structure's circular observation decks made a cameo as extraterrestrial landing pads for flying saucers. On the ground beneath the steel structure are the cracked and crumbling remains of a giant 130-foot-by-166-foot terrazzo road map commissioned by Texaco. Funding has been secured to restore the site in the coming years (fingers crossed). Nearby, find the two time capsules sites which contain writings by Albert Einstein, scientific instruments of the atomic age and other everyday materials, not to be dug up for 5000 years.

But did you hear about the legend of the underground home buried in the park? At the height of nuclear paranoia, the 1964 fair exhibited a subterranean luxury fallout shelter, which some urban historians believe is still there; a Cold War-era time capsule home. After the fair closed, to avoid demolition costs, the theory is that organizers just trucked in some topsoil and left it to be buried underground. Despite numerous attempts to find it, the mystery remains unsolved. If you're up for a treasure hunt and can get ahold of vintage map of the exhibit, here's a hint: *Block 50, Lot 5, Underground World Home. (New York City Building, Queens, NY 11368; +1 718-592-9700; Wed-Sun 11am-5pm; Queensmuseum.org)*

The New York State Pavilion
at the 1964 World's Fair
© Joe Haupt

Lovers of History, and New York, Start Here

The city's oldest museum is probably one of its most overlooked. Hidden away behind a rather uninviting Beaux-Arts building outside Central Park, the **New York Historical Society** has an amazing collection of historical artifacts to tell America's story, with New York City being at the heart of it. But our favourite part? It's also home to one of the oldest reading rooms in the country. Half museum, half library, scholars, novelists and the merely curious are welcome to discover one of the most important research facilities in the country, holding millions of unique and priceless books and manuscripts. Of particular interest to us was the sizeable collection of New York City guidebooks dating back to the early 19th century. The society's mission is and always has been to collect as many documents and ephemera, from momentous occasions to everyday happenings, as possible so that we're not just spinning myths for future generations. In the 1990s, New York's first museum was on the verge of bankruptcy after more than 200 years and the institution was forced to auction off old master paintings to pay the utility bills. The city had nearly lost its most precious society when it was rescued by emergency grants and fundraising which made its much-needed 21st-century renovation possible.

Only a small portion of the museum's collection is on display at any one time, but there are periodical behind-the-scenes visits to the archives organized by the New York Adventure Club *(Nyadventureclub.com)*. Always hosting interesting exhibits, give this one a chance next time you're wondering which museum you should visit this weekend. They've got a camp bed used by George Washington, a stunning collection of Tiffany lamps and an entire basement dedicated to making history relatable and interactive for children. *(170 Central Park West, New York, NY 10024; Tues-Thurs 10am-6pm, Fri 10am-9pm, Sat 10am-6pm, Sun 10am-5pm, closed Mon; Nyhistory.org)*

But don't stop there. Continue schooling yourself across the park at another equally underrated museum. If you want to be able to spew interesting anecdotes about the past, present and future of NYC like a true New Yorker, the **Museum of the City of New York** tells its incredible story through a terrific archive of everyday historical items, clothing, possessions, photographs and documents. Often overshadowed by the other giant institutions on museum mile, skip the crowds at the Met and the Guggenheim and find out what makes New York the city it is. *(1220 5th Ave & 103rd Street, New York, NY 10029; Open daily 10am-6pm; Mcny.org)*

The Skyscrapers Explained

It's hard not to be impressed by the size of the skyscrapers in New York, and whether you're an architecture fan or just fascinated by how on earth these things got so damn high, then head to a little-known museum that helps explain how these giants came to exist. **The Skyscraper Museum** might be small in size but is full of information and neat design models that show the evolution of the NYC skyline. If you have an hour to kill around Battery Park, you'll be glad you knew it was there.

(39 Battery Pl, Battery Park, New York, NY 10280; +1 212-968-1961; Wed-Sun 12pm-6pm; Skyscraper.org)

New York City architects wearing the buildings they designed at the 1931 Beaux Arts ball.
Courtesy of the Office for Metropolitan History.

 Also see: the house museums in "Snooping around other people's houses", pg 135, the Tenement Museum pg 321, New York Transit Museum pg 246, the KGB Spy museum pg 333, Museum of the American Gangster pg 70, and some excellent family-friendly museums in "The Kids are Coming too", pg 224.

History Hiding Behind the Facade

Who knows what overlooked treasures you might uncover if you just wander inside...

If those Art Deco Walls Could Talk

Down in TriBeCa is the former headquarters of the **AT&T Long Distance Building**, where once upon a time, if you needed to place an international phone call, you would have made it in this building. Today, a silent monument to a bygone era of communication, just imagine how this stunning Art Deco lobby must have buzzed with activity as the center of international communication in Manhattan, home to 2,200 long distance lines. But the walls are still talking. In 1932, a talented female artist, Hildreth Meière, was commissioned to create a vast and stunning mosaic mural she named "Continents Linked by Telephone and Wireless". Just walk in and give a nod to the lobby attendant (who usually has some interesting anecdotes to share) as you ogle the Jazz Age mosaics showing continents linked by golden telephone strands. It's one of the very few interior landmarks in Lower Manhattan that welcome casual visitors wandering home from dinner out in trendy TriBeCa.

(32 Avenue of the Americas, New York, NY, 11013)

AT&T Long Distance Building

Thomas Edison's Pharmacy

When you're in need of a magic cure, step into Greenwich Village's **C.O. Bigelow's**, America's oldest apothecary, which has remained relatively unchanged since the days when customers could fill their opium prescriptions or purchase a jar of leeches. Bigelow's has provided their own range of "healing therapeutic preparations" since 1838 for the likes of Mark Twain (they still have records of his charge account) and Eleanor Roosevelt. Legend has it that when Thomas Edison burnt his fingers testing his light bulb, it was to Bigelow's, in hurried search of a soothing balm, he went. This family-owned living museum still stocks their own tried and tested elixirs today, housed in a sumptuous old store with a storefront mosaic, gilded gothic-style gas chandeliers, marble pillars, scrolling library ladders and 19th-century oak cases.
(414 Avenue of the Americas, New York, NY, 10011; +1 212-533-2700; Bigelowchemists.com)

Saving the 1920s Movie Palaces

When **Kings Theater** was built in 1929, talking pictures were the latest and greatest in modern entertainment. Nearly 50 years later, the Brooklyn movie palace screened its last film, *Bruce Lee: The Man, The Myth*. After the final curtain, its lavish Jazz Age interiors, almost entirely intact in 1977, began a slow and steady deterioration in the decades that followed. One of the five historic Loew's "wonder theatres" was on the brink of collapse when a $95 million dollar renovation project saved Kings at the 11th hour. The original lobby furniture, which had been safely stored at the expense of the theater's old manager for over 40 years, was reinstalled, while the severely decayed 1920s auditorium was entirely refurbished and restored to its original state. Diana Ross was the headlining act for the grand reopening in 2015. Kings Theatre has reclaimed its title as one of the most exquisite theatres in the nation, playing host to a diverse cultural program from a hip hop interpretation of the Nutcracker ballet to a Beach Boys reunion. Join one of the regular historic tours of the theatre before taking your seat for a truly ornate spectacle. Dine out in the area at the Sycamore Bar & Flower Shop, see pg 172, 190.
(1027 Flatbush Ave, Brooklyn, NY 11226; Kingstheatre.com)

The first of the five "Wonder Theaters" built in New York by Loews during the heyday of early motion pictures was the **Valencia Theatre** in Queens, the glittering jewel in the crown. Architect John Eberson designed something truly breathtaking; from the ornate facade that resembles a centuries-old Spanish church, to the interior; opulent and lavishly decorated in gold, teal and crimson with a painted night sky out of the Arabian Nights soaring above the auditorium seats. The Valencia is closer in atmosphere and style to a cathedral than a modern multiplex, so it is perhaps appropriate that after the last picture was

shown here in 1977 following a steady decline, it was handed over to Tabernacle of Prayer For All People church for restoration. The Tabernacle is a working, thriving community church, with high energy services on Sundays at 11.30am, which means you can still wander in and enjoy the greatest cinema of them all.
(165-11 Jamaica Avenue, Queens, NY, 11432; +1 718-657-4210)

Kings Theater
© Moucheraud

The Secret Archives of Carnegie Hall

Ever heard that Carnegie Hall joke? A pedestrian on 57th Street sees a musician getting out of a cab and asks, "how do you get to Carnegie Hall?" To which the artist wearily replies, "Practice!" Is there any music venue as famous as the illustrious, storied concert hall on 7th Avenue and 56th? Built with beautiful red brick as a gift to the city from steel millionaire, Andrew Carnegie, the Hall has hosted performances by the world's greatest artists, from Tchaikovsky through to George Gershwin to the Beatles. It is also home to one of the most astonishing archives in New York. From conductors' batons and concert programmes to a handwritten score by Beethoven, the collection tells the story of over 45,000 events that have taken place here since 1891. Faithfully overseen by long-time employee Gino Francesconi, many items revolve through the Rose Museum inside Carnegie Hall, where you can see such treasures as Benny Goodman's clarinet. But the museum displays just a fragment of the wonderful collection. The **Carnegie Hall Archives** are available to researchers upon request.
(881 7th Avenue, Midtown, NY, 10019; +1 212-247-7800; Carnegiehall.org has details about upcoming events, as well as tours. If you're interested in the archives, they are open by advance request, Mon-Fri 10am-5pm, call +1 212-903-9629)

The Disappearing Street where they made American Music History
Walk down West 28th Street between 5th and 6th Avenues today, and you'll
find mostly low-grade retail stores selling mobile phone accessories, hair
extensions, wholesale import-exporters and the like. The smaller, older
buildings are dwarfed by a constant construction of modern day high rise
apartments and hotels. It is hard to imagine, but just over a century ago, this
small street was once the beating heart of the American music industry. Known
the world over as the legendary **Tin Pan Alley**, music publishers and composers
wrote some of the most famous tunes in the American songbook here. Theater
impresarios, vaudeville acts and film producers would flock to Tin Pan Alley,
trying to find the next hit song for their new production. Some of the greatest
names in American musical history once worked here, amongst them Irving
Berlin, George & Ira Gershwin, Hoagy Carmichael, Scott Joplin, Johnny Mercer
and Oscar Hammerstein II. The music publishers would hire piano players,
known as 'song pluggers' to perform their songs in the storefronts. Popular
legend has it that the name Tin Pan Alley came from the non-stop, cacophonous
din coming from the open windows.

Today, Tin Pan Alley has no historic landmark status, and the increasingly
dilapidated buildings are in danger of being demolished and lost for good.
Starting on the corner of 5th Avenue and West 28th streets towards 6th Avenue,
keep an eye out for the older 3-4 story buildings, which are original to the
heyday of Tin Pan Alley. It is well worth going in the shops and up the stoop
stairs. You'll often find a small notice on the wall, such as at No.45, saying this is
where George Gershwin used to work. *(5th Avenue & West 28th, Koreatown, NY)*

Snooping Around Other People's Houses

When homes become museums

Manhattan's Oldest (and Haunted) Home

Perched atop one of Manhattan's highest hills in Washington Heights, the beautiful **Morris-Jumel Mansion** was originally built as a grand summer villa for a British colonel, then seized as a headquarters for George Washington during the Revolutionary War, when it hosted distinguished dinner guests such as Alexander Hamilton and Thomas Jefferson. But the history of the oldest home in Manhattan turns macabre when it comes to Mistress Eliza Jumel, an American socialite born into poverty, who came to live at the mansion with the wealthy French husband she was later accused of murdering. The grand and colorful matriarch who claimed to be a friend of Josephine Bonaparte was soon remarried in the mansion's front parlor, this time to the controversial ex-Vice President Aaron Burr, infamous for murdering Alexander Hamilton in a duel. Just four months later, their divorce was finalized on the day of Burr's death. For her divorce lawyer, she had chosen none other than Alexander Hamilton Jr.

Eliza became an eccentric recluse and died in the house at the age of 90. For over a hundred years, the Morris-Jumel Mansion has been open as a museum where she is said to still haunt the corridors. You can sign up for paranormal investigations, attend concerts and film screenings, or just poke around one of New York's most beguiling old homes. Afterward, just on the doorstep is one of Manhattan's most photogenic streets, Sylvan Terrace (see pg 46) which has remained virtually unchanged since the 1800s. *(65 Jumel Terrace, New York, NY, 10032, +1 212-923-8008; Morrisjumel.org)*

Inside the World of a Victorian Feminist Photographer

Alice Austen did everything a Victorian woman shouldn't. She smoked, dressed up like a man, and took to the NY streets to photograph the people who gave it heart and soul: the janitors, organ grinders and fishmongers; the street sweepers, sailors, and shoestring peddlers. She lived with a kind of ferocious joy and fell deeply in love with a woman who would become her muse in life, love and photography for over 50 years. With some 8,000 images to her name, it's remarkable that Austen is only just receiving the recognition she deserves as both a pioneer of documentary photography and a remarkable figure in the LGBTQ community. Luckily, her legacy is tended to at **The Alice Austen House**, the quaint 17th-century farmhouse by the water she called home and now operates as a small museum. Pack a picnic lunch and visit this gem in the spring, when the vines start to crawl across the white porch. It's also worth noting that you can rent the museum's al fresco space with sweeping views from the Statue of Liberty to Coney Island for an intimate garden party or wedding reception. *(2 Hylan Blvd, Staten Island, NY 10305; +1 718-816-4506; Tues-Fri 1pm-5pm, Sat-Sun 11am-5pm; Learn about its many upcoming events at Aliceausten.org/events)*

A Minimalist Dream Home

Wander the multi-floor industrial loft of the late, great king of American minimalism at the **Donald Judd House**, where the artist lived and worked from the 1960s until his death in 1994. The Spartan layout is very much as he left it in the heart of Soho. Judd bought the entire 1870 cast-iron building in 1968 and you can whizz through his world in about 90-minutes, checking out his kitchenwares, his perfectly bare bedroom, and of course, his art collection. Keep an eye out for pieces by not only Judd but his friends and mentors. Marcel Duchamp's shovel is hanging on the wall. Book in advance online. *(101 Spring St, Soho, NY 10012; + 1 212 219-2747; Juddfoundation.org/visit)*

Flâneur of the Frick Mansion

Did you know that the library reading room at the **Frick Collection** is open for public use? It's a gem too, and no appointments necessary, just enter through the back of the museum, bring a photo ID and they'll make you a library card.

Winter Courtyard at the Frick

Don't forget there's also a Louvre-worthy dose of 18th-century portraits in the building, and a winter garden court where you could sit for hours listening to the water trickling from the fountain, sketching, people watching and feeling like you're at Paris' *Petit Palais*. The Frick Collection has been one of the nation's grandest little museums since 1930. Mr. Henry Clay Frick was one of 20th-century New York's biggest business tycoons, with union-busting tendencies that gave him the tabloid moniker of "Manhattan's Most Hated Man" at the peak of his success. In an attempt to leave behind a legacy that was a little less scathing, he began collecting world-class paintings and decorative art pieces at his lavish home in the hopes of turning it into a museum after his passing. Today, his awe-inspiring abode is like a step back in time to the Gilded Age. Enjoy a room full of Fragonard, several Vermeers and Rembrandt in complete calm and serenity (no children under 10 allowed). First Fridays of the month are free, and on Wednesdays, there's a pay-what-you-wish window from 2pm-5pm. *(1 E 70th St, New York, NY 10021; +1 646-248-5547; Tue-Sat 10am-6pm, Sun 11am-5pm; Library open Mon-Fri 10am-5pm, Sat 10am-2pm; Full opening hours on Frick.org)*

The Kitschiest, Glitziest House in New York

From the dozens of cherubs balancing gold pots in the front garden to the life-sized camel on the rooftop and the Cinderella carriage by the back door, you'll be hard pressed to find a house as delightfully gaudy as the **Garabedian House** in the Bronx. The candy pink suburban home is a kitschy spectacle of Liberace meets David Lynch surrealism, crammed with mannequins, and ablaze with lights all year round. But it's after Thanksgiving that the real magic begins, when the Christmas lights turn on and the rest of the Garabedian family mannequins come out, running a surreal spectrum of the nativity scene starring everyone from Michael Jackson to Miss Universe playing Cinderella in a 1980s ball gown. No one quite knows why the Garabedian family started decorating their front lawn in such a manner, but it swiftly became a local holiday tradition to go and gawk at it each year. Forget the lighting of the Christmas tree at the Rockefeller Center – even Mariah Carey shot parts of her music video for "All I Want for Christmas" in front of the Garabedian house. You can stop by 24 hours a day, but the house is at its most spectacular after Thanksgiving, and at night. The house is about a 15-20 minute walk from the Pelham Parkway subway stop on the 5 train. Occasionally you can catch glimpses of the Garabedian family quietly pottering around inside their home, seemingly unbothered by the crowds gathered outside to stare at the majestic spectacle they've created. *(1605 Pelham Parkway North, Bronx, 10469)*

A Real-Life "Miss Havisham" Time Capsule

Seekers of 19th Century New York should head to straight to the **Merchant's House Museum**, the only place in the city where you can discover a townhouse of the era that's been perfectly preserved both inside and out. This was home to wealthy merchant Seabury Tredwell, but most notably, to his youngest daughter Gertrude, who was embroiled in a forbidden *Romeo & Juliet* love affair of sorts with a young Catholic man who lived nearby. Her Episcopalian father disapproved of the romance and she never found true love again. Gertrude died in the upstairs bedroom at the age of 93, having never married. She'd been living alone at the house for over two decades, becoming more eccentric and reclusive as the city changed around her and the Great Depression took its toll on the neighbourhood. The late Federal-style brick house, filled with the family's original possessions, furniture and decor, became a museum just three years after Gertrude's death in 1936. It was deservedly one of the first buildings in New York to be designated with landmark status. Gertrude is said to still be watching over the home. *(29 East 4th Street, New York, NY, 10003; +1 212-777-1089; Thurs 12pm-8pm, Fri-Mon 12pm-5pm. Particularly recommended are the Candlelight Ghost Tours, check the website for further details; Merchantshouse.org)*

Unexpected Art Galleries

The Hidden Room of Earth

On an island where the average price of real estate is over $1,700 per square foot, 250 cubic yards of pure soil has been occupying a 3,600 square foot loft in Soho since 1977. The pampered pile of earth (all 250 cubic yards of it) is a permanent interior sculpture by artist Walter de Maria, who never actually gave an explanation for the work. It was only supposed to last for three months, but the exhibit has now surpassed 40 years of existence, publicly accessible, five days a week, for free. Walter de Maria died in 2013, but the Dia Foundation has vowed to keep the **Earth Room** around forever if it can, using heavy duty rakes to keep things in order. Visitors can buzz themselves in and walk up to the second floor to view the art but no touching. Instagrammers are also kept at bay with a no photography rule. Just be at one with the earth ... or something like that. *(Ring buzzer 2B, Second Floor, 141 Wooster St, Soho, NY; Wed-Sun 12-6pm, closed for 30 minutes at 3pm; Diaart.org)*

The Asylum That Gave Lou Reed Electroshock Therapy Is Also an Unforgettable Art Museum

Creedmoor is the largest live-in mental asylum of its kind in New York, as well as its most infamous; it's where the American singer-songwriter Woody Guthrie died, and where Lou Reed went through electroshock therapy. At its peak in the 1950s, it housed 7,000 patients. By the 1980s, it was literally killing them. Dr. Janos Marton dove head-first into that hell, combatting it with the creation of his **Living Museum**. Founded in 1983, the museum is an active studio space for patients to sculpt, sew and paint their stories. It's also welcoming of anyone curious enough to enter Creedmoor's labyrinth, and find its entry at building #75. Just look for the door plastered in faces. Inside, the senses go into overdrive. Vintage lamps light up row after row of brightly colored workstations, while painted pathways and arrows guide you through an eternally green jungle room, a reading nook with endless copies of National Geographic, and corridors wallpapered with poetry. There's no corner that isn't for art. A lot of it is beautiful, a lot of it is scary, but none of it is boring. This is a place where everyone is an artist before they're a patient, which isn't to say Dr. Marton doesn't recognize the importance of that duality, he just doesn't want anyone to feel contained by their illness. He has both a Ph.D. in Psychology and an MA in Fine Arts from Columbia, but you could say his concept also has its roots in Eastern Europe, where Marton's memories of growing up with communism in Hungary steered him towards art as a tool for liberation.

Creedmoor Psychiatric Center was once the city's most controversial inpatient mental hospital, and by the mid-seventies, it was crumbling in every sense of the word. Building #25 was completely abandoned (and still is). But today, the Living Museum of Creedmoor is home to a community that will heartily welcome you into the massive, 2-floor space where no brick is left unpainted. The true highlight is meeting and observing the artists at work, and it all feels a bit like stepping into the tunnel scene of Gene Wilder's *Charlie and the Chocolate Factory. (79-25 Winchester Blvd, Queens Village, NY 11427; +1 718-264-3490; Visit hours are 10am-12pm and 2pm-4.30pm, Mon-Thurs)*

Living Museum

Museum in an Elevator

A tiny museum housed in a 20ft freight elevator accommodates no more than 3 people at a time. Hidden down an inconspicuous alley, every single object in **Mmuseumm** is entirely banal, but each has its own fascinating story that will challenge the way you look at everyday objects. Just as curious, is the nearby window that operates as a type of gift shop for visitors. Dial +1 (888) 763 8839 for the free audio guide while there. *(4 Cortlandt Alley, New York, NY 10013; Sat & Sun 12pm-6pm, visible 24/7 through viewing windows)*

Dig Through the World's Largest Sketchbook Library

There's a library in Brooklyn where anyone and everyone can be a contributor to the collection. The **Brooklyn Art Library** has existed for 10 years and yet it's fittingly one of those wonderfully unusual things that few New Yorkers know about. As we write this, The Sketchbook Project currently has over 41,000 sketchbooks in its library, making it the world's largest (free) sketchbook collection. Each creation is readily available to the public, waiting to be discovered on the shelves of their storefront space in Williamsburg. The concept is simple: contributors start with the same blank 32-page sketchbook available online or in-store (where they also sell some beautiful sketchbook supplies). Sketchers are given complete freedom from there. Draw, write, doodle, cut, print, photograph, scribble, scrawl, whatever you must. When you're done, send it back and voilà. The works are divided into obscure themes such as "Secret Codes" or "It's raining dogs and cats." To avoid the books being damaged, an online search system is installed in the library so visitors can pick a specific book, theme, or simply jump to a random sketchbook. The librarian then locates the book for you, along with another personal choice that they think you might be interested in. The creator receives a notice every time their book is checked out, a little reminder that their work matters.(28 Frost St, Brooklyn, NY 11211; +1 718-388-7941; Wed-Sun, 10am-6pm; Sketchbookproject.com)

Art Classes with Winston Churchill's Chums

What began humbly in 1871 as the *New York Sketch Club* became the storied **Salmagundi Art Club**, where renowned painters, sculptors and other talents have vied for membership. Over 1500 masterpieces fill the historic brownstone's walls, which are also covered in easels and art supplies belonging to the bygone, bohemian-bourgeoisie of New York. William M. Chase, Louis C. Tiffany and even Winston Churchill were all members. For $20, you can walk right into their historic brownstone mansion in Greenwich Village and bask in it with your own sketchpad and paintbrushes for a class, no reservation required.*(4396 47 5th Ave, Greenwich Village, NY 10003; +1 212-255-7740; daily 1pm-5.30pm; Visit Salmagundi.org for more info)*

When Books Become Art

How to keep the printed word alive? Turn it into art. The **Center for Book Arts**, est. 1974, was the first non-profit of its kind, created to teach both traditional book-making methods, and turn them on their heads. An immense, rotating gallery space shows off works of serious intricacy, while their classes beckon you to learn everything from hand typesetting basics to paper marbling and tooling with real gold. *(28 W 27th St, Flatiron District, NY 1000; +1 212-481-0295; Mon-Fri 11am-6pm, Sat 10am-5pm, Closed Sun; Centerforbookarts.org for classes)*

Centre for Book Arts

Ceci n'est pas une ... art gallery

Well actually it is, but the bright, white contemporary gallery at 131 Chrystie St in the East Village also happens to be hiding a secret entrance to a chandelier-lit cocktail bar, **Fig 19**. It's an impressive way to start a date; confidently leading them through the modern art space, only to reveal an old-world speakeasy hiding in the back. Take a moment to browse the artworks for sale at this legitimate gallery space, especially on a Wednesday evening from 6-8pm when the bar's opening hours overlap the gallery's. Give a nod to its curator before disappearing behind the unmarked door where they serve a particularly fragrant Rose Selavy cocktail that would make Marcel Duchamp proud. *(131 Chrystie St, East Village, NY 10002; Sun, Tues, Wed 6pm-2am; 8pm-2am Thurs-Sat; Instagram: @Figure19)*

Becoming the Artist in the Art Gallery

At America's most famous art museum, be inspired by their iconic collections with **Drop in Drawing at the Met.** Evening sessions take place on selected Fridays within the museum's galleries. Open to all visitors, free with museum admission, materials are provided, but you may bring your own sketchbook. Pencils only. *(1000 Fifth Avenue; Central Park, NY 10028; +1 212-535-7710/ Metmuseum.org/events/programs/met-creates/drop-in-drawing)*

Over in Gramercy Park, discover the clubhouse confines of the **National Arts Club**, founded by New York Times' arts and literary critic Charles de Kay in 1898. Filled with sumptuous bars and Gilded Age glamour, the art galleries are open to the public during the day, as are the drawing classes held on Monday, Wednesday and Friday evenings, meaning that one of Manhattan's Gilded Age private clubs, can be enjoyed by all.

(15 Gramercy Park South, New York, NY, 10003; +1 212-475-3424; Mon-Fri 10am-5pm. Drawing classes are usually between 7pm-9pm from $15, bring your own materials; Nationalartsclub.org)

The glass ceiling
at the National Arts Club
p141

A 1920s Secret Society Clubhouse

If you happen to take an interest in Masonic conspiracy theories, head three
blocks from Central Park to 253 West 73rd where you'll notice a facade dripping
in Freemason symbolism. Spot the all-seeing eye, the hourglass, the beehive,
square & compass and an emblem with the letters "LC" – all traces of the
building's fascinating history as the **Levelers Club**, America's first masonic hotel.
According to one of the original residents who wrote an entire book about the
building, the Neo-Romanesque temple was designed as the only true-to-size
replica of King Solomon's Jewish Temple in the world – smack in the middle
of New York City. The vast clubhouse/ hotel was, in fact, the first of its kind in
the United States, with a total of 225 bedrooms, plenty of secret meeting rooms,
luxurious Turkish baths, an indoor pool, bowling alleys, barber shop, ballroom,
banquet hall, auditorium, roof garden – pretty much everything you could need
to accommodate one of the most ancient and clandestine fraternities in the world.
The secret clubhouse only served its original purpose for two years, however,
before it gave into the Great Depression. If you're discrete about entering, you'll
find the astonishingly well-preserved ornate lobby of the original clubhouse.
Last we heard, the old swimming pool and Turkish-baths are still there in the
basement, in ruins. *(253 W 73rd St; Upper West Side, 10023; residential)*

 Also see what's "Hiding in Plain Sight" on pg 268.

Bibliophile's Paradise

Libraries & Rare Bookshops

Take Refuge in a Mansion of Books

A family of Irish immigrants once lived in an apartment inside the **New York Society Library**, the oldest cultural institution in the city. They were the caretakers that slept amongst the books after the library closed, which was quite a common arrangement until the late 20th century. Libraries all over town had secret apartments for the bookkeepers and their families, who were free to roam the aisles of historic print after hours. The literary guardians of that generation have since retired and today the hidden home inside the New York Society Library serves as the rare book room. You don't have to be a member to use the reference reading room with its beautiful mahogany desks surrounded by antique card catalogs. The library founded in 1754 is open to all, so don't be intimidated by the fancy Upper East Side facade – walk in and make yourself comfortable in what looks like an English gentleman's club where George Washington once racked up some pretty hefty late return fees. If you can spare the annual $270 membership fee or $350 for a family membership, you'll have access to the ultra-luxurious member's reading room where you can cozy up on weekends in an armchair with the papers by the fireplace or hibernate through winter in their private study rooms. We'd take that over a gym membership any day. *(53 E 79th St, Upper East Side, NY 10075; Sat-Sun 11am-5pm, Mon-Fri 9am-8pm; Nysoclib.org)*

Brooklyn's Mini "Hogwarts" Library

Founded in the middle of the Civil War, **The Brooklyn Historical Society** is the queen of Brooklyn libraries. In the magnificent reading room on the second floor, with its carved wooden columns and stained glass lunettes, you can camp out for the afternoon on one of the antique tables to work on your memoirs or dive into the most comprehensive collection of Brooklyn-related archives on the planet. They've got everything from family papers, letters, maps and diaries to an extensive photography collection, as well as over 1200 interviews of oral history. This is also a wonderful place for budding historians to gain after-school work experience. The Teen Council gets together two days a week after school to curate the society's next public exhibition. Students receive a stipend, school credit and it sure looks great on a college application. In the evening, the society is also a lively place for debate and discussion about social and historical issues with weekly community speakers, round tables and screenings (see page 108). Take a workshop with an archivist to discover how they preserve history or join the fight to save historic NYC with an urban activist. Admission to the library and its facilities is free for members, $10 for adults, $6 for students and senior citizens. *(128 Pierrepont St, Brooklyn, NY 11201; +1 718-222-4111; Open Wed-Sun 12pm-5pm, library open Wed-Sat 1pm-5pm; Brooklynhistory.org)*

Dr. Frankenstein's Room of Rare Books

At the age of 18, a headstrong young woman by the name of Mary Shelley began writing the story of a scientist who brings to life a hideous creature from stolen body parts. *Frankenstein* was published anonymously in 1818, inspired by a macabre new world that was discovering modern medicine. Scientists like Luigi Galvani were experimenting with electric currents on dissected frogs and observing them twitch and spasm, while his nephew Giovanni Aldini graduated to working on human cadavers in public demonstrations, where audiences watched lifeless limbs rising from the operating table. Such subsequently named "galvanized" experiments are laid bare at the **New York Academy of Medicine**, home to an incredible 19th-century rare book room that could stand in as Dr. Frankenstein's secret study. In between the pages of centuries-old texts kept inside this Fifth Avenue jewel box, history's most ghoulish scientific experiments are carefully illustrated in surprising, unsettling detail. The archives include half a million records and medical ephemera, from original texts by Galvani and Aldini to works by Sigmund Freud. There's even a frightening 19th-century surgical kit to ogle at and a prototype of George Washington's dentures constructed from actual teeth. Amazingly, this veritable cabinet of curiosities has been available to the public since 1878, and all you need to do to visit is book an appointment a few days in advance. If you have anything particularly rare you'd like them to bring out for

Argosy Bookstore

you from the closed stacks, give them a head's up (*reserve by phone: 212-822-7315 or Email: library@nyam.org*). Alternatively, meet in the lobby of the library on the first Monday of the month at midday when they offer drop-in tours to see highlights from the collection.
(1216 5th Ave, Upper East Side, NY 10029; Tues, Thurs & Fri 10am-4.45pm, Wed 10am-6.45pm; Nyam.org/library)

Mr. Morgan's Mini Palace of Rare Books

There's a fairytale library hiding in Manhattan that was founded in 1906 by a certain J. P. Morgan (yes, *that* J. P. Morgan). You're thinking banking baron rather than book lover, but this was the tycoon's storage space for his world-class collection of rare books, manuscripts, and antiquities. Mr. Morgan had secret doorways installed in the walnut bookshelves that tower up to the painted ceilings, revealing a more playful side to "America's greatest banker". Today the **Morgan Library & Museum** is a public space, open to all. Make your way past a modern glass lobby and through a Raphaelite rotunda into Morgan's study, a space swallowed in deep red velvet walls and the inimitable smell of old New York money. The special vault for his most prized selections is open to researchers by appointment. Find the main library, the East Room (pg 144), which looks more like the Vatican than any place in Midtown, holding rare copies of Dickens, a lovesick letter from Alexander Hamilton and even an ancient Egyptian amulet. Grab an audio headset from the information desk if you want to know everything about this hidden cultural gem. *Psst!* Wander around for free on Tuesdays 3-5pm, Fridays 7-9pm and Sundays 4-6pm.
(225 Madison Ave, Midtown, NY 10016; +1 212-685-0008
Open Tues-Thurs 10.30am-5pm, until 9pm on Friday and 6pm Sat & Sun)

New York City's Oldest Independent Bookstore

Remember that bookstore Audrey Hepburn worked at in *Funny Face*, before she left Manhattan for Paris? You'll think you've walked into the real thing at **Argosy Bookstore**, or something close to it.

 Founded in 1925, it's now in its third generation of family ownership with an enormous stock of antiquarian and out-of-print books, as well as art, antique maps and prints, and the history of science and medicine. Sat behind desks piled high with antique books and glowing green library lamps, here is where you'll find the last true booksellers, busying themselves with client inquiries about the whereabouts of rare editions and generally restoring your faith in the book trade. Argosy is the founding member of the Antiquarian Booksellers Association of America and has about 60,000 out-of-print books on all subjects. They also have another 80,00 rare and unusual books hidden up on the 5th floor, which can be accessed if you have a serious inquiry.

Just minutes from the Plaza Hotel, seek out this old world gem in the midst of the concrete jungle. It really is exactly how you imagine it in the movies. *(116 E 59th St, Midtown East, NY 10022; +1 212-753-4455; Mon-Sat 10am-6pm, until 5pm on Sat; Argosybooks.com)*

Argosy Bookstore

The Salacious History of the Village Library

Take the stairs at the **Jefferson Market Library** and climb the spiral steps up the Victorian Gothic bell tower, taking your time to admire the stained glass windows and soak up the history of what was once a central courthouse built in the 1880s. This is where Harry K. Thaw went to trial for the murder of famed architect Stanford White in 1906: a crime of passion that gripped New York and became known as the 'trial of the century', involving a love triangle between the most celebrated 'It' girl of her day, Evelyn Nesbit, her deranged husband, Harry Thaw, and the architect of the original Madison Square Garden, Stanford White. Its more salacious aspects were laid bare for the press, including details of a certain red velvet swing hanging from a ceiling in White's townhouse where he allegedly seduced young Evelyn, often referred to as "the world's first supermodel". In the summer of 1906, her jealous multi-millionaire husband Harry Thaw fired three pistol shots into White's head while he sat at his private table enjoying the rooftop theater at Madison Square Gardens. Thaw would be sentenced to a hospital for the criminally insane while the infamous case involving "The Girl in the Red Velvet Swing" would go on to inspire its own Hollywood movie starring Joan Collins in the 1950s. By that time, the Manhattan courthouse which had been voted one of the most beautiful buildings in America was abandoned and facing demolition. Thankfully, the New York Public Library stepped in, and what was once a holding area for criminal's became the library's reference room. Looming above it all was, and is, the hundred-foot lookout tower with uninterrupted views of Greenwich Village. Once used as a firewatcher's lookout, the bell would summon the rival gangs of volunteer firemen competing for glory in 19th-century New York. The bell was restored in the 1990s after 135 years of silence and still strikes on the hour from 9 am to 10 pm, making Greenwich Village once again feel more like a village. It's free to walk in the Jefferson Market Library, pick a desk and get on with some work with all that history surrounding you. There's also free film nights during the winter, book discussions and arts and crafts for the kids.

(425 6th Ave, New York, NY 10011; Mon-Thurs 10am-8pm, Sat 10am-5pm, Sun 1pm-5pm)

▶ Three Things to Seek out at the New York Public Library

1   **Mysterious World War II Propaganda**: In the 1980s, a librarian in the NYPL's Rare Book room discovered camouflaged Anti-Nazi pamphlets inside a dusty old box. The label attached to the box said: "*Do not open until war is over*". Inside, he found vintage sample packets of tea and seeds, tourism pamphlets, advertising leaflets for beauty products and cheap editions of the classics. On closer inspection, the librarian discovered that this seemingly innocent collection of WWII era advertising was, in fact, hiding hundreds of camouflaged anti-Nazi booklets slotted inside sample packets of seeds, as well as many miniature editions of anti-Nazi newspapers printed on tissue paper or photostatted in minute print. You know, the stuff librarians' dreams are made

of. It's not exactly clear how these pamphlets ended up in a remote corner of the NY Public Library's rare book room, but one of the envelopes found in the box was addressed to the library from Germany in 1941. Around 80% of this cleverly disguised propaganda was produced by the German Communist Party, although very few of the publications have survived. The material is available for viewing by appointment.
(Register for access: nypl.org/about/divisions/rare-books-division)

2   **The Last of New York's Wooden Phone Booths**: While the Rose Reading room gets the most tourists snapping away at its grandeur, down in the basement, you can still find a row of vintage wooden phone booths, a rare sighting indeed for modern day NYC. As one might expect from such an illustrious locale, the phone booths have a lovingly polished and elegant veneer, and several still have their pay phones inside.

3   **The real Winnie-the-Pooh**: The original stuffed animals that were given to Christopher Robin Milne by his father (and creator of the beloved characters) when he was a little boy in the 1920s have been living at The New York Public Library since 1987. Winnie, Kanga, Piglet, Eeyore, and Tigger, are on display in the children's center. *(476 5th Ave, Midtown, NY 10018; Mon & Thurs-Sat 10am-6pm, Tues & Wed 10am-8pm,, Sun 1-5pm; discover their after hours at the library events on Nypl.org/locations/schwarzman)*

Patron of the Arts in Training

In an era of widespread budget cuts for public art education and facilities, the world needs more enthusiasm and appreciation for the arts. It also needs more donors, budding philanthropists and aspiring Peggy Guggenheim's, but for the 21st-century patron, being useful needn't be limited only to *buying* the art. And you needn't be a millionaire to support creators during their creative process...

Meeting Artists in their Studios

At the **Museum of Art and Design**, visitors can meet working artists in residence as they produce work in their studios on the 6th floor of the museum. Ask questions, start a dialogue about their creative process; it's all part of an innovative model of interactivity with the art community. One full-time fellow and six daily students are selected for six-month sessions and given financial support, studio space, as well as access to all the tools of the museum. In return, the public is allowed into the artist's world. *(2 Columbus Cir, Midtown, NY 10019; Studio hours: Tues, Wed, Fri, Sat: 10am–5pm Thur: 10am–5pm, 6–8pm, Sun: 10am–1:30pm, 2:30–5pm; To apply as a student: Madmuseum.org/artist-studios)*

Beethoven for Breakfast & Mozart for Lunch

Start the day off at the **NY Philharmonic Open Rehearsals** watching one of the world's greatest orchestras hone its craft. Their morning rehearsals are open to the public for the bargain price of $22. They wrap up just in time for the **Gotham Early Music Scene**'s free lunchtime concerts of classical music in a 19th century, Byzantine-esque chapel in Midtown. The nonprofit corporation supports and promotes the artists and organizations in New York devoted to the music of the Medieval, Renaissance, Baroque, and early Classical periods.
(NY Philharmonic Open Rehearsals, 10 Lincoln Center, Upper West Side, NY 10023; +1 212-875-5656; Thurs 9.45am-12.30pm in David Geffen Hall; Nyphil. org/openrehearsals; Gotham Early Music Scene, The Chapel at St. Bartholomew's Church, 325 Park Ave, Midtown, NY 10022; +1 212-866-0468; Thurs 1pm-2pm; Gemsny.org)

New York City's best-kept gastronomic secret

What Carnegie Hall is to musicians, the **James Beard Foundation** is to chefs. Five to six-course meals with wine pairings are held at this historic home almost nightly, open to members and non-members. Attending a James Beard chef dinner is a chance to experience America's finest culinary talent, go inside the kitchen, meet the chefs and share your enthusiasm with other food lovers. The late American cook, James Beard, was a celebrated peer of Julia Childs, mentor to generations of professional chefs and author of over 20 cookbooks. His home in Greenwich Village has since become a non-profit society for the celebration of cuisine. The only way for a chef to "perform" here is by invitation, and the foundation has always been a trusted barometer of rising stars in the culinary arts, connecting the world's top restaurants with undiscovered food artisans at the top of their game. If you're looking for the perfect gift for an aspiring chef or food lover, a gift certificate at a James Beard chef dinner will go down a treat *(Jamesbeard.org/james-beard-house-gift-certificates)*. The foundation is also on a mission to make America's food culture more sustainable for everyone through its educational programs. If your world revolves around food, memberships are less than $2.50 a month and get you a discount on all chef dinners. There's a kitchen volunteer program for young chefs looking for hands-on experience beside some of the best culinary minds in the world, and scholarship applications can be found on the website.
(167 W 12th St, Greenwich Village; NY 10011; +1 212-675-4984; Mon-Fri 9am-5pm; Jamesbeard.org)

A Members-only Gilded Age Theatre Club where time stands still
Hidden away in New York, there is a certain club that stands alone, created as
a private haven for performers and lovers of the arts ever since it first opened
on New Year's Eve in 1888. **The Players** is a living museum full of secrets,
containing an unparalleled collection of theatrical artifacts and costumes, many
over a century old. Discreet drawers open to display Victorian death masks, and
the walls are covered with striking portraits of members past. On the top floor,
a perfectly preserved 19th-century apartment, frozen in time under lock and
key, was once the home of the club's founder, Edwin Booth, the most famous
American actor of his day (and coincidentally, the older brother of the man who
assassinated Abraham Lincoln).

The Players can be found at number 16 Gramercy Park, where residents of the
well-to-do area were less than thrilled at the prospect of an actor's club opening
on their doorsteps. At the time, acting was considered a louche profession for
second-class citizens with dubious morals. But this was one of Booth's main
aims: to raise the profile and respectability of the acting profession. He opened
membership to all those in society who loved the arts, where actors might
mingle with elite Victorian society and patrons of the arts. Mark Twain was
among the founding members, whose billiard cue can be found mounted above
the mantelpiece in the billiard room. Later, the portraits of Katharine Hepburn,
Bogart and Bacall were added to the members paintings that cover the walls,
and now you can even spot Jimmy Fallon's portrait. There's a 'Sarah Bernhardt
Room', named after the iconic actress who visited the club, and legend has it,
got stuck in the elevator for over an hour, and left in a huff, swearing never to
return again. The Players is steeped in theatrical history, and while many private
clubs have floundered in recent years, the Players is thriving. Packed with
members of all ages almost every night, all devoted to the arts, the Players is the
oldest social club in Manhattan that still operates from its original home.
(16 Gramercy Park S, New York, NY 10003; membership details Theplayersnyc.org)

Amber Maykut, Founder of Brooklyn Taxidermy,
Photographed by Sheila Barabad

05
I'm Not a Hipster But...

New York is filled with "hipsters" in that there's so many makers and art appreciative people here … people really into music, film, cuisine, fancy cocktails, painting, vinyl record collecting, writing, printmaking, jewelry making, or whatever niche they're passionate about. And often these people take that same hyper-attentiveness and apply it to their physical appearance too. They fashion themselves to signal that they are part of a subculture: tattoos, vintage clothes, pins or shirts proclaiming their favorite bands. They live here for the variety and convenience: delis open 24/7, bars open until 4am, every type of food imaginable at your fingertips, endless things to do. They live here to go out, to be on the grid, to see their favorite bands, to work at the best restaurants, to take part in or see art openings, museums, and other happenings. Like how Los Angeles is filled with models and actors hoping to be discovered, New York is full of artists trying to grow themselves, make a name for themselves, or just make it in one way or another- maybe just to prove to themselves that they can survive here for a bit. And like Paris or Los Angeles, everyone is passing though at some point, to live here or just to visit, and to experience the millions of things this city has to offer.

– Amber Maykut, Founder of Brooklyn Taxidermy (pg 278)

Saturday Night Fever

Bars & Nightclubs

Hipsters and Hip Hop

Loosie Rouge is a fabled vagabond femme fatale who roamed the streets of Paris and New York in the 1980s. "She's rumored to have dated Christopher Wallace and Liza Minnelli at the same time," say the creators of the South Williamsburg bar named in her honor, "Today she lives in spirit in Brooklyn". Tucked down an alleyway framed by string lights under the Williamsburg Bridge, start with dinner at the very Instagram-friendly setting of Loosie's Kitchen, celebrating the diverse roots of contemporary American home cooking (also open for breakfast and lunch). In the summer, the dining area under the atrium becomes an open-air set up. Head through the back of the restaurant to access the jazz & blues club next door where Brooklyn PYT's line the bar, vibing to live Hip Hop jam sessions several nights a week. The energy is high at the weekend with old school beats, salsa or freestyle rhyming accompanied by trumpets, guitar and drums, reminiscent of catching an intimate show by "The Roots" in the early days. On Monday there's a good jazz night to soothe your weekend hangover. The entire joint is also available to hire for private parties. *(91 S 6th St, Brooklyn, NY 11249, USA; +1 718-309-0231; ope n everyday 7am-2am; Loosierouge.com)*

Cocktail Hour with Indie Fashion Editors

Fashion's movers and shakers are the primary clientele at **Mr. Fong's**, an understated but suave dive bar with a hint of "Twin Peaks" that serves excellent Bloody Mary's under the Manhattan Bridge. There's a jukebox, dark red leather booths and creative cocktails with a punch. Who exactly is Mr. Fong? He's a bit of a local legend: a Chinatown real-estate agent who can be credited in part for the hipsterfication of the Lower East Side. After he helped the owners find this space for their unassuming "It" bar, they gratefully named it after him. Get there early to watch the room fill up with cool kids and see where the night takes you. *(40 Market St, Chinatown, NY 10002; +1 646-964-4540; open everyday 5pm-4am; MrFongs.com; Instagram:@mrfongsnyc)*

Boogie in Line with Your Roller Disco Tribe

The city's most welcoming and fashionable collective for roller disco, **Roller Wave NYC**, pays homage to NY's storied Empire Skate Club from the '70s. Where else can you skate around with a beer, fall on your butt to ABBA, and fully expect a stranger to help you up? Their sequined crew brings pop-up skate parties to school gymnasiums and local boutique hotels on a near-weekly basis. Tickets (including optional skate rental) run around $30 – a small price to pay for the kind of feel-good energy worthy of *The Sonny and Cher Show*. *(Check Eventbrite.com and Instagram:@rollerwavenyc for details)*

Indie Pop Dance Party

Shake off the week's tension at **Baby's All Right**, an unpretentious three-room and two-bar venue that can give you a most memorable dance party one night, introduce you to an eclectic new band the next, and serve you a solid brunch the following morning. Check the calendar for your preferred music, whether it be Hip Hop or Indie Pop.
(146 Broadway, Brooklyn, NY 11211; +1 718-599-5800; Mon-Fri 6pm-2am, Sat-Sun 11am-4am; Babysallright.com; Instagram:@babysallright)

That '70s Show

There's a groovy 1970-something time warp in Chinatown that could easily become your favorite bar. Comfy, kitschy and cool, **The Flower Shop**, is a good-time retro bar-and-grill with $1 oysters at happy hour upstairs and a pool table in the den downstairs.
(107 Eldridge St, Lower East Side; +1 212-257-4072; Sun-Wed 5pm-12am, Thurs-Sat 5pm-2am; Theflowershopnyc.com)

Drinking Games at the East Village Tiki Bar

When you and your friends just want to get together at a big round table, sipping eye-popping cocktails while feeling like you're on vacation, **Mother of Pearl** is your spot. Designed to look like a Postmodern Polynesian hotel lobby, the ambiance is immediately uplifting and has the drinks to match. Make your way through flammable cocktails and 2-3 person sharing drinks that we bet you can't finish. Keep your strength up with the mushroom pot stickers and Pupu platters for two from the all-vegan menu.
(95 Avenue A, New York, NY 10009; +1 212-614-6818; Mon-Wed 5pm-1pm, Thurs-Sat until 2am, Sat & Sun open from 3pm; Motherofpearlnyc.com)

Let's Try That Bulgarian Place

Ever danced to folk-techno Chalga? You will after a few vodka shots in the ice cage at **Mehanata Bulgarian Bar**, one of Manhattan's most outrageous nightclubs where you can kick up your heels like a Cossack and maybe run into Macaulay Culkin at the bar, all grown up (and hipster). Hang out on the mezzanine in their bohemian Romani vardo wagon, complete with traditional clothes for you to dress up in for a group photo. Guaranteed to be one of the best, weirdest nights you've had in a while. Too bad you won't remember it.
(113 Ludlow St, Lower East Side, NY 10002; +1 212-625-0981; Open Thurs-Sat 8pm-4am; Mehanatanyc.com)

Secrets of the Bodega

Mezcaleria La Milagrosa is hiding behind a sparsely-stocked bodega in Brooklyn. A host sitting at the counter with a clipboard indicates that there's something hiding behind the refrigerator door. Password given (your reservation name), proceed through the freezer door to an intimately designed space, somewhere between a Mexican bar and an old -school '70s disco. Start with the Mezcal, sample the old-fashioned Negroni and move on to the Margarita Jamaica. The owner has an extensive record collection that he shares on the old '45 jukebox through a sound system that does the music justice. Note: It's reservation only, which keeps the crowds at bay.

(149 Havemeyer St, Brooklyn, NY 11211, +1 718-599-1499; Open daily from 7pm)

Dining with the Cool Kids

Trendy eateries

The Pizza Bunker

Poke your head behind **Roberta's** unassuming door through a cement wall and see if you can resist the smell of their freshly baked pies wafting around you. But there's so much more to discover if you venture further inside. Roberta's is made up of repurposed shipping containers (one of which houses an in-house radio station), a rooftop greenhouse that grows about 20% of the pizzeria's ingredients, a bakery, an outdoor playground for adults, a tasting kitchen — and the compound continues to expand. Come on a hot Sunday night in the summer for a wild "Pizza Tiki Disco Party" in the garden or warm yourself up during winter in their surprisingly cozy shipping containers with the famous "bee sting pizza" that comes with a side of hot honey.

(261 Moore St, Brooklyn, NY 11206; +1 718-417-1118; Mon-Fri 11am-12am
Sat-Sun 10am-12pm; robertaspizza.com)

Roberta's, Brookyln

A Taste of Summer in Europe

The facade is confusing because the sign is written in Chinese (this is Chinatown), but the cuisine at **Kiki's** is all Greek. The vibe: good-looking 30-somethings wishing they were back in Santorini. The food is just as they remembered it from their summers on the Greek isles too. Expect a wait on busy nights later in the week (and they don't take reservations) but Plan B is to head down the block to its sister restaurant **Forgetmenot** for a laidback fairy-lit faux dive bar where you can order food from Kiki's. *(130 Division St, Chinatown, NY 10002; +1 646-882-7052; everyday 12pm-12am/ Forgetmenot: 138 Division St, +1 646-707-3195; everyday 10am-1am)*

Just around the corner, for a romantic taste of the Algarve with design cues from Portugal's increasingly-hip capital city of Lisbon, book yourself in at **Cervo's**. Intimate and dimly-lit, serving outstanding melt-in-your-mouth seafood plates, this is a prime spot for a second date – after you've verified they like seafood. *(43 Canal St, Chinatown, NY 10002; +1 212-226-2545; everyday 5.30pm-11pm; Cervosnyc.com)*

Beautiful People eating Kung Pao Pastrami

At **Mission Chinese Food**, it always feels like you're at the after-party dinner of a new trending fashion designer. Now with two locations in NYC, each entirely tailored to its loyal, super cool clientele, the Bushwick establishment is a neon-lit warehouse with a "Matrix" look about it while the Manhattan restaurant has a more David Lynch vibe. In both cases, the Sichuan cuisine is excellent with our favorites being the green tea noodles and the mouth-numbing Mapo tofu. *(171 E Broadway, Lower East Side, NY, open everyday 5.30pm-11pm, also open for lunch Sat & Sun 12-4pm; +1 917-376-5660 / 599 Johnson Ave, Brooklyn, NY 11237; +1-718-628-3731; Mon-Sun 5.30pm-11pm, Missionchinesefood.com)*

French Girl Hangout

When she's not swanning around the 11th arrondissement in Paris, French It-girl Jeanne Damas' home away from home is **Lucien**, a chic little bistro with frisée salads that go heavy on the *lardons* (that's bacon bits in American), and fading French advertisements peeling off from the walls. *(14 1st Avenue #1, East Village, NY 10009; +1 212-260-6481; everyday 11am-12pm, until 1pm Fri & Sat; Luciennyc.com)*

For the Millenial Carrie Bradshaw

Call up the girls after work and meet at **Sel Rrose**, the coolest oyster bar in Manhattan. The weathered walls, marble counters and pink Rococo accents make for romantic surroundings while catching up and eye flirting with strangers across the room. Order a dozen fresh oysters for $30 (or $1 oysters at

Happy Hour), truffle fries and a round of the house Spritzs. Reserve a table or come early for happy hour (everyday 4-7pm) and stay seated around the bar. *(1 Delancey St, Lower East Side, NY 10002; +1 212-226-2510; Café open Mon-Fri, 9am-3pm, bar & restaurant everyday 4pm-late; Selrrose.com)*

Sel Rrose

© Courtesy of Sel Rrose

Nolita by Night

With vintage floral wallpaper and cozy leather diner booths, **Lovely Day** feels like a homey smalltown café from the deep south during the day. By night, it's a buzzy, dimly-lit Nolita hotspot where we found ourselves dining next to London It-girl Alexa Chung. The Thai(ish) comfort food plates are usually under $10 and the pineapple fried rice might just be the closest you'll ever get to eating sunshine. Head down to the underground cocktail bar for a night cap. *(196 Elizabeth St, Nolita, NY 10012; +1 212-925-3310; Sun-Thurs 11am-11pm, Fri-Sat 11am-12am; Lovelydaynyc.com; Instagram:@lovelydayny)*

Live Music Upstairs. Secret Supper Club Below Ground

Sip absinthe to the sounds of a Django-worthy guitar duo, or a live flamenco performance at **St. Mazie Bar & Supper Club**, whose antique charm feels like it fell out of some nondescript, Latin-tinged European village. Small stage side tables surrounding the evening's entertainment can be booked on Eventbrite (eventbrite.com/stmazie) but for dinner, you can book a table in the cavernous

Flamenco nights at St. Mazie Bar

secret cellar supper club or the overgrown back garden in summer. *(345 Grand St, Brooklyn, NY 11211; +1 718-384-4808; Mon-Wed 6pm-2am, Thurs-Fri 6pm-4am, Sat-Sun 12pm-2am; Stmazie.com)*

Tartare with a side of Tarot

Still buzzing after several decades, **Raoul's** is the ultimate throwback to 80s and 90s New York in its prime. It's been Soho's celebrity hangout since 1975 when artists still lived in illegal lofts and no one came downtown at night without a good reason. Founded by two brothers from Alsace, the only French bistro in an all-Italian neighborhood stuck out from the rest, and the up & coming artists took notice. By the 80s & 90s, it was at the heart of the Soho after-hours scene where you could find anyone from Andy Warhol to Sarah Jessica Parker getting up to no good. Nancy Stark, the house tarot reader,

witnessed most of it. She's been reading the destiny of customers there for over 20 years at the top of the spiral staircase (Sun-Wed, 7-11pm). With a gossip-filled history in its walls to keep the conversation flowing, pick Raoul's for a double date spot and slide into Johnny Depp's or Robert De Niro's old booths. Treat yourselves to a white tablecloth, *steak au poivre* dinner before tempting fate with a tarot reading after dessert. Most tables are close together, so expect to get friendly with your neighbors.
(180 Prince St #2924, SoHo, NY 10012; +1 212-966-3518; open for dinner Mon-Fri, lunch & dinner on weekends)

Gather the whole Gang at …

Decoy: A Peking duck & pancake feast on long communal tables in a former Greenwich Village laundromat. Accommodates large groups, arrive hungry/ starving and committed to paying the prix-fixe of $79 per head which includes one whole duck per 5 persons or less, and a variety of appetizers, mains and sides of your choice.
(529-1/2 Hudson St, Greenwich Village, NY 10014; +1 212-691-9700; Open everyday 5pm-11.45pm; Decoynyc.com)

Bunker: Before a night out in Bushwick at one of the buzzing bars or clubs on Troutman Street (Lot 45) or Wyckoff Avenue (House of Yes), get some really decent Vietnamese street food in your belly at this playfully converted industrial warehouse. The straw hut bar and tropical foliage make it feel like the beach could be waiting around the corner after you finish your *Bánh mi* sandwich.
(99 Scott Ave, Brooklyn, NY 11237; +1 718-386-4282; Sun, Tues, Wed 12pm-10pm, Thurs-Sat 12pm-11pm; Bunkernyc.com)

Carthage Must Be Destroyed: There's no street sign for this hard-to-find secret brunch mecca hiding amongst the warehouses of East Williamsburg. They don't take reservations for their 10-seater communal farm tables but show up before midday or after 2 pm and you'll beat the rush. The color palette is millennial pink and terra cotta, and the open kitchen serves up organic goat feta lunch boxes and delicate plates of heirloom breed eggs. How to find it: march through the parking lot and take a right at the end where you'll see the pink pastel pipes. It's worth the hunt. Know before you go: this restaurant has a no-Instagram policy, which means no photos outside of your personal space. Ironically, they do have their own Instagram account *@CarthageMustbeDestroyed*. *(222 Bogart St, Brooklyn, NY 11206; +1 917-488-1844; everyday 9am-4pm; Carthagemustbedestroyed. com)*

Brooklyn Crab
pg 202

Social Playgrounds in the Sun

Bars & restaurants with outdoor spaces

Cuban Block Party

When the heart feels like South American cuisine on a lovely day in Brooklyn, it heads to **Habana Outpost**, an al fresco lot where the good vibes are flowing and the Cuban sandwiches are on point. Order at the counter, pull up a chair and let the salsa music transport you to another world (one not too far from a beach). Check the website for special music and art events, alfresco movie nights and kids 'creativity days'. While the block party is for the warmer seasons only (April to October), the outpost is part of a non-profit organization called 'Habana Works', committed to fostering community, promoting urban environmentalism and spreading love, "the Brooklyn way."
(17 Prince St, Brooklyn, NY 10012; +1 212-625-2001; Open daily 9am-12am; Cafehabana.com; Instagram:@cafehabana)

A Ranch in the Clouds

The McKittrick hotel is an emporium of curiosities waiting to be discovered, including the theatrical "Sleep No More" experience (see pg 278), but at the very top of this building in Chelsea you'll find the rooftop playground, **The Lodge at Gallow Green**. In summer, it's one of the city's most gratifying sky-high bars, transporting you to an overgrown garden or a rustic 1930s farmhouse in the countryside, open for lunch, cocktails and dinner. In winter, it becomes a rooftop ski chalet nestled amongst the sky scrapers with rocking chairs, blankets, firepits and mulled wine. We'd advise signing up to the McKittrick guestbook to be among the first to know about seasonal openings, events and happenings throughout the building.
(542 W 27th St, Chelsea, NY 10001, USA; +1 212-564-1662; mckittrickhotel.com/ guestbook)

Rooftop People Watching with Margaritas

From the roof of an Airstream trailer, **Zona Rosa** has a great space for watching Williamsburg go by; heated in winter and open in summer under the string lights. The restaurant is built over and around a vintage Airstream trailer where chefs prepare fresh tacos, Queso Fundido and ceviche plates. At Happy Hour (Mon-Fri 5pm-7pm), they offer $6 Margaritas, shots and Mexican snacks.
(571 Lorimer St, Brooklyn, NY 11211; +1 917 324-7423 ; Open early evening to midnight on weekdays, and afternoon to midnight on weekends; Zonarosabrooklyn.com)

A Hipster's Paradise is an Empty Lot in Brooklyn

A place that only Brooklynites are likely to understand the appeal of, **Lot Radio** is literally a small empty lot in North Williamsburg. Here, a nonprofit radio

station has taken up residence inside a shipping container and live streams music 24/7 while serving coffee in the winter and $5 beers in the summer. The gravel yard is furnished with some benches, crates, tables and hammocks; and on a sunny day in Brooklyn, this very basic concrete slice of unused real estate attracts locals and passersby who appreciate the good vibes courtesy of the DJ, the affordable beverages and the simple pleasures of city life.
(17 Nassau Ave, Brooklyn, NY 11222; Mon-Fri 8am-12am, Sat & Sun, 10am-12am; Thelotradio.com)

The Clam Shack That Came to Bushwick

On the corner of a barren industrial landscape between Bushwick and East Williamsburg, **Cape House** almost looks like a mirage: a clam shack plucked straight from the beaches of New England and dropped here. Bring your friends and spread out on the ample patio space with plenty of communal tables to go around. Snack on clam strips, shrimp rolls or an excellent clam chowder. The staff are friendly, and regular nightly DJ sets make it a fun pre-game stop before a night out.
(2 Knickerbocker Ave, Brooklyn, NY 11237; +1 718-821-2580; Open daily 12pm-4am)

 Also see "Hidden Back Gardens" pg 188.

The back garden at Sunny's bar in Red Hook
pg 205

The Little Black Book of a New York Shopaholic

Bars & restaurants with outdoor spaces

Online shopping has weakened the 21st-century woman's natural instinct for that age-old practice of leisurely perusing actual boutiques, touching things and trying before you buy. But where do you even start with a city like New York? Sure, there's always the famous department stores for a rainy day, but did you really come to this city to ride the escalators? Whether your style muse is Carrie Bradshaw all the way or more of a classic Audrey Hepburn circa *Breakfast at Tiffany's*, get to know the city's fashion pockets and shop like a true local...

Malin Landaeus vintage boutique, Williamsburg

Girls Day Out in Nolita:

Sequestered away from busy Broadway, noisy Canal St., and high-end Soho boutiques, Nolita is a boutique shopping haven for both the boho-chic and the classic dresser. At the center of it all, Prince Street is home to the **Nolita Outdoor Market** on weekends between Mott St and Mulberry St, offering Etsy-type accessories, quality leather bags and homemade goods in a mass-produced world (bartering acceptable, open March-December). Down Mott Street, you'll discover **Warm**, where you can start shopping for your hippie retirement in Mexico, while **Creatures of Comfort** on Mulberry Street is a more eclectic alternative to the often over-hyped Opening Ceremony store a few blocks down. Take a turn on Elizabeth St. where you'll find rows of small accessory boutiques, apothecary stores and fashion jewelry shops like **Love Adorned** and the expertly curated **In Support Of**, which showcases some of the industry's best-undiscovered fashion designers. Shop 'til you drop, but do the latter at the **Elizabeth Street Garden**, a beguiling urban paradise hiding in the heart of Nolita with old statues rescued from all over the city and haphazardly left here in this public greenspace where a school once stood. On your way out, pop into the **Elizabeth Street Gallery** next door selling giant antiques to fill your imaginary chateau. *(Subway: Prince Street Station / Spring Street)*

Find the shops on Instagram: #NolitaMarket, @TheWarmStore, @ LoveAdorned, @CreaturesofComfort, @InSupportOf, @Elizabethstreetgallery_ nyc

Stepping it up a gear in the East Village:

The ever-gritty streets of the East Village, in spite of downtown fancification, are your next stop for seeking out new American fashion talent. Any girl who cares about fashion too much will start with the beautifully curated **Maryam Nassir Zadeh**; not always affordable, but always fun to browse and borrow styling tips from. Along with **The Rising States** over on Ludlow Street, both carry unique fashion you won't find online and emerging designers that remind you why once in a while you should shop IRL (in real life). Also on Ludlow Street, you have your "LA cool girl" staple stores like **The Reformation** and **Frankie Shop**, always coming through with unique winter coats around the corner on Stanton Street. A few blocks north to East 9th, **Cloak & Dagger** is where Jane Birkin meets Wes Anderson in a fashion boutique. And you must pop into **Cobblestones** a few doors down at number 314, a long-standing little vintage store circa 1981 that's bursting with vintage accessories, run by Delani Koppersmith, one of the friendliest New Yorkers around. *(Subway: Second Avenue Station/ Delancey Street)*

Find the shops on Instagram: @maryam_nassir_zadeh, @TheRisingStates, @Reformation, @TheFrankieShop, @CloaknDaggerNYC, @CobblestonesVintageNYC

Sussing out Gentrified Williamsburg:

On Brooklyn's Bedford Avenue, the weekend escape of choice for Manhattanites, you'll want to keep your eyes peeled for the vintage stores in between the stroller-filled cheesecake shops and encroaching "boutique" fashion chains. Look out for **Amarcord**, the thrift store that has its pulse on the latest trends but curates pieces from its vintage stock to create new fashion-forward looks for the mannequins. Just next door, fill up your jewelry box at **Catbird** with stackable rings, dainty chain necklaces and ear cuffs. For a rainy day, across the road is **The Mini Mall**, which is exactly as the name implies: a miniature indoor mall with pop up vintage stores and small shops selling non-touristy NYC souvenirs. Around the corner, hidden in the shade of a big old tree on North 6th street, discover Betsey Johnson's favorite vintage store, **Malin Landaeus.** Run by the über cool Swedish mother & daughter duo, Malin and Nova Landeaus, they host afternoon tea every Sunday and bake vegan goods behind the counter which doubles as their weekend kitchen. You won't be able to resist the hand-dyed vintage silks, dreamy lace blouses and one-of-a-kind finds. Further up the street is **Space Ninety 8**, where three floors plus a rooftop of hipster offerings make up this Williamsburg concept store, brought to you by the same folks behind Urban Outfitters. Finally, head back a few blocks in the other direction away from the river and deeper into Brooklyn to seek out a carefully curated vintage superstore. Word on the street is that New York's best-fit vintage Levis jeans are found at **10 Ft Single by Stella Dallas**, an enormous vintage emporium that also boasts a coveted collection of concert-tees, Nordic-sweaters, shoes for days and all the plaid you can imagine. Owned by vintage dealers from Japan, there's a separate room hidden at the back where they keep the rarest and most special pieces. *(Subway: Bedford Ave Station)*

Find the shops on Instagram: @AmarcordVintage, @CatbirdNYC, @MalinLandaeusVintage, @SpaceNinety8, @10FtSingleByStellaDallas

On the Thrifter's Trail from Greenpoint to Bushwick:

For a "his & hers" day out in Brooklyn, start by heading up Wythe Ave, where hip young startups are gradually occupying old industrial Brooklyn, and and brands paying big money for local street artists to paint their logos on warehouse walls. Stop at the corner of Dobbin Street where you have both **The Dobbin St. Vintage Co-op** (see pg 157), specializing in vintage homeware and clothing, and the Insta-ready **Feng Sway** (the one with pink palm trees). Score a silk jumpsuit, fringe dress or a stack of 70s graphic t-shirts. You might also end up leaving with one of their giant tropical house plants on sale. Just a warning. A block down, pay a visit to the Mecca for New York vintage, **Beacon's Closet**. It's the only place where the city's most fashionable elite can bear to part with their clothing after a Spring clean, which means there are some real gems to be found here. *(Subway: Nassau Ave Station)*

   Hop from the G to the L train to fuel up at Roberta's with a legendary "bee sting" pizza over in Bushwick (see pg 157) and take a stroll around the corner to **Friends NYC**, a concept store where you feel like you might bump into one of the characters from *Girls* trying on a pair of pink velvet dungarees. It's a great spot for gift-shopping for your girlfriends and sister witches; Frida Kahlo socks – check, occult jewellery – check, sage smudge bundles to ward off the evil b*tches – check. *(56 Bogart Street, Ground Floor, Brooklyn, NY, +1 718-386-6279; everyday 11am–8.30pm; FriendsNYC.com)*

Head two blocks east to Knickerbocker Avenue where yet another giant Brooklyn vintage emporium awaits. At **Urban Jungle** (L Train Vintage) you can find the *Top Gun* flight suit you never knew you needed, as well as everyday pieces like denim, shirts, dresses, skirts etc, all of which hover between $6 and $10. It could take you an hour to get through all the racks in this store so if you're in a hurry, save it for another day, or if you're shopping with a buddy, split up to cover more ground. *(118 Knickerbocker Ave, Brooklyn, NY 11237; +1 718-381-8510; everyday 12pm-8pm).* On your way out, poke your head around the back of the store on Thames Street to get an eyeful of the backstage sorting areas where all the clothing arrives in giant sacks from vintage wholesalers. It gets you wondering where all of this stuff really comes from. *(Subway: Morgan Ave)*

Find the shops on Instagram: @DobbinStCoop, @FengSway, @BeaconsCloset, @FriendsNYC, @LTrainVintage

How to Dress Like a New York Gentleman

Bars & restaurants with outdoor spaces

For the practical man, shopping entails revisiting only a handful of trusted establishments that can ensure he doesn't have to repeat the process again for a substantial amount of time. Those trusted establishments can be broken down into two very simple categories: Smart and casual.

Smart:

There used to be an ad on the MTA subway in the 1950s that ran "Bet You Do Better In A Hat (84 out of 100 women prefer men who wear hats)," showing a well-dressed *Mad Men*-looking fellow in a fedora surrounded by goggle-eyed women. Vintage hat wearing is becoming ever more popular in New York City, with shops like **Goorin Brothers** (Goorin.com) running three neighborhood stores in the city, but the elegant grandfather of them all is the **JJ Hat Center**, which has been making men dress snappier since 1911. An incomparable range of exquisitely hand-crafted and properly-fitted hats, run from Fedoras to Panamas, with debonair old New York names such as the Gramercy, the Grand Central and the Bowery awaits you there. Suitably located on swish Fifth Avenue, the JJ Hat Center is the first port of call for the man about town. *(310, Fifth Avenue, New York, NY, 10001; +1 212 239 4368; jjhatcenter.com; Mon-Fri 10am-7pm, Sat 10am-6pm, Sun 12pm-5pm)*

To complete the look, the timeless art of dressing like a gentleman has never been easier than a visit to **Fine & Dandy** in Hell's Kitchen. Elegance is in the details, and a superlative collection of all things swish awaits inside. Everything

from silk pocket squares to custom tailored shirts, from felt hats to hip flasks, are on hand to equip the dapper dandy.
(445, West 49th Street, New York, NY, 10019; 212 247 4848; fineanddandy.com; Mon-Sat 12pm-8pm, Sun 1pm-8pm)

Casual:

For that rugged, outdoorsy, Theodore Roosevelt look, the **Filson New York Flagship** is in a league of its own. Step inside a 6,000-sq-ft cozy hunter's cabin in the middle of downtown Manhattan, made from a reclaimed 1850s Douglas Fir barn in Oregon. Take your time trying on the world's most durable wax jackets, fleeces, flannel shirts, worker boots, duffel bags and more. Expensive? Half the price of brands like Barbour and you get what you pay for. On Saturdays, the store often sets up a hands-on workshop where you can bring in your jackets for re-waxing or leather in need of reconditioning. They'll even serve you whiskey while you shop.
(876 Broadway, Gramercy Park, NY 10003; Mon-Sat 10am-8pm; +1 646-975-9855; Filson.com)

For the serious sneakerhead, ring the bell of the super secret streetwear brand **Alife**, marked by a small bronze plaque on the Lower East Side. Inside it looks like an English gentleman's Saville Row tailor that might reveal a 007 gadget room behind one of the dark wood-paneled shelves. Rather than brogues and bowler hats, however, here you'll find an incredible wall-to-wall collection of sneakers from hand-painted tennis kicks at around $50 a pair to Air Jordan

Space Jam sneakers going for upwards of $500. They have the athletic streetwear to match, from Varsity jackets to hoodies and sweatpants with attractive design graphics.

(58 Rivington St, Lower East Side, NY 10002; +1 212-432-7200; Mon-Sat 12pm-7pm, Sun until 6pm)

Social Clubs for the Humble Gent

Ode to the old Sicilian Social Club

In Brooklyn's Carroll Gardens, a plain black door with a small plaque reads "Non-Members Welcome." This was once the home of a Sicilian social club, the 'Society Riposto', back when the neighborhood was still predominantly Italian, where club members would come to sip grappa and play cards. After the club folded due to dwindling membership in 2003, it was turned into **Brooklyn Social** a year later. Decorated with mementos of the original Society Riposto back in Sicily, and pre-war sepia photos of past members, the bar has retained a friendly and cozy character. Stop by for a game of pool and enjoy an afternoon daiquiri in the backyard.

(335, Smith Street, Brooklyn, NY, 11231, +1 718 858 7758; Sun-Thur 5pm-2am, Fri-Sat 5pm-4am; Brooklynsocialbar.com)

Fred Astaire's Barbershop

Essential to a gentleman is a long-standing relationship with his local barber, and no barbershop has been around quite as long as **Paul Mole**. A neighborhood staple on the same Upper East Side block since 1913, three of the dozen chairs are over a century old, which means that chances are, you might well sit in the same chair that Fred Astaire, John Steinbeck, Tennessee Williams or Bing Crosby once did. The surroundings are comfortingly old fashioned, but the service and haircuts are as elegant and modern as any gentleman could wish for.
(1034, Lexington Avenue, New York, NY, 10021; +1 212 535 8461; paulmole.com;
Mon-Fri 7:30am-7:30pm, Sat 7:30am-5:30pm, Sun 8am-4:30pm;
appointments are recommended, but walk-ins will always be made welcome)

The Art of Whiskey

If you're over in Long Island City for the afternoon visiting MoMA PS1 (only the largest platform for contemporary art in the country), you might feel inclined to go somewhere slightly more intimate to debrief afterwards. Take a short walk down the street to find **Dutch Kills**, an excellent bar in Queens specializing in a multitude of whiskeys varying wildly in price. Your eyes will have to adjust to the darkness, but the attentive bartender will welcome you with a metal glass of cucumber water with hand cut ice upon arrival. Unload your opinion on PS1's thought-provoking art over an old fashioned and a delicious pork belly sandwich with 1940s tunes playing from the jukebox in the back.
(27-24 Jackson Ave, Queens, NY, New York; +1 718-383-2724;
open every day from 5pm to 2am)

▶ Planning a Party

From birthdays and work parties to city weddings and formal dinner parties, we've got a few tricks up our sleeve...

Turning 21 again in a Legendary Secret Wine Cellar

The **21 Club** is a legendary New York restaurant and former speakeasy. Upstairs it's filled with secrets and vintage Hollywood glamour, meanwhile downstairs, an underground vault hides behind fake walls and a two-ton door to fox Prohibition-era Feds. Behind the brick foundation with a cleverly disguised lock, is the 21 Club's storied wine cellar, home to over 20,000 bottles including the private stash of Frank Sinatra, Joan Crawford, Richard Nixon and Elizabeth Taylor, some of whose bottles are, incredibly, still there. Make your way through the maze-like cavern that runs beneath the neighboring brownstone, and you'll find a long wooden dining table for private hire, surrounded by fine wines, with seating for 12 to 22 people. At the end of the room is one of the club's last

surviving original dining booths, which was used by former NYC mayor Jimmy Walker and his mistresses during Prohibition. Dinner down here consists of a seven-course meal and a five wine pairing. Is there anywhere more fitting to celebrate turning 21 than at the 21 Club?
(21 West 52nd Street, Midtown, NY, 10019; +1 212-582-7200; Be aware of the strict dress code at 21.club.com)

Flower Shop in the Front, Party in the Back
From low-key weddings in the city to big summer birthday parties, you won't have to worry about the flower arrangements because the **Sycamore Bar & Flower Shop** is as the name implies: a flower show in the front and a bar & restaurant in the back. In the warmer months, their tented bar area and gorgeous backyard with ivy climbing up the walls would make a great place for any party, BBQ included. For smaller gatherings like a baby shower lunch or bachelorette dinner, you can also book a flower arranging workshop with the resident florist, Honeysuckle Hill Flowers.
(1118 Cortelyou Rd., Brooklyn, NY 11218; +1 347-240-5850; Open Mon-Wed 3pm-2am, Fri 3pm-4am, Sat 1pm-4am, Sun, 1pm-2am; Events info on Sycamorebrooklyn.com)

Picture Perfect Brownstone Weddings
Imagine the most elegant, Pinterest-perfect garden wedding in the city under string lights and **Maison May** can very likely make it a reality in their historic Brooklyn brownstone. For daytime and evening celebrations for up to 110 guests, they'll take care of everything from the catering to the entertainment, all tailored to each couple's individual style. Founded by the talented French restaurateur Catherine May, trust her to throw you an effortlessly chic European wedding or private event you didn't think you could pull off in New York City. To get an idea of her style, discover the Maison May café around the corner at 270 Vanderbilt Ave, open daily for lunch.
(246 Dekalb Ave, Brooklyn, NY 11205, +1 718-789-2778; Maison-may.com)

Maison May townhouse in Brooklyn,
courtesy of Maison May

Game Night Cabana Party

Victorian splendor is reborn with a dash of tropical kitsch at **Royal Palms Shuffleboard Club**. The charming attendants wear old-timey coveralls, pink flamingos pop up out of nowhere, and the sunken, aquamarine shuffleboards make you feel like you're poolside on some 1880s cruise ship. Then there's the game itself, which is simple and addictive. Strictly 21-and-over, with walk-ins welcome, and for medium-to-high roller groups of 10 or more, you can reserve one of their striped cabanas for $50/hour with beverage packages starting at $25/hour per head for unlimited beer and wine. For Sunday parties, they'll waiver the $50 court fee. You can also enquire about renting half the venue or all of it.
(514 Union St, Brooklyn, NY 11215; +1 347-223-4410; Open early evening to midnight on weekdays, Fri-Sat til 2am, Sun til 10pm; Royalpalmsbrooklyn.com/parties)

Taco Party in a Garage

The **Tacombi** restaurant in Nolita really nailed that vintage taco truck aesthetic, with gorgeous Mexican typography, string lights and kitschy tableware. Pretend like you're having a backyard party in Cali with a bunch of friends, great tacos (prepared inside a vintage VW van, no less) and frozen margaritas by the barrel. The restaurant can accommodate small groups and large parties and even create custom menus for your event. The staff is always cheerful and chatty – one waiter told us tacos were actually invented by Lebanese immigrants in Mexico. *(267 Elizabeth St, Nolita, NY 10012; +1 917-727-0179; Sun 11am-11pm, Mon-Wed 11am - Midnight & Thurs-Sat til 1am; Tacombi.com/events)*

Romantic Candlelit Dinner Parties

If you can't get enough of New York's most romantic restaurant, Palma (see pg 51), step things up a notch and hire out their **Palma Carriage House**. built in 1810, for intimate private dinners of up to 12 people. Start with cocktails in the second-floor library before heading downstairs to a cozy Italian kitchen and dining room to share a magnificent homemade feast. For bigger parties, their garden restaurant under the stars can be privatized too. *(28 Cornelia St, Greenwich Village, NY 10014; +1 212-691-2223; open Mon-Fri, closed for lunch on Monday; Palmanyc.com/ Events)*

Tacombi, Nolita

Joanne Hendricks Cookbooks

06

I Know This Great Little Place

In New York City real estate is sacred. Undeveloped green space is like gold dust and the small family-owned restaurants and shops are a dying breed. You'd better believe New Yorkers value their secrets. But here's the thing about secrets: they don't help people stay in business and they don't save precious spaces from turning into a brand new block of condos. Our philosophy: if you find someplace special, tell a friend.

Mom & Pop Shops

Bars & restaurants with outdoor spaces

They're little museums in their own right, preserving the character and traditions of the city's past, while facing the continuous threat of modernization and rising rents...

The Little Red Brick House of Rare Cookbooks

If Manhattan has a portal to a literary Narnia, we believe **Joanne Hendricks Cookbooks** might be it. Hiding behind the weathered old wooden door of this two and a half story red brick house built in the 1820s is the kind of bookshop you just didn't think existed anymore. It might read "cookbooks" on the brass plaque outside, but even if you've never managed to cook anything more elaborate than an omelet, don't make the mistake of not giving that rickety old door a nudge and stepping inside Joanne Hendrick's home. Yes, that's right, you're stepping into Joanne's home. Mr & Mrs. Hendricks live inside this historic house on Greenwich Street above the bookshop. Joanne is quiet and shy, but with the right questions, you can end up sharing stories in her little bookshop for over an hour. Each of her books is a treasure to behold. There are books about how to tell one's fortune from tea leaves and priceless antique first editions. You'll gush over her beautiful wallpaper and the dinner table trinkets and collectibles that sit on the shelves in between hundred-year-old books. Art Deco cocktail cups, vintage ladles, prints and porcelain for the kitchen; you'll want it all, but never once will you feel like you're in a shop. Joanne welcomes you into her home like they do in storybooks; where the lead character on a long journey gets invited in by the wise woman for some much-needed respite from the big scary world out there.

(488 Greenwich Street, West Soho 10013; +1 212-226-5731; opening hours vary, call ahead to check Joanne is in town)

The Last Soda Fountains of New York

If you happen to be on a mission to document the city's last diners, luncheonettes and soda fountains, don't miss **Anapoli Ice Cream Parlor and Family Restaurant**. A little off the grid, out in Bay Ridge, Brooklyn, this one is over 100 years old, frozen in time with its original stools and mosaic floor tiling, stained glass and cherry wood fittings. Most of the clientele are locals that have been coming here since their youth, but some of them might never have noticed they have a back garden open during summer. Much like Hildebrandt's Ice Cream and Soda Fountain outside of Queens (see pg 50), it's worth the field trip, even if it's just for a good old fashioned malt.

(1351, 6920 3rd Ave, Brooklyn, NY 11209; +1 718-748-3863; Mon-Thurs, 7am-7:30pm, Fri & Sat 7am-9pm, Sun 8am-7.30pm)

A Time Capsule Barber Shop

"The one charm about the past," wrote Oscar Wilde in his masterpiece *The Picture of Dorian Gray*, "is that it is the past." Clearly, he never met Tony Garofalo. We can safely assume that the sign above **Tony's Park Barbershop** hasn't been updated since 1930-something. The lettering above the door, a cursive mantra reading, "Any Style...You Like," is fading. Yet, when we step inside, the warmth and life of the space are almost tangible. Time has softened its paint into shades of pastel blue. It's hard to believe this place has managed to remain exactly the same for so long with its faded clocks, antique barber chairs, pastel Formica cabinetry, pressed-tin ceiling and don't forget that old New Yawk hospitality. The vintage cash register is so old it only rings up customers in $2 increments. Tony Garofalo emigrated to Brooklyn in 1964, got a job at this Park Slope barbershop and became the owner a year later when he bought the business for just under $2,000. Several years later, he bought the apartments above too. Garofalo has now been behind the wheel – or barber chair, rather – of the little Brooklyn Barber Shop that could for over half a century. He just turned 80, so if you manage to get there in time, you might just have the pleasure before it's too late and another piece of old New York disappears. It's the epitome of the New York you see in the movies, but better. It's real. *(4409 5th Ave, Brooklyn, NY 11220; Mon-Sat 8am-4pm)*

> What makes you happiest in New York?
> — Well, every time I get a paycheck,
> how's about that?

– Tony Garofalo, Barber and owner of
Tony's Park Barber Shop since 1965

Tony's Park Barbershop

An Antique Purveyor of Rare Teas & Coffee since 1895

They say New York is the city that never sleeps, which might explain why New Yorkers are crazy about coffee, but also, why **McNulty's Tea & Coffee Co.** is still a thriving local business after 125 years. Stepping inside this dark and cozy emporium in the West Village is deliciously nostalgic as the aroma of Ceylon Silvertips, Guatemalan beans and New York history curl around your senses. As the story goes, the original owner was Judge McNulty, an Irish immigrant affiliated with the notorious political corruption of Tammany Hall that rigged elections to get the Irish in power. The shop still sells a 'Secret Judge Blend' coffee that was allegedly created just for him. Today McNulty's is owned by the genteel Wing H. Wong and his son David, who have run the shop for nearly forty years as guardians of a vital supplier of rare teas and coffees for the connoisseur. Underneath the low tin tile ceiling, burlap sacks of beans imported from all over the world are piled on the gently sloping wooden floorboards. Cabinet drawers and apothecary jars are filled with every sort of tea and coffee your heart could desire, from highly prized Jamaican Blue Mountain roasts to China Black Gunpowder tea. For caffeine addicts, McNulty's must seem like as veritable modern-day opium den.
(109 Christopher St, Greenwich Village, NY 10014; +1 800 356-5200; Open Mon-Sat 10am-9pm, Sun 1pm-7pm)

The King of KA-CHING

The **Faerman Cash Register Company** has somehow survived from another age, selling and repairing cash registers and scales for over a century. When the Faerman's started out in 1910, ornate brass cash registers were necessary showpieces in order for shops to indicate they were a high-end establishment. Back then, this block of the Bowery was home to four other cash register companies, and still had an elevated railroad with trains thundering overhead. Bernie Faerman had been repairing and selling machines at his family's shop

Faerman Cash Register Company

after returning from World War II. Since his recent passing, his son Brian is now manning this tinkerer's paradise on his own and will continue lovingly rebuilding the machines, as his father did, so they can be used for another hundred years. Brian's a talkative one and a real softy on the inside (once you get through that working man exterior), so expect to linger a while. As electronic registers and cashless payment systems make it increasingly harder for a business like this to exist, this is a slice of old New York City that you have to see before it disappears forever.
(159 Bowery, New York, NY, 10002; +1 212-226-2935; Mon-Fri 9am-5pm, Sat 9am-3pm, closed Sundays)

If Bob Dylan and Bernie Sanders opened a Bookshop

Jim Dougras is a New York wise man with long silver hair topped by a cowboy hat, who runs **Unoppressive Non-Imperialist Bargain Books**, a small Mom & Pop bookshop with a big presence since 1992. Why Unoppressive? Because you can still afford a book here if you're stone-broke. Non-Imperialist? "Because it's not Amazon and it's not trying to take over the world", says Dougras. Allen Ginsberg regularly browsed these shelves in the last few years of his life, and there's an entire corner dedicated to Bob Dylan books. In 2016, this tiny Greenwich Village bookshop moonlighted as a Manhattan HQ for the Bernie Sanders campaign. After the election results in 2016, Dougras put up a sign up on the door offering free therapy. Jim works every day of the week with his wife, staying open until midnight on weekends to keep his bookstore alive during difficult times. He can come across a little grouchy on his occasional off day, but let it be known that he just wants you to come in and find something impactful on his shelves; something that will move you and restore your faith in humanity after a long day in a dog-eat-dog world.
(34 Carmine St, New York, NY 10014, +1 212-229-0079; Mon-Thurs 11am-10pm, until midnight Fri & Sat; Unoppressivebooks.blogspot.com)

Century Old Sewing Machine Repairs

A curious relic from when the Garment District dominated this part of Manhattan, **Hecht Sewing Machine & Motor Co** is part industrial sewing machine repair shop, and part treasure trove of antiquities and artifacts from America's past. Stretching back much further than the small incongruous storefront on West 38th would have you believe, the Hecht family business has been around since about 1910. Seek out this unexpected Aladdin's Cave when you're feeling overwhelmed in the heart of busy Midtown. It's hard to know just what is for sale and what is decoration, but Hecht's is one of those small, niche businesses that has somehow survived the vast swathes of change that have taken most of the old Manhattan away forever. Be sensitive to the fact that the owner is trying to run a business, so if you're in the market for a sewing machine, you'll get to stick around longer.

(304 West 38th Street, New York, NY, 10018, +1 212-563-5950; Mon-Fri 9am-5pm)

Hecht Sewing Machine & Moto Company

Secret Restaurants

Lunch at the United Nations

If more people thought to poke their head into the United Nations building, they would know that the public is welcome to dine with delegates for lunch, from Monday to Friday. Politicians, ambassadors, emissaries, translators, spokespeople, humanitarians – they all need to eat right? So should we really be all that surprised that the United Nations has its own restaurant offering an international *prix-fixe* buffet with stunning views of the East River? **The Delegates Dining Room** isn't exactly the trendiest of restaurants, but it's certainly "where the world meets," and one of the most unusual places to say you've had the pleasure of dining in New York City. Reservations are required in advance as is a business dress code (this is a white-tablecloth kinda joint and the prix-fixe is $40). Visitors for lunch should also show up 15 minutes early for security and ID check-in.

(First Avenue & 43rd Street, New York, NY, 10017; +1 917-367-3314;
Mon-Fri 11.30am-2.30pm; Delegatesdiningroom-un.com)

Don't Tell Them We Gave You the Phone Number

Bohemian is "not open to the public" and you're supposed to be recommended by existing patrons. Apparently, it's "a thing" in Tokyo and this is the secret New York base of a Japanese collective called Play Earth, which has a few referral-only restaurants already in Japan and around the world. We'd like to say we think it's pretentious, but we're always suckers for a challenge. The phone number is unlisted and the restaurant is hidden down a dimly-lit corridor inside of a building in Noho that used to be owned by Andy Warhol. Jean-Michel Basquiat also had his live-in studio here. Ring the doorbell and the first thing you'll realize as you enter is that this "super exclusive restaurant" is actually just a very relaxing place. The second thing you'll notice is there's nothing really that bohemian about Bohemian. The atmosphere is a minimalist's dream with modern art on the walls, nooks of mini zen gardens and plush mid-century armchairs surrounded by low tables for low eating — Japanese style. If you're lucky, there might be a long-haired Japanese guy on hand at the bar serenading you through dinner with his Spanish guitar. The menu is an original blend of Japanese x French (all the rage in Paris) but with an added American twist. The chef does an excellent beef short rib sashimi, Foie gras soba and they even have their own take on macaroni and cheese. Share the Uni croquette to start and don't miss the Yuzu soufflé for dessert. Also an option: the tasting menu at $55 per person. Okay, now for that all-important phone number. Yes, we have it and we're going to give it to you, but promise you won't tell them you got it from us. In theory, you have to be recommended by a regular who gives you the phone number and in turn, you provide that regular's name to book a table. But we'll let you in on a little secret: when they ask how you got the number just say "a friend gave it to me", which in our experience, is all you need to pass the test. If you prefer to do it without cheating, they suggest first-time visitors email them through their website with a full introduction of yourself and "should the stars align", they'll get in touch. Or you could just skip that part. Here's the number: 212-388-1070. And the address for that matter: *(57 Great Jones Street, NoHo, 10012, NY; Playearth.jp/eng/bohemian_ny)*

Break Naan in an Underground Indian Temple

Arguably the best South Indian cuisine in the state of New York and possibly the entire country, is served in a no-frills canteen in the basement of an ornate, practicing Hindu temple in Queens. Everyone is welcome at the **Ganesh Temple Canteen**, a bustling underground cafeteria serving $3 Dosa pancakes (shaped like wizard hats) and five-star quality South Indian cuisine served on humble plastic trays. Get that mango Lassi to drink in case you pass your spice threshold, the onion Uttappam (another type of pancake) with chutney and *sambhar* sauces and those delicious Vada donuts. You can go all out here on sampling the menu because it's all scandalously cheap. After lunch, you can even step inside the temple. Remember to be respectful. Leave your shoes at the door and heed to the "No Coconut Breaking" rule; a measure put in place to regulate the ancient practice of breaking coconuts to remove obtacles (*45-57 Bowne St, Queens, NY 11355; Open everyday 8:30am-9pm; +1 718-460-8484*).

The Ganesh Temple of Queens

Brooklyn's Secret Japanese Supper Club

Inside a nondescript residential building in Williamsburg, there's a secret Japanese restaurant behind one of the apartment doors. This is not just another supper club with a dilettante chef, but a seriously gifted host whose level of cooking is being whispered about as a talent which far surpasses anything you can find in many of New York's most revered restaurants. Japanese-born New Yorker, Ai, invites you to eat at her **Ajito: The Hideout**, an enchanting loft space she shares with her husband Matt, an all-around creative guy who builds his own bicycles and has an endless supply of fascinating and friendly dinner table conversation. While he plays the role of the charming host, introducing everyone to everyone, Ai has the magic food hands, conjuring up dazzling Japanese fusion dishes using fresh Japanese herbs and ingredients from the small urban farm they built on their loft's rooftop. The secret of Ai's hideout began to spread amongst in-the-know lovers of Japanese cuisine when she began using the online platform, *Eat With*, the website that invites people to dine in homes around the world, a.k.a., a foodie's version of 'Airbnb'. Ai offers several different menu experiences (she's known for seamlessly accommodating guests with special dietary needs) and can also accommodate for a private party. (*Find upcoming dates on Facebook.com/ajitofood or find & reserve with Ai on Eatwith.com/users/439987*)

A French Bakery hiding in the Lobby of a 1920s Office Building

Behind the heavy doors of the Merchants Building in TriBeCa, **Arcade Bakery** exists in a series of alcoves that we suspect might have been home to a shoe shiner's shop, or something of that nature, once upon a time. The cleverly designed café popped up in this Art Deco lobby in 2015, designed by acclaimed baker Roger Gural in collaboration with the Workstead studio, but it feels like it could have been here long before. Gural serves up delicious ham breakfast sandwiches, traditional French pastries and the revolutionary "Laminated Baguette": a doughy baguette wrapped in a butterfly, flaky croissant crust. Seat yourself in one of the alcove nooks with fold-down tables, open your newspaper and stay a while.

(Arcade Bakery, 220 Church St, Tribeca, NY 10013; +1 212-227-7895;
Open Mon-Fri 8am-3pm)

Secret Soba

The funny thing about **Sakagura** is that it's located in the basement of a humdrum business block, but once you find it, you'll feel like you've found an authentic and tranquil portal to Japan. Kitted out like a traditional *Izakaya* (informal tavern), you'll find good sashimi and sushi here, but not just. The homemade soba noodle bowls hit the spot, the tempura is always a safe bet for fussy eaters, but for something adventurous, let the ox tongue stew surprise you.

(211 E 43rd St, B1, Midtown, NY 10017; +1 212-953-7253;
Open for lunch Mon-Fri 11:30am-2:20pm, dinner from 6pm everyday; Sakagura.com)

Estonian Soul Food

In the 1920s, a group of Estonian sailors in the city wanted a place to put their feet up, and reminisce about the old country over a hot bowl of *lõhesupp*. Thus, the **Estonian House** was born and thrives to this day as a semi-private social club for one of New York's smallest, but most welcoming immigrant communities. The stunning, four-story *Beaux-Arts* building is a sight for sore eyes in Midtown, and the inside doesn't disappoint either. Sounds of the Estonian choral group, study groups and various other events drift down its dark wooden staircase. You'll want to make a straight shot back to its restaurant, which is not at all ornate, but covered in nostalgic, Impressionist-style paintings of Baltic lakes and monuments, and whose resident barmaid, Vivika, will steer you towards a good stiff drink. Nothing on the dinner menu is over $10, so you can go all out sampling *ühepajatoit* (meat stew), *pelmeenid* (dumplings) and *kringel* (cinnamon bread). Cash-only and no reservations required.

(243 E 34th St, Midtown, NY 10016; +1 212 684-0336; Thurs-Sat 5pm-10pm)

Hidden Enclaves & Garden Restaurants

Where to find your own little piece of urban paradise away from the crowds...

A Family Feast with Views of the Empire State Building

There's nothing trendy about **Marchi's**, which is probably why it's often overlooked, and why their beautiful, fairy-lit garden with a remarkable view of the Empire State Building is one of the city's best-kept secrets. Situated on a tree-lined street in Manhattan at the bottom of a brownstone with no real sign outside, this place is nothing but old school Italian: still family-run, and still serving the same 5-course Italian meal since it first opened in 1929. There's no menu, so no pressure, just sit back and let the Marchi family feed you, starting with an overflowing plate of fresh crudité. They'll likely come out with the house lasagna next, which melts in your mouth, followed by fish, then a meat dish and dessert. It's all homemade. How does a place like this still exist in central Manhattan? The family owns the building. On a hot summer's day when all the popular terrace spots are overflowing with people, treat yourself to a casual *al fresco* family feast at Marchi's.

(251 E 31st St, Murray Hill, NY 10016; +1 212 679-2494; Open daily 5pm-10pm)

The Cloisters,
pg 191

The Village Restaurant

In the heart of a 400-year-old cobblestone village in the city, bound together by a tight-knit community whose homes look like they've been teleported in from old Europe (see page 45), you'll find **Vinegar Hill House**. Bring anyone from your mother to your lover here for some whiskey and cornbread and farm fresh seasonal plates in a relaxed, antique setting. In the summer, an urban paradise awaits in the back garden under the cherry tree.

(72 Hudson Avenue, Brooklyn, NY 11201; +1 718-522-1018; Mon-Fri 6pm-11pm, weekend Brunch is served Sat-Sun 10.30am-3.30pm; Vinegarhillhouse.com)

South American Pit Stop

If you've never tried a Venezuelan arepa, start at **Caracas Arepa Bar** with a Hot Queen arepa (traditional corn pancake filled with Sautéed pulled chicken) and a side of tequeños (fried cheese sticks). Don't forget to dip them in the secret spicy sauce they have at every table. The Williamsburg location has a charming hidden backyard with picnic tables and colorful parasols for a Venezuelan barbeque ambiance in the heart of Brooklyn.

(291 Grand St Brooklyn, NY 11211; (718) 218-6050; Open every day from noon to near midnight)

Mother's Day Treat

Charmingly opulent to the point of kitsch, **Barbetta** is where women of the 1950s expected to be taken for a fancy dinner date. In Manhattan's Theatre district, this is another of New York City's oldest family-owned Italian restaurants, which took up residence in this brownstone townhouse over a century ago. The Baroque-style interiors have remained the same over the decades, and the back garden with its century-old trees and wisteria make you feel as if you're dining on a fancy country estate. Barbetta happens to own their own truffle hounds that search the Piemonte countryside in Italy during truffle season – so anything with truffles on it is a good choice. The restaurant claims to be the first restaurant in New York to serve white truffles. In fact, they keep an entire list of Barbetta firsts on their website including, first to serve risotto, sun-dried tomatoes and Tuscan Extra-Virgin Olive Oil, first to have a pre-opera menu and the first restaurant with a garden (outside Central Park). Make it a first for mother dear and treat her to a delightful Mother's Day lunch.

(321 W 46th St, Manhattan New York, NY 10036; +1 212-246-9171; open every day for lunch & dinner, bar open until midnight; Barbettarestaurant.com)

Gorgonzola in the Greenhouse

La Lanterna di Vittorio has a very charming lantern-filled winter garden for dining under the stars all year round. Calzones, candlelit tables, fireplaces ablaze, nightly jazz in the adjacent bar – this little trattoria in Greenwich Village ticks all the right boxes, especially when they welcome you without a reservation after you couldn't get that table at Palma (pg 51) around the block. *(129 Macdougal St, Greenwich Village, NY 10012; +1 917-639-3236; Sun-Thurs 10am-2am, Fri-Sat 10am-3am).*

We'd also like to give an honorable mention to another Italian eatery in the village, **Frankies 457 Spuntino,** for their gorgeous little back garden open during the summer months that'll have you feeling like you're on summer vacation in Tuscany (and you can even hire it out for garden parties). Someone at the table should always order the house specialty: cavatelli with hot sausage and browned sage butter. *(457 Court St., Brooklyn, NY 11231; +1 718-403-0033; Open Mon-Fri 11am-11pm, 12am on weekends.)*

 For more gardens, rooftops and terraces, see Social Playgrounds in the Sun pg 163, Night of Joy, pg 32, St. Mazie Bar, pg 159, Grand Prospect Hall, pg 63, Sunny's Bar, pg 205, Loosie Rouge, pg 155, Maison May and Sycamore Bar & Flower Shop, pg 172.

A Secret Graveyard in the Heart of the Manhattan

Here's one we found while scanning satellite images of the city. **New York Marble Cemetery** is a rare slice of green, half a hectare exactly, invisible from the street and surrounded by old tenement buildings behind the Bowery. The historic graveyard is entered through an alleyway with an iron gate at each end, located between 41 & 43 Second Avenue. The burial ground counts former

The New York
Marble Cemetery

mayors, notable merchants and congressmen, whose names are listed on the walls rather than on tombstones, as its permanent guests. An enchanted oasis out of time and place, the hidden garden is blooming come spring. The cemetery is open at least once a month; April through October on Saturdays or Sundays from 12pm-4pm. Not to be confused with the nearby New York City Marble Cemetery one block east, which is entirely separate and visible from the street. Check the website for the scheduled days.
(41 1/2 2nd Ave, New York, NY 10003; Check website for opening days and hours; Marblecemetery.org)

Elevator to an Oasis Amongst the Skyscrapers
In the busy Financial District, a discreet escalator leads to the **Elevated Acre**, a secluded leafy oasis in the midst of our concrete jungle. Several stories above the pandemonium of Downtown is an entire acre of natural beauty overlooking the East River. Winding paths, surreal views and picturesque flower beds make it a perfect, secret place for a peaceful lunch.
(55 Water Street, New York, NY; +1 212-747-9120; 55water.com)

Dinner in a Fairy-lit Hideaway
Tucked away at the end of a graffiti-covered alley in Manhattan, the inviting French windows, twinkling string lights and green potted plants of **Freemans Restaurant** welcome you to a cozy little hideaway offering an old-world ambiance, and rustic American cuisine on the menu. What was once an abandoned and dangerous dead-end alley, has become a reliably charming Lower East Side destination since opening in 2014 and looks set to stay. A future classic, this is a restaurant that we wager a book much like this one could be talking about in a hundred years time.
(Freeman Alley, Lower East Side; +1 212-420-0012; open everyday for lunch & dinner, and brunch on Sundays)

A Medieval Garden transported from Europe
Nestled into a hilltop overlooking the river, Manhattan hides a veritable medieval oasis, older than the United States itself. **The Cloisters** is a museum comprised of a labyrinth of ancient French archways, turrets and Gothic chapels that traveled across the Atlantic in the 1930s to find a new home here. The cavernous site could pass as a ruin from Rome's Trastevere, but it's actually an extension of the MET Museum. Its heavenly halls boast some of the most remarkable medieval artifacts in the world, from actual papal garments to those famous unicorn tapestries, but somehow it's remained a bit of an overlooked New York secret. The cloisters were another of John D. Rockefeller, Jr.'s elaborate fantasies come-to-life, a composite of Medieval structures brought from European monasteries and abbeys and reassembled in Manhattan. From

Bellocq Tea Atelier

the ancient variety of roses to star-shaped mole plants, the spindly floriculture look like it's been flourishing here for centuries. Designed to promote communion with God, every sprout in the garden is meticulously selected to make sure nothing other than *ye olde* varieties take root. Pack a picnic. *(99 Margaret Corbin Dr, Manhattan, NY 10040; +1 212 923-3700; Open daily from 10am-5pm; metmuseum.org/visit/met-cloisters)*

The Cloisters

Baby, it's Cold Outside

Come in from the snow storm and warm up at New York's coziest spots......

Narnia's Secret Tea House

Discovering the **Bellocq Tea Atelier** is a bit like finding Narnia in this industrial part of Greenpoint, Brooklyn. Ring the doorbell of an inconspicuous black door and step into the very definition of zen. Exotic hanging plants, weathered walls lined with shelves of beautiful tea cases and antique measuring instruments catch the eye, while an aromatic feast of top-tier herbal artistry wafts around you. Ease your winter suffering on the pink velvet vintage couches with a tasting of some of the finest and rarest teas in the world, guided by your personal tea guru who can help you find the perfect brew. Discover Marjorelle Mint and High Mountain Oolong tea alongside a beautifully curated collection of tea wares, incense, honeys and candles for sale. Try to stop yourself from curling up and taking a nap in what has to be the world's most beautiful hidden tea house.

(104 West St, Brooklyn, NY 11222; +1 800-495-5416; open Wed & Thurs 12pm-6pm, Fri & Sat 12pm-7pm, Sun 12pm-5pm; Bellocq.com)

Up: Bellocq Tea Atelier
Right: Tea & Sympathy

A Very British Little Tea Room

Oh, we do hope this one is still around by the time you're reading this. Afternoon tea as it should be at **Tea & Sympathy** — welcoming British accents, perfectly cut cucumber sandwiches, photographs of the Queen and her corgis on the walls, this place truly feels like a Maggie Thatcher-era time warp. Even in London, places like this are hard to find these days. It's been a Greenwich Village favorite for over two decades, but in late 2018, the owners were forced to start a crowdfunding page to raise money to keep it in business. "We have stood by and watched all of the local businesses who made the West Village what it is today lost to landlords and buyouts and profit losses. We are trying so hard not to be added to that list," wrote the owner, Nicky Perry, who also runs an authentic fish & chips shop next door, **A Salt & Battery** (see pg 90). We very much hope for all our sakes that they manage to stick around. Go for the tea & scones, stay for the Shepherd's Pie and come back for the home away from home. *(108 Greenwich Ave, Greenwich Village, NY 10011; +1 212-989-9735; Mon-Fri 11am-10.30pm, Sat 9.30am-10.30pm, Sun 9.30am-10pm; Teaandsympathy.com)*

A Lumberjack's Brooklyn Cabin

One of the rowhouses on Union Street is not like the others. The ground floor of the corner block has been converted into a wood-fronted cabin, complete with rustic Adirondack chairs and chopped firewood in the yard. Swing open the barn door of **Black Mountain Wine House** to find a roaring fireplace, a hearty list of gastropub dishes and wines that are almost all offered by the glass. Whatever the time of year, this cozy spot feels like an escape to rural Vermont. *(415 Union St, Brooklyn, NY 11231; +1 718-522-4340; Open daily 3pm-12am)*

Hidden Fondue Spot

On winter nights when you're longing for gooey cheese comfort food, preferably served inside a European ski chalet, head to **Café Select**. The Swiss-themed café cooks up their staple "après ski fondue" in a hidden room at the back for a *fromage* feast under the twinkle lights. *(212 Lafayette St, New York, NY 10012; +1 212-925-9322; Mon-Fri 8am-2am, Weekends 9am-2am)*

Your Forever Irish Sweetheart

When the windows at **Neary's** start fogging up in winter, it's time to head inside and warm up with an Irish welcome and outstanding roast beef. This east side gem opened on St. Patty's Day in 1967 and has been thriving ever since. Jimmy Neary himself is there every night and can lift the spirits of any "sourpuss" suffering from the winter blues. Not just another Irish pub, Neary's prides itself on being a down-home, unpretentious experience while offering a classic red tablecloth ambiance to wine and dine your longtime sweetheart. *(358 E 57th St, Midtown, NY 10022; +1 212 751-1434; Open daily from 11am-2am; Nearys.com)*

Cinnamon Toast Brunch

All is swell at **Allswell**, a cozy cottage tavern on Bedford Avenue outfitted with warm wood interiors and inviting windows framed with twinkle lights. More brunch spots should offer Cinnamon Toast on their menus, a simple but delicious old American breakfast staple – but they don't, which is the number one reason you should discover Allswell. The friendly service and wide choice of comfort food will lure you back for dinner on a cold winter's night. *(124 Bedford Ave, Brooklyn, NY 11211; +1 347-799-2743; Mon-Thurs 12pm-12am, Bar open until 2am on Friday, Sat 10am-2am, Sun 10am-11pm; Allswellnyc.com)*

OAK SQUARE

3303

Escaping the City Without Really Trying

We all need a timeout and in under an hour, you can find yourself in sleepy "small town America", vacation like you're in New England or hike like you're in Yellowstone Park. No car? No problem. You won't believe how far your metro card can take you.

Pulling Carrots out of the Ground in New York City

The **Queens County Farm Museum** is the only historic working farm left in New York City, and it's open to the public seven days a week, all year round, free of charge. Roam 47 acres of farmland where tomatoes, eggplants, asparagus and other fruits and vegetables are thriving. From Spring through Fall, you're invited to drop by and volunteer alongside the farmers every Tuesday and Sunday anytime between 10am and 4pm. Volunteers must be 18 or older, no need to sign up or plan ahead, but be prepared to get your hands dirty. There's a fresh farm salad on the house for lunch in exchange, but of course, spending your Sunday in an 18th century time capsule of farm life in New York City is the real reward. Kids love it here too (see pg 234) especially for the animal feeding and the weekend hayrides. *(73-50 Little Neck Pkwy, Queens, NY 11004; +1-718-347-3276; Open everyday 10am-5pm; Queensfarm.org)*

June 1944, Meyer, Edward

Rooftop Dinner in a Sunflower Field

When it comes to rooftop farms, **Brooklyn Grange** is king. Tour acres of vegetable patches and take a selfie with a sunflower; sign up for a natural dye workshop, or intro to beekeeping. But above all, do one of their family-style farm dinners, where they invite guest chefs to cook using ingredients from the harvest and lay a feast out at twilight. There are two farms, one in Long Island City and another by the Brooklyn Navy Yard but tickets sell out fast. Be sure to sign up for their newsletter to book well in advance. *(BrooklynGrangeFarm.com)*

Brooklyn Grange

▶ Meet the Brooklyn Grange Beekeepers

— Can you recall the last moment when NYC made you think – "damn, I love this city"?

Danielle: I was inspecting a hive in the Financial District and I looked over the edge of this 30 story building, and the light was just hitting the bees in this way that illuminated them as they flew up from the street to the roof. It was a special moment seeing these little insects make their way home to this tiny hive in the middle of bustling Manhattan.

— What's your favourite place to "escape the city" within the city?

Geraldine: I love libraries, especially the map room at the New York Public Library, off to the side and less visited than the main hall. The decor is so lush and you can take out maps from across the world and centuries back.

Beekeepers Danielle Knott and Geraldine Simonis,
at Brooklyn Grange Brooklyn Navy Yard Apiary,
photographed by Valery Rizzo.

Search for the City's Busy Little Beehives

As fate would have it, some of the dreamiest real estate in New York City is also its tiniest. The beekeeping villages of America's premier metropolis aren't always where you'd expect, and it can take a keen eye to spot them amongst the skyscrapers. A stone's throw from the insanity of the Stock Exchange is the **Battery Park** bee village, whose architectural style is an adorable nod to the area's Dutch roots. The houses are painted a custard yellow and would have a great view of the Statue of Liberty if it weren't for their pint-sized proportions. (*Financial District, NY, 10004, across from the U.S. Coast Guard Recruitment Centre*)

On the doorstep of Columbia University there's the holy honey of **St. John the Divine**, whose bees are busy pollinating the cathedral's veritable Garden of Eden, which boasts cherry blossom trees, a fountain, and even peacocks. The cathedral's grounds reign over 11-acres of the otherwise hectic Uptown area and a visit to its gardens is a welcome respite. (*1047 Amsterdam Avenue at 112th Street New York, NY 10025; +1 212-316-7540; Open 24/7*)

While you're uptown, stop by the **Bryant Park** apiary where they even offer classes in beekeeping. (*Between Fifth and Sixth Avenues and between 40th and 42nd Streets, Midtown, NY, 10018; +1 212-768-4242; Bryantpark.org/programs/ beekeeping*). Finally, while discovering the "Brooklyn catacombs" (pg 280) listen out for the bees of **Green-Wood Cemetery** whose honey, aptly named "The Sweet Hereafter" is made for sale in small batches, available onsite at the graveyard. (*500 25th Street, Brooklyn, NY 11232; +1 718-768-7300; Open every day 7am-7pm; Green-wood.com*)

Battery Park bee village

A Rose by Any Other Name

A sprawling Japanese cherry tree esplanade, a glass aquatic plant house and a fastidiously tended "Fragrance Garden" are just a few of the exotic splendors of the **Brooklyn Botanical Garden**, founded over 100 years ago in Prospect Park. Its 52-acres even boast an art gallery, a rare book room that houses collections of European herbs and a Shakespeare Garden (charming cottage included) exhibiting more than 80 plants mentioned in the playwright's work. Entry is free Fridays before noon.
(990 Washington Ave, Brooklyn, NY 11225; +1 718-623-7200; Tues-Fri 8am-6pm, Sat-Sun 10am-6pm; Bbg.org)

A Parisian alternative to Central Park

Opened in 1891 at the heart of working-class Brooklyn, **McGolrick Park** is a small respite in Greenpoint, Williamsburg with a Parisian feel thanks to the 18th-century colonnade, antique statues and winding pathways reminiscent of *Parc Monceau* on the Left Bank. Come for the Sunday farmers market, from 10am -3pm and play with pups in the Dog Run area.
(Russell Street &, Nassau Ave, Brooklyn, NY 11222)

10 Very Convincing Reasons to Hang out in Red Hook

You could say New York City's Red Hook neighbourhood is a bit of a ghost town, albeit a delightful one, compared to how it was 50 years ago. Local old-timers remember when it was a bustling shipping port; thousands of people walked the streets and there were restaurants on every corner. Red Hook's renaissance is already underway as this sleepy corner of south Brooklyn welcomes young businesses eager to revive old workshops and warehouses. And yet, this still feels like a place where pirates could retire. There's a bohemian, nautical charm about the area that makes you feel like you're vacationing in a renegade community of New York. It's also one of the most lovable neighbourhoods in the city and here are a few reasons why...

1   **The Chocolate Factories**: Red Hook is home to not one but two chocolate factories. First, there's **Raaka**, which means "raw" in Swedish, and boy, does that raw smell of cocoa bean hit you on your way into this old metalworking factory. They welcome walk-in visitors all day and are always very generous with doling out samples that give you a taste of their adventurous flavor pairings (and you can purchase right there from the factory). But you can also book a factory tour and tasting for $15 or even a chocolate making class at the weekend for a creative group outing. *(64 Seabring St, Brooklyn, NY 11231; +1 855-255-3354; Mon-Fri 9am-5pm; Sat & Sun 12pm-6pm; Book online at Raakachocolate.com)*

Closer to the water there's the enchanting **Cacao Prieto** which shares its chocolate factory with a whiskey distillery, meaning you get to combine your chocolate tasting with a whiskey flight. Oh, and chickens. They keep chickens in their courtyard. *(218 Conover St, Brooklyn, NY 11231; +1 347-225-0130; Mon-Fri 9am-5pm, Sat & Sun 11am-7pm; Book online at Cacaoprieto.com)*

Red Hook

2 **The Waterfront Barge Museum:** Meet Red Hook storyteller, David Sharps, who lives on a retired wooden barge that's now a listed historic landmark. Everyone is welcome aboard his floating 'museum', better described as a bohemian showboat lost in time. Decorated with old-timey props and nautical antiques, the barge has its own theater with hand-painted backdrops that set the scene for pirate shows, live music concerts, operas and David's very own showboat circus (he's an accomplished juggler and performer). Even if you stop in on a day without any scheduled performances, Mr. Sharp will sit with you around the stove fire on his rocking chair and tell stories about his days living on the Seine in Paris on a houseboat, or recount the waterfront tales of Brooklyn. Admission is free, but a donation is suggested. A must-visit when in Red Hook. *(290 Conover St, Brooklyn, NY 11231; +1 718-624-4719; Thurs 4pm-8pm, Sat 1pm-5pm; Waterfrontmuseum.org)*

3 **Brooklyn Crab:** *Have we just pulled up to a crab shack in Montauk?* You won't believe you're in New York at this Red Hook fun house with a vast terrace and outdoor bar, crab barrels and string lights hanging from the ceiling and mini golf in the back. Come for cocktails in the sun with a side of fried shrimp. *(24 Reed St, Brooklyn, NY 11231; +1 718-643-2722; Wed-Sun 11:30am-10pm; Brooklyncrab.com)*

Clockwise from top left: Waterfront Barge Museum, Sunny's Bar, Brooklyn Crab and Cacao Prieto

4   **Steve's Authentic Key Lime Pies:** We mentioned earlier in this book that if someone you know just got dumped (see pg 88), the best thing you can offer them is one of Steve's fresh-squeezed, fresh-baked key lime pies. But what we didn't mention was the Mom & Pop shop's delicious chocolate-dipped key lime tarts to go, known as "The Swingle." Frozen on a stick and dipped in a molten pool of rich Belgian chocolate, don't miss the classic key lime pie, but if you like to challenge your taste buds, try the Chipotle flavor Swingle. Enjoy your sweet treat in the little park right next door with excellent views of the Statue of Liberty at Louis Valentino, Jr. Park & Pier, where the salty waves crash against the rocks on a windy day. Just don't leave Red Hook without a pie to take home for the fridge. *(185 Van Dyke St, Brooklyn, NY; +1 718-858-5333; Mon-Thurs 12pm-6pm, Fri until 7pm, Sat 11am-7pm, Sun 11am-6pm; Keylime.com)*

5   **Red Hook Winery:** These guys are working with the best vineyards in New York state – that's right, local wine made from local grapes that grow in Long Island and the Finger Lakes. Surrounded by old wine barrels in a cozy tasting room, enjoy generous pours at a reasonable price. Go on, order a cheese plate while you're at it. *(175 Van Dyke St, Brooklyn, NY 11231; +1 347-689-2432; everyday 12pm-6pm; Redhookwinery.com)*

6   **The Story behind the Forgotten Red Hook Trolley:** Feeling light on your feet out of the winery, take the waterfront path towards that big old storehouse with the Dutch windows. Stay by the waterfront until you get to the Fairway Market terrace and you'll spy an abandoned trolley (pictured on pg 196), sitting out in the open, catching the spray of the water by the Red Hook dock. There used to be a whole collection of trolleys here until they were removed in recent years after the city pulled the plug on the ill-fated dream of an adventurous New Yorker. In 1980, a 20-year-old urban explorer by the name of Robert Diamond discovered the world's oldest subway tunnel buried beneath the streets of Brooklyn. He entered the underground through a manhole at Atlantic Avenue and Court Street and crawled for 70 feet in the darkness until he hit a wall that sealed off the main portion of a forgotten tunnel. Originally built in 1844, it was written about by Walt Whitman himself during his time as a writer for Brooklyn periodicals. *"The old tunnel, that used to lie there underground [...] and soon to be utterly forgotten [...] For it was here you started to go down the island, in summer. For years, it was confidently counted on that this spot, and the railroad of which it was the terminus, were going to prove the permanent seat of business and wealth that belong to such enterprises. But its glory, after enduring in great splendor for a season, has now vanished–at least its Long Island Railroad glory has. The tunnel: dark as the grave, cold, damp, and silent."* (Walt Whitman for Brooklyniana, No.36, 1862). A determined Robert Diamond broke through the concrete wall with the help of a local gas company, winning a contract with the Department of Transportation to give tours of the fabled tunnel. On a

roll, he then embarked on a monumental project to acquire seventeen antique trolley cars from around the world, in an attempt to bring back the trolley service to the streets of Brooklyn. Lack of funding, lack of action and disputes with local volunteers saw the experiment lose favor with the city after 10 years of building tracks around Red Hook. The Department of Transportation paved over most of Diamond's tracks in 2010, confiscated his trolleys that were rusting out in the open and even canceled his contract for the popular underground tours of the Atlantic Avenue Tunnel (also known as the Cobble Hill Tunnel) citing safety concerns. All that's left of Bob Diamond's dream is one remaining skeleton of a 1951 PCC car that ran on Boston's Green Line for decades, and some overgrown trolley tracks going nowhere. Even those may be gone by the time you visit, so get to Red Hook quickly before this little-known trace of obscure Brooklyn history disappears.
(Red Hook Dock, 500 Van Brunt St, Brooklyn, NY 11231)

7   **Freebird Books**: By the water's edge, there's a charming used bookshop with a wooden storefront that could have been plucked from a ghost town out West. There are reading pews, likely salvaged from a church and a great selection of reads for around $5. Befittingly for this renegade community, they host a monthly post-apocalyptic book club. (See book clubs pg 105).

8   **Somewhere Pop-Up**: On a sunny day in Red Hook, take your newly acquired read from Freebird Books over to a romantic glasshouse setting where the French windows are flung open, and the cold brew coffee is made to perfection. They also serve tea, fresh lemonade, pastries and lots of natural sunlight. We're hoping this pop-up sticks around for more seasons to come, but we're pretty sure something pleasant will always exist inside this glass box on a sleepy corner of Red Hook.
(220 Conover Street, Brooklyn, 11231; open seasonally Mon-Fri 7am-5pm, Sat & Sun 8am-2pm; Instagram: @somewhere_redhook)

9   **Sunny's Bar**: This legendary dive bar is reason alone to come to Red Hook. It's been here since 1895 – the one with the old pick-up truck parked out front waving an American flag. If you come out to Red Hook in the evening just for Sunny's, it'll be like venturing to an eclectic little bar in the middle of nowhere (which makes it all the more fun). There's usually a bluegrass band playing at the weekend but tons of character any night of the week. They have a cozy little backyard with string lights and a garden shed. On sleepy Sundays, you'll share the bar with the local pirates and their pets. Sadly, Sunny Balzano himself, the Red Hook-born bohemian artist turned local legend, passed away in 2016 at the age of 81, but his spirit certainly lives on at his beloved Red Hook bar.
(253 Conover St, Brooklyn, NY 11231; Mon 5pm-12am, Tues 4pm-2am, Wed- Fri 4pm-4am, Sat 11am-4am, Sun 11am -12am; Sunnysredhook.com)

10   **The Free Ikea Water Taxi that Gets You There:** Getting to Red Hook is easier than you think. The subway and metro train ride might be a little tricky, but there's an unlikely saving grace thanks to IKEA's water taxi, which is free on weekends and runs a daily service every 45 minutes between Wall Street's Pier 11 in Manhattan to the Red Hook store – just a 10 minute walk along the water to Sunny's bar. They also have a free shuttle bus that runs every 30 minutes from the Smith & 9th, 4th & 9th and Borough Hall subway stations. When returning to the city late at night, spring for a car service, you'll be glad you did. An uber Pool will get you back to central Williamsburg for under $10.

A Stroll through the Forgotten Garden of Eden

Pack a picnic! You're leaving the busy city behind for a fairytale day trip to Yonkers. Allow yourself to be whisked off your feet by **Untermyer Gardens** with its walled Persian paradise, natural botanical beauty, early *Beaux-Arts* follies and far-stretching ponds. Take a summer snooze under the majestic weeping beech trees or take in the romance at the Temple of Love overlooking a waterfall with the Hudson River in the distance. Lo and behold, you'll also find the world's largest sundial here. Even more impressive, is that not so long ago, these historic gardens were entirely overgrown and forgotten. Only in 2011, did a nonprofit step in to restore the splendor of this early 20th-century estate. Getting there involves a short train ride from Grand Central Terminal on the Metro North. If more New Yorkers knew about this place, they would flock *en masse*, so maybe keep this one close to the heart, deal?
(945 N Broadway, Yonkers, NY 10701; open every day from 7am to 7pm)

Untermyer Gardens
© Kristine Paulus

The Tenenbaums' Island Getaway

Take the northbound 6 train as far as it will go, then hop on a short bus ride through Pelham Bay Park and over the water to find yourself in the small neighborhood of **City Island**, a small New England-like fishing village. Technically part of the Bronx, this seaport island has its own remote charm that makes you feel a sleepy world away from New York. Just a mile and half long and half a mile wide, City Island is famed for its seafood restaurants, mostly clustered down the southern tip of the island. In the summer, places like Johnny's Reef, Tony's Pier and Sammy's Fish Box are buzzing with day trippers driving down from the Bronx, most of whom simply drive back again, without exploring the tiny island's hidden treasures. Most of the island's life is centered around the main street, City Island Avenue, filled with antique shops, but much of City Island's charm lies in wandering down the side streets off the main Avenue. Head down to the end of Tier Street, where at number 21 you'll find a quaint house with a spire overlooking the water. Not only was a *Long Day's Journey Into Night* filmed here in 1962, but it was used as the family summer house in *The Royal Tenenbaums* where Gene Hackman's character shoots at his own children with a BB gun from the roof.

Head down Reville Street, and you'll find the historic Pelham Cemetery overlooking the water and passing sailboats. Similar in style to the early New England graveyards found in Colonial fishing villages, it's the final resting place of Revolutionary War soldiers and intrepid seafarers. The cemetery also gives the closest look you'll get at the mysterious and off-limits Hart Island, used as a Civil War prison, Victorian sanatorium, reformatory school and Cold War missile base. Tended by inmates from nearby Riker's Island, Hart Island is an eerie, desolate and abandoned place, filled with the graves of the city's unknown and unclaimed.

Around the corner on Fordham Street, is an old schoolhouse that houses the delightful **City Island Nautical Museum** (open mid-April to mid-December, every Sat & Sun 1pm-5pm; Cityislandmuseum.org). Wander around the old classrooms and hallways to discover the island's long-standing relationship with the surrounding water, back when City Island was a bustling community of Victorian mansions, boatyards, saloons and clubs that produced over half a dozen of America's Cup-winning yachts.

(Take the 6 train to Pelham Bay Park, walk south toward Wilkinson Avenue. Take Bus 29 from Bruckner and Wilkinson Avenue toward City Island)

Edgar Allan Poe's Cottage

Finding it there seems improbable. Absurd, even. Yet, on a sunny day way out in Sector G of the Bronx, amidst cheap Thai massage parlors and "99¢ Only" stores, stands the 221-year-old home of the king of American macabre, **Edgar Allan Poe's Cottage**. It's been a quiet witness to revolution, urban sprawl, abandon and Poe's greatest heartbreak. "He wrote some of his best work here," says Vivian Davis of the Bronx Historical Society, "But a lot of people don't know the love story side." She's talking about Virginia Clemm, Poe's ill-fated wife who died in the back bedroom in 1847. Her bed is still there, along with two other Poe family relics: a golden mirror and a rocking chair. We'll let you guess which room is haunted.

(2640 Grand Concourse, Bronx, NY 10458; +1 718-881-8900; Thur-Fri 10am-3pm, Sat 10am-4pm, Sun 1-5pm; Admission is $5/adult, $3 for students & seniors)

Edgar Allan Poe's Cottage

Downton Abbey in the Bronx

In the far reaches of Pelham Bay, or rather, just ten miles from Manhattan, the 348-year-old **Bartow-Pell Mansion** in the Bronx was once one of many retreats built for affluent New Yorkers to hang up their top hats and relax in Downton Abbey-level splendor. As with many old American mansions, the estate has her fair share of extravagant artifacts, ghost stories and, particularly here on the East Coast, early Native American history. Every inch of the home is still dripping in family antiques and the "upstairs-downstairs" dynamic has been left intact, including the old servants' bells that can still be found hanging from the wooden beams in the attic

bedrooms. Downstairs, one can imagine Ms.Bartow and her children needle pointing in the various drawing rooms while behind the scenes, servants were busy keeping the house running like a well-oiled machine. Regardless of the season, Bartow-Pell is heavily involved in the community, with a calendar that overflows with Teddy Bear Tea Parties for the kids, pop-up brass band nights and candle-lit tours.
(895 Shore Rd, Bronx, NY 10464; +1 718-885-1461; Wed, Sat, Sun 12pm-4pm; Bartowpellmansionmuseum.org)

A 15-minute drive west towards the Hudson, Van Cortlandt House is the oldest building in the Bronx, among the oldest in America, as well as one of its finest examples of high Georgian stone homes. If walls could talk, the near three-century-old bricks of the **Van Cortlandt House** would whisper secrets of both its high society founders, and its use during the Revolutionary War by both Lafayette and Washington. Entry is $5 for adults.
(6036 Broadway, Van Cortlandt Park, Bronx, NY 10471; +1 718-543-3344; Wed-Sun 10am-4pm, from 11am on Sat & Sun; Plan your visit at Vchm.org)

 Day Planner Tip: **Make a Downtonesque day of it in the Bronx, starting with Edgar Allan Poe's Cottage and Van Cortlandt House in the morning, stopping by the New York Botanical Gardens for lunch (pg 61) and make it to Bartow-Pell before the gates close at dusk.**

Picnics at Mark Twain's River House

With spectacular views of the Palisade cliffs across the Hudson, **Wave Hill** country estate is one of the most spectacular escapes on a warm summer's day. The neo-Georgian manor was built in the 1800s and leased by Mark Twain for several years, and before him, Theodore Roosevelt used to summer here with his family. The country estate in the Bronx has landscaped terraces worthy of a Gatsby lawn party, greenhouses, botanical gardens and up to 28 acres of woodland to wander; home to 4000 species of plants and trees. In the summer months, the public gardens host live music concerts, and guests are welcome to sit on the lawn while gazing up at those magnificent cliffs. There's an on-site café offering afternoon tea and a designated picnic area. Wave Hill also trains future gardeners as interns and for a small donation, you can adopt a bee from the Wave Hill colony. A quick trip on the metro north from Grand Central will take you all the way to Riverdale. A free Wave Hill shuttle bus meets passengers from northbound trains every hour from morning until 5 pm. *(675 W 252nd St, Bronx, NY 10471; Tues-Sun 9am-4:30pm, closed on Mon; see website for more details: Wavehill.org)*

A Subway Ride over Water to Bootlegger's Bay

Take the A train past the stop for JFK airport, look out the window and wait to find yourself riding right over the water. Get out at **Broad Channel** to discover the only inhabited island in Jamaica Bay with its wild marshy coastline, houses on stilts and rickety bridges reminiscent of a fishing village in Newfoundland. About as remote a place you can reach with a Metrocard and still see the Manhattan skyline in the distance, Broad Channel has a friendly, small-town feel, so cut off from the metropolis that during Prohibition, it was a thriving haven for bootleggers and saloons.

(The A or S to Broad Channel. The island is best explored on foot. Drop in at the Ruffle Bar to chat with the locals! 919 Cross Bay Blvd, NY, 11693; +1 718-318-2300)

Retire like a Sailor for the Day

Thousands of sailors once lived out their days on the north shore of Staten Island's **Snug Harbor** under the retirement home's motto "we who are weary seek a harbor." A glimpse into New York's seafaring past, the 19th-century site includes 130 acres of sculpted gardens, Victorian cottages and grand Greek Revival buildings that resemble Masonic temples. After a period of neglect

Broad Channel

and abandonment following the rise of the social security system, today much of this old retirement home has been repurposed into a cultural center, with enough museums and art spaces to fill a whole day of exploration. Start across the street from the main entrance, where down a set of stairs, you'll find the original abandoned platform and tracks from the long-gone North Shore Railroad. Much of Snug Harbor's charm lies in its cultivated grounds, which include a breathtaking Chinese Scholar's garden, a lush Tuscan fountain garden, and a secret walled garden with a maze and castle turret. The jewel in the collection though is the **Noble Maritime Collection**, occupying one of the old Beaux Arts buildings. You'll find an entire houseboat waiting inside, once home to artist John Noble, who for forty years, sailed around Staten Island capturing the waterfront through his lens. Climb aboard and explore Noble's restored 19th-century yacht cabin at this excellent Smithsonian-affiliated museum. *(1000 Richmond Terrace, Staten Island, NY, 10301; +1-718-425-3504; opening hours vary by season but usually 10am-5pm Tues-Sun during the summer, Fri-Sun only the rest of the year; Snug-harbor.org)*

A Perfect Day Trip Upstate

Hunting for Antiques & Ruined Mansions

Fall has arrived, Central Park is ablaze with shades of yellow, red and orange, but you'd be doing yourself a huge disservice if you didn't venture out of town to see what the great state of New York has to offer at this time of year. Just 50 miles from New York City is the charming village of **Cold Spring**. Regular trains leave Grand Central Terminal and take approximately 70-80 minutes. Make sure to find a seat on the left-hand side of the carriage leaving New York, as the track hugs the Hudson River, often just a few feet away from your window. Cold Spring's Main Street is a delightful example of "small town America," known for its well-preserved 19th century buildings, antique shops and incredible views of the Hudson River. Make sure to poke your head behind the picture perfect storefront of **Once Upon a Time**, where loveable old timers Bob and Barbara sell their antique miniatures, vintage toys, costume jewelry and other oddities. *(12 Main St, Cold Spring, NY 10516; +1 845-265-4339; open Mon-Fri 10am-4pm, Sat & Sun 10am-5pm).*

Stop for lunch at the colorful French saloon **Le Bouchon**, with its red chequered tablecloths and commendable faux French cuisine that makes you think of the old pioneer towns that tried to bring some French flair out to the Wild West.If the weather permits, sitting out on the porch with a bowl of French onion soup and a glass of port is a very agreeable way to watch this small town go about its day. *(76 Main St, Cold Spring, NY 10516; +1 845-265-7676; everyday 12pm-9pm)*

For something a little more American, get a hearty country-style brunch at the cute-as-a-cupcake **Hudson Hil's Market & Café** *(129 Main St, Cold Spring, NY 10516; +1 845-265-9471; Mon-Fri 8am-4pm, Sat & Sun until 5pm).* For a pint, you'll head to **Doug's Pretty Good Pub** at number 54 Main Street, claiming to serve "the best burger in town, voted by some guy who likes burgers." And if you're tempted to stay in this fairytale little town overnight, there's the historic **Pig Hill Inn** *(Pighillinn.com).* Established in 1825, its a perfectly cozy bed & breakfast with wood burning stoves in the rooms, and rates starting at $160 a night. But above all, do not leave this town without walking down to the water on West Street by the pergola to take in those views of the Hudson Valley. This land: what peace and beauty it has to offer!

Once Upon a Time
in Cold Spring

Hiding in the woods outside Cold Spring is one of the most captivating, and easily accessible, ruins in New York. The once magnificent **Cornish Estate** was built in 1917 for Edward Joel Cornish, President of the National Lead Company, and his wife Selina. The couple died tragically within a fortnight of each other in 1938, leaving the mansion empty, and a fire in the 1950s saw the grand home abandoned for good. Ever since, it's been slowly reclaimed by nature. But you can still get a clear picture of how beautiful this home once was. From the sweeping driveway to the greenhouses, to the long, tiled front terrace that ran the length of the mansion, and the steps that led down to an outdoor swimming pool. The central chimney stack is still standing, exposing the home's numerous fireplaces that once belonged to a living room, upper bedrooms and an attic– all vanished. The ruins are so remarkably intact and accessible, it is easy to wander in and picture the weekend cocktail parties that were once held here back in the 1920s and 30s before the Cornish Estate was lost to the forest. Standing on what was once the front lawn, Google a photograph of the house taken from the same spot before the fire and hold your phone up for a jarring 'before & after' view.

If you're traveling by foot, it's an easy-going hike to the mansion. Turn right on Main Street, following Fair Street out of town for approximately 15 minutes, until it joins NY-9D. A minute further on and you'll find a small car park and the beginning of the Cornish Estate Trail Loop. The mountains surrounding Cold Spring offer first-rate, non-too taxing hiking, and are a popular destination for hikers in the City. Take the trail that follows the direction of the river, and the Cornish Estate Ruins can be found to your left after about 20 minutes. They are easy to spot and incredible to explore.

If you're travelling by car and using GPS, search for "Northgate, Cornish Estate" and park by the side of the road just opposite the trail entrance. (Here are your parking space coordinates: N 41.4390505, W 73.973283). Careful not to mistake your destination with the "Cornish Estate Ruins", which will take you on a long and winding, but beautiful, detour through the woods in all its Autumn glory (the perks of getting lost). Edward Cornish kept a dairy farm to raise his prized Jersey cows deeper in the woods, which is also in ruins. If you'd like to visit this too, the closest you can park your car is around a 40 minute hike from the site and a further 20 minutes to the mansion. *(Bike and kayak rental are available from the town of Cold Spring on Main Street).*

Cornish Estate

07
Parents are Coming to Town

So the family is coming to check up on you in the big city. You'll want to keep them entertained but most importantly, create some great memories together. The perfect host should consider not overwhelming first-time visitors, be open to trying some of the classics and take the opportunity to plan a little family adventure, especially if the kids are coming too...

Jazz-Obsessed Dad

His record collection is filled with the who's who of the Harlem Renaissance, carefully alphabetized next to his collection of Scotch whisky. He hides a stash of Cuban cigars from your mother in his golf bag, but you'll never tell on Pa...

Real Basement Jazz in a Harlem Brownstone

Harlem's secret recipe for ridding yourself of the Sunday scaries, the brownstone home to **American Legion Post #398** looks like a regular local veterans organization, but venture down into the basement to discover a legendary, underground jazz jam session in full swing. Transported back to the Harlem of the 1940s, enjoy a comforting Southern soul food dinner on the cheap with phenomenal live jazz. Mingle with the local cool cats and smiling veterans with great stories over at the next table while sipping on $4 beers. Entrance is free, but cash is king for the bar and don't forget to sign in to the book first before entering. (*248 West 132nd Street, New York, NY, 10027; +1 212-283-9701; entrance is free, but as it is a branch of the American Legion, you'll have to sign in to enter. From 6pm, Sundays*)

Late Night Undiscovered Talent

A thriving bohemian basement bar, **Smalls** is a throwback to the era when Greenwich Village was filled with jazz clubs that stayed open until the sun was up. Almost every night they have an "after hours jam session" from midnight until 4am – a chance to get up close to some of the rising talents of New York's jazz scene, or perhaps even show off your own talents as a musician. A cover charge gets you in all night ($20), drinks are cheap ($3 beers) and you'll get a great view of the stage no matter where you sit. Go alone, with friends or with family; everyone will be happily bobbing their heads and having a good old time at this cozy little club. (*183 West 10th Street, Greenwich Village, New York, NY, 10014; +1 646-476-4346; Mon-Fri 7.30pm-4am, Sat 4.30pm-4am, Sun 1pm-4am; Smallslive.com*)

The Pizza Joint That Serenades You with Live Jazz

You can't really go wrong with pizza and jazz at **Arturo's Coal Oven Pizza**, a locally-owned Greenwich Village institution for over half a century. Its Neopolitan coal-oven-fired pies really only come in one size: *big*. Bring the whole family in on this one or a very hungry date. Timeworn leather booths, quirky decor and walls covered in old photographs make this a lowkey, locals' keepsake, but the nightly jazz makes it an extra special Village gem. Jimmy, the head waiter, also does a pretty good rendition of Frank Sinatra while bringing out those 16-inch pies. (*106 W Houston St, Greenwich Village, NY 10012; +1 212-677-3820; open daily 4pm-12am. No reservations on weekends*)

Time Traveller on Stage

He looks like Clark Gable and plays his instrument like Bix Beiderbecke; Michael Arenella's smooth style evokes the bygone era of the crooner that made 1920s dance music for the glittering Jazz Age. To catch him singing and performing with his Dreamland orchestra, head over to Brooklyn's exquisite, dark-paneled **Clover Club** on Wednesday nights and find yourself tapping your feet to the scintillating and energetic repertoire with some of the best cocktails in the borough. Michael is also the man behind the summer's most wonderful event, the swish Jazz Age Lawn Party (see pg 298) on Governor's Island. *(210 Smith Street, Brooklyn, NY, 11201; Wed 8.30pm-11pm; +1 718-855-7939; Cloverclubny.com)*

Michael Arenella with his Dreamland Orchestra at the Clover Club

One of the Grand Ol' Sit-Down Clubs of the '50s

Jack Kerouac called it "the bop joint" in his novel *On the Road*, and Ray Charles sang, "See the girl with the red dress on, she can do the Birdland all night long..." Founded in 1949, **Birdland** has remained one of the most active jazz clubs in New York City, and despite having moved a few blocks up from its original spot, this joint still gives the stage to the most talented artists in town, the old fashioned way. In a room bathed in red light, you'll be seated at a table and offered a dinner menu proposing small plates, sandwiches or main courses, all Southern style with a Cajun flair. Guests are asked to order a minimum of $10 each for the table. Sip your gimlet while getting to know a singer with vocals as smooth as Nat King Cole or a talented Grammy-nominated quartet – you might even catch Rod Stewart's touring band dropping in for a night of big band jazz. Unless you see other guests take the lead, it's a general *faux pas* to get up and dance or talk loudly throughout the performances. Think of it as a jazz concert with dinner. Tickets usually run between $25-$30, and it's advised you book in advance.

(315 W 44th St #5402, Midtown, NY 10036; open daily 5pm-1am; +1 212-581-3080; Birdlandjazz.com)

Beat the Monday Blues with the Oldest-Running Jazz Band in Town

There's a small steakhouse in the West Village where the kitschy holiday decorations stay up all year long and there's music every night of the week from 7 pm. But on Mondays, **Arthur's Tavern** is home to the Grove Street Stompers, who claim to be the oldest-running band in town, playing Dixie jazz here since 1959. On weekends, you can practically become part of the house band, huddling around the musicians on their stage, grooving to some Motown, bebop & blues until the early hours.

(57 Grove St, New York, NY, 10014; +1 212-675-6879; Arthurstavernnyc.com)

Sinatra's Cigar Supplier

Perhaps you remember, or at least long for the return, of an era when men wore pressed three-piece suits, two-tone shoes and regularly smoked cigars. If so, nestled amongst the skyscrapers and bustle of 42nd Street, just steps from Grand Central Terminal is a small, elegant townhouse of note. A surviving relic of bygone Manhattan, today it's the flagship store of **Nat Sherman**, makers and purveyors of fine tobacco products since 1930. Dark polished woods, comfy couches, elegant Art Deco touches and charming staff make you feel more like a guest in a gentleman's well-appointed living room than a customer at a tobacconist. The company began in suitably clubby style during Prohibition when Nat Sherman won a small tobacco manufacturer in a game of cards. And when a friend ran out of money building a skyscraper on Broadway, Nat stepped in to lend the necessary funds, in return for the lobby space that would become his first tobacco store. In 2007, the still family-owned company relocated to what is affectionately known as "The Townhouse." Inside you'll find a grand piano, framed letters from past illustrious customers such as Winston Churchill, Sammy Davis Jr. and Ol' Blue Eyes himself, Frank Sinatra, and a private members clubhouse smoking room downstairs. Old fashioned wooden counters display endless cigars, pipes, loose leaf tobaccos and two dozen or so brands of Nat Sherman cigarettes. Whilst public attitudes towards smoking have moved on, a visit to the friendly Townhouse is more like an indulgent trip to a time long vanished, when, as current owner, Michele Sherman says, "you could tell a man's worth by the shoes he wore and the cigar he smoked."

(12 East 42nd Street, New York, NY, 10017; +1 212-764-5000; Natsherman.com)

Pop Loves His Whisky & Moonshine

Take a little field trip with Pa down to the Brooklyn Navy Yard and pull up to the 19th century castle-like gates of the city's first distillery since Prohibition. It was founded only a few years ago in 2010, but **King's County Distillery** is ranked as one of America's most immersive whiskey experiences, calling the 119-year-old Paymaster Building home in the heart of Brooklyn's forgotten "Irishtown" where the legendary Whiskey Wars waged in the 1860s. Drop in any day of the week and order a drink from the leather-bound menus in their beautiful bar at the Gatehouse tasting room, which looks like the set of a Civil War-era movie. Co-founder Colin Spoelman's upbringing in the moonshine-making hills of Kentucky is reflected in the menu which offers moonshine margaritas, daiquiris

King's County Distillery

© Ian Bartlett

and martinis as well as the house whiskey and bourbon. Distillery tours with tastings are offered in the afternoons from Tuesday to Sunday, showing guests how they mash, ferment, distill - and most importantly, drink - all the whiskey, bourbon and moonshine that's made here seven days a week, 16 hours a day. Their copper whiskey still is imported from Scotland and heck, they even have an on-site corn and barley patch. Tours are a very reasonable $14, which includes the tasting and admission to the onsite "Boozeum." Come summer, enquire about their secret whiskey garden.

(299 Sands St, Brooklyn, NY 11205; +1 347-689-4211; Mon-Fri 10am-10pm, Sat 12pm-10pm, Sun 12pm-8pm; Learn more about tours at Kingscountydistillery.com/tours)

America's Oldest Public Golf Course is in the Bronx

When you want to play a relaxing round of golf, probably the last place you'd would think to look for lush fairways and verdant greens would be in the Bronx. But tucked away in the corner of **Van Cortlandt Park**, is the oldest public golf course in America. Opened in 1895, what better place to treat a golf-loving father, than this historic course where Babe Ruth and Joe Louis once played. The Clubhouse is a picturesque "19th hole," overlooking Van Cortlandt Lake, and still contains the original wood-paneled locker rooms, dating back to 1902.
(Van Cortlandt Avenue South & Bailey Avenue, Bronx, NY, 10471; +1 718-542-4595; for reservations check in with Golfnyc.com)

Meet the Parents

When it comes time to introduce yourself to potential in-laws, tread very carefully when choosing the battleground to win their hearts...

Take them to Paris

New York's well-oiled powerhouse of French cuisine, **Balthazar**, attracts all walks of life, from fashion week models to your cultured aunt from Minnesota. To recreate the charm of the Left Bank's Brasserie Lipp or Café de Flore for the in-laws, head here to get your fill of *Steak au Poivre*, waiters in all-white, red leather banquettes and the sounds of clinking aperitivo glasses to fill those awkward silences.
(80 Spring St, Soho, N NY 10012; +1-212-965-1414; open every day all day; Balthazarny.com)

A Legendary Table

Manhattan's iconic **21 Club** will see to it that you're properly dressed to meet the parents. Gentlemen are required to wear jackets, which should go without saying that wearing shorts or flip flops is not permitted on the premises. Upon entering the Bar Room, you'll notice that every inch of the ceiling is covered in vintage toys donated by guests; a model boat from JFK hangs by a toy Air Force One plane from Bill Clinton. Jackie Gleason's pool cue from *The Hustler* is displayed above the bar, which has collapsible shelves to send liquor bottles down a chute in case of a raid from the days of Prohibition. Each table is numbered, and what could be grander than sitting at number 30, where Humphrey Bogart used to court Lauren Bacall. Or number 21: that's where Tony Curtis and Burt Lancaster sat in *The Sweet Smell of Success*. John Steinbeck and Ernest Hemingway also had their favorite tables, while Robert Benchley of *The New Yorker* had his own entire corner, marked today by a plaque, where he would hold court with Dorothy Parker and their other peers from the Algonquin Round Table. The menu is exceptional, matched only by the sense of stepping back in time to old Manhattan sophistication. But to *really* impress your future in-laws, enquire with your waiter about visiting the secret wine cellar which hides behind a two-ton brick wall door and a covert locking system. Home to over 20,000 rare bottles, the underground cellar has a cavernous dining room for private hire, surrounded by fine wines (see pg 171). Hopefully, the parents will be so impressed with their time at the 21 Club, you won't have to worry about picking up the check.

(21 West 52nd Street, Midtown, NY, 10019; +1 212-582-7200; Be aware of the strict dress code at 21.club.com)

The Loeb Boathouse

Out-of-Towner Parents

On a beautiful day in Manhattan, the view from the terrace of **The Loeb Boathouse** in Central Park is hard to beat. Suggest an early brunch at 11 am to ensure you get seated on the patio beside the lake where couples paddle gently by on rowboats. Homemade banana bread comes without asking to warm the table while you wait for generous servings of Eggs Benedict and maple waffles. Daintier options like crab cakes, ceviche and Quiche Lorraine are also on the menu. The fancy lakeside brunch might not be the lightest on the pocket, but this romantic haven, just a short stroll into Central Park, has been winning folks over since the 1950s. Booking is advised.

(Park Drive North, E 72nd St, Central Park, NY 10021; +1 212-517-2233; Mon-Fri lunch & dinner, Sat & Sun brunch from 9.30am-3.45p & dinner, Thecentralparkboathouse.com)

The 21 Club
courtesy of Belmond

The Kids Are Coming Too

Almost everything you can do in this book, you can do with your favorite little rascals, but if they're really well behaved, you might just take them on a special adventure...

Meet the Neighborhood Slot Car King & Queen of Brooklyn

Dolores and Frank 'Buzz' Perri are the heart and soul of **Buzz-a-Rama**, the city's last slot car arcade, est. 1965. Quite a cast of characters come through its hallowed doors: doe-eyed eight-year-olds with cars in need of repair, old-timers who hang by the counter, and classic arcade machine addicts. Every inch of the joint is covered in materials and memorabilia from Buzz's past. He has one of the most impressive collections around, and guards his most prized machines at a location we can't even disclose. "The '60s and '70s were the peak years" for racing, says his wife Dolores, "People would come to hang out all day." The lines were so long to get in, they'd often spill outside the door. The slot cars can hit some pretty high speeds, all of which are controlled with the simple gesture of toggling a headless 'pistol' hooked up to the track with wires. Buzz-a-Rama is also the go-to hospital for toy race tracks and cars in need of some TLC. "It's just as much about the building of it all as it is the racing," Dolores explains, "It teaches kids patience." You'll find us by the kitschy "Refuelling Center" in the back, snacking on Kit-Kats and 35-cent coffee. Bring the kids, the roommates, or a date who's really worth his or her salt.
(69 Church Ave, Brooklyn, NY 11218; +1 718-853-1800; Sat 2pm-7pm, Sun 2pm-5pm)

Buzz-a-Rama

Dolores and Frank 'Buzz' Perri
of Buzz-a-Rama

Splitting a Sundae circa 1923

You'll realize what whipped cream is supposed to taste like at **Eddie's Sweet Shop**, a Forest Hills institution since 1909, where every last detail is authentic, from the vintage menu boards to the 80 year-old refrigerator (one of the earliest electric models available in the United States), which still works, keeping that hand-whipped cream cool. Enjoy a sundae at the counter the way your grandparents would have, with homemade ice cream and homemade toppings. The hot fudge, butterscotch and syrups are all made in house too. Ice cream aside, it's the local people watching that makes this place feel like a time warp into Forrest Gump's hometown, from the shy high school kids on first dates to families packing in after church.

(105-29 Metropolitan Ave #1, Queens, NY 11375; +1 718-520-8514; Tues-Sun 1pm-11.30pm)

Eddie's Sweet Shop

The *OTHER* Yankees

So you want tickets to see the Yankees play and relive the golden age of New York baseball like it was in the 1950s. Going to a Major League Baseball game can be a major expense, not to mention a tad overwhelming for beginners. That's where the other Yankees come in, the **Staten Island Yankees** that is – one of the city's Minor League clubs that still have all the fighting spirit of the big leagues, with the loveable nostalgia of the small-town underdog teams. Tickets for the so-called "Baby Bombers" are a fraction of the price of a trip to Yankee Stadium. Not just that, one of the best parts of going to the Richmond County Bank Ballpark is the scenic boat ride to Staten Island, where you'll discover the local's secret to seeing the Statue of Liberty up close and personal – forget the long lines waiting for the official tour boats and just take the free Staten Island ferry instead, which sails right by with a front row view. Spend the day being transported back to a more innocent time in baseball history, catching foul balls to take home for the memory and watching teenage rookies becoming future stars. Relive old rivalries when the famed New York Yankees and Giants dueled regularly with the Brooklyn Dodgers; rivalries which are alive and well down in the Minor Leagues. Fierce competition for local pride takes place all summer long between the Brooklyn Cyclones and the Staten Island Yankees. They even have cheerleaders, mascots and often fireworks. After the game, score some autographs from the friendly players and let the kids run the bases with views of the Manhattan skyline behind them. It's an all-American family day out, just like they used to make 'em.

(Richmond County Bank Ballpark, 75 Richmond Terrace, Staten Island, NY, 10301; +1 718-720-9265; milb.com/staten-island. Minor League baseball runs on a shorter scheduled season to the Majors, normally mid-June to the first week of September. The Staten Island Ferry is free, and runs regularly from Battery Park)

Where the Superheroes Shop

For the burgeoning caped crusader in your family, the first port of call should be the **Brooklyn Superhero Supply Company** in Park Slope. Purveyors of everything needed to fight crime, from night vision goggles and invisible ink pens to masks, gauntlets and silk capes. "Ever Vigilant, Ever True" is the motto of these headquarters designed to look like a mad scientist's laboratory. But the whimsical shop floor only tells half the story: enter a secret door to discover a wonderful hidden library where the nonprofit 826NYC runs workshops and meetings to encourage your child's creative writing. They also organize field trips and host after-school programs (*826nyc.org*) and the store can be rented out for birthday parties.

(372 5th Avenue, Brooklyn, NY, 11215; +1 718-499-9884; Tues-Sun 12pm-6pm; Superherosupplies.com)

Night at the Museum

The most important thing to know about the iconic **taxidermy collection at the American Museum of Natural History** is that it's by no means the result of a killing spree by a bunch of rich old guys that liked to hunt. It starts with the museum's co-founder, Theodore Roosevelt, America's first conservationist President, who regarded Earth as one giant pulsing organism. Scientists and explorers were sent all over the world to study the animal kingdom, but with film technology still in its infancy and no sophisticated telephoto lenses, only the lucky few were able to see its beauty up close. The industrial revolution was threatening entire species of animals, so it was decided that the best way to get the general public to care about saving the environment and its wildlife, was to bring it home and recreate what the scientists themselves had witnessed in the field.

Diorama at the American
Museum of Natural History

Two hundred and fifty of the world's most accurate dioramas were made between 1902 and 2007, and although animals were killed to create these time capsules, conservationists maintain their deaths were a means for urging preservation, conveying to the audience that this is the last place where people may see some of these creatures. It all started with the birds. In an effort to put an end to plume hunting, the museum's first dioramas displayed birds on the brink of extinction, hunted for fashion and folly. Curators and artists traveled together across continents to select individual animals, study them in their natural environments, and duplicate the exact place in nature they were observed. The artists used old Renaissance methods to paint the masterful curved background scenes, and real plants and insects were incorporated into the foreground. While Theodore Roosevelt's conservationists were trying to preserve these species, today the museum also faces the task of conserving the dioramas themselves, many of which are now well over a century old. The dioramas are very tightly sealed and the only way to get inside many of them is to remove the front glass. It's an ongoing but fascinating task for the museum's artists, taxidermists, archivists, scientists and historians – the sort of people we need more of in the modern world.

The museum has several programs to encourage young learners. Stop by the Sackler Educational Lab anytime from noon to 5pm on Saturdays and Sundays to talk to a scientist, learn about the latest discoveries in human evolution, handle key fossil hominins such as Lucy the 3.2-million-year-old ape, and see a real human brain. To really immerse them in this library of life on Earth, consider booking them in for a **Night at the Museum Sleepover**, open to 6–16 year olds twice a month. When the doors close and the lights dim, overnighters take out their flashlights to explore the museum after dark in search of a variety of adventures before falling asleep next to the polar bears, or beneath the belly a 94-foot-long blue whale. *(amnh.org/plan-your-visit/amnh-sleepovers)*

But why should the kids have all the fun? There's also a sleepover for grown-ups, where you'll sip champagne, roam the empty halls, enjoy live music and a buffet dinner before unrolling your sleeping bag under the blue whale. *(Central Park West & 79th St, Upper West Side, NY 10024; +1 212 769-5100 ; Open daily from 10am-5:45pm. amnh.org/plan-your-visit/amnh-sleepovers/sleepovers-for-grown-ups)*

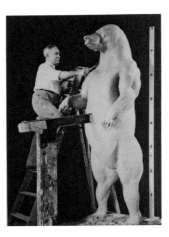

Taxidermist Robert Rockwell making an Alaska brown bear clay model, 1972

Survival Training in central Park

If we lost the resources, supplies and technology we take for granted – how would you, or more importantly, your children, survive? Modern-day caveman Shane Hobel teaches ancestral living skills at his **Mountain Scout Survival School**, which holds classes across NYC's boroughs. You can learn the art of starting a fire from scratch, take an animal tracking class in Cold Spring (see pg 221), or prepare for urban emergencies in Central Park. For the latter, students will learn communication protocols, how to pack a "Go Bag," paths of travel, rendezvous points and available resources, all of which lead to the survival school's other wilderness classes, skills we might need after say, the apocalypse. There are courses for kids and adults almost every weekend throughout the year. Sleep better at night knowing your kid is a survivor. *(143 Main St, Beacon, NY 12508; +1 845-629-4866; More info via Mtnscoutsurvival.com)*

Miniature Yachting in Central Park

The earliest boats to set sail on Conservatory Water made it into the *New York Times* when an article reporting on "Miniature Yachting in Central Park" was published in 1875. The pond itself was inspired by Paris's Grand Basin in the Luxembourg Gardens, another famous spot for model boating, and both sites have been creating magical childhood memories for generations on either side of the Atlantic. **The Central Park Model Yacht Club** was founded in 1916 to "encourage those interested in designing, building and sailing model yachts." Some of the sailboats floating today were built by young skippers, members and trustees of the early 20th century. In those days, model yacht racing was a "free-sailing" sport, where the boats were launched with little more than a nudge and a word of good luck. But as early as 1885, Nikola Tesla developed a wireless radio-controlled "robotic boat" that he exhibited at Madison Square Garden in 1898. When the technology reached the general public much later in the 1960s, a tug-of-war ensued between the traditionalists and radio controllers, whose high-tech models were still powered by the wind, but could now determine the direction in which the breeze would take them. If you haven't a clue how to sail a toy boat, let alone teach a kid how to, fortunately, the yacht club is still around to help both children and adults learn the basics of sailing. You can rent mini-sailboats at $10 an hour and mini-yachtsmen can store their own models in the boathouse for $20 a season. There are races every Saturday from 10 am to 1 pm which are a delight for spectators and skippers alike. Surrounded by Central Park's most beautiful views, there is something absolutely necessary and nostalgic about getting bundled up in the fall to enjoy one of New York's most beloved past times near the Alice in Wonderland statue.
(E 72nd St, Conservatory Pond, Central Park, NY 10021; +1 917-522-0054, Mon-Thurs 11am-5pm, Fri 11am-7pm, Sat 1pm-7pm, Sun 10am-6pm, closed during coldest months; Cpmyc.org)

The Central Park Model Yacht Club

A Marionette Show in a 143-yr-old Swedish Cottage

You'll feel like Hansel & Gretel when you happen upon the **Swedish Cottage Marionette Theatre**, a wooden chalet that was literally transplanted from Scandinavian soil to Central Park in 1877. Since then, it's become a storied marionette theater run by Harlem-born local legend Bruce Cannon, who'll tell you his own fairytale story of how he discovered his talent for puppetry that changed his life and gave him the platform to build a community unlike any other in the city. Come for a classic production or one of the company's many original shows. Every puppet, backdrop and snowflake is designed and made in-house in the workshop at the back of the cottage. This world of handcrafted puppets and hand-painted sets will tug at your heartstrings. *(W 79th Street, Upper West Side, NY 10023; +1 212-988-9093; For info on shows & tickets, visit Cityparksfoundation.org/swedish-cottage-marionette-theatre/)*

Swedish Cottage Marionette

Training for the Hunger Games

In the heart of Queens, **Pro Line Archery Lanes** has been the "home of archery champions" since the 1970s, where both Olympic-level professionals and novices hone their bow and arrow skills. It's also a lovably unfussy, family-friendly archery range with old club posters hung under the glow of fluorescent lights, and 75¢ coffee that works on an honor system. Bond with Dad while learning how to shoot like Katniss Everdeen, just $20 for a 2-hour session, equipment rental included, or $15 for kids aged 8-17. *(95-11 101st Ave, Queens, NY 11416; +1 718-845-9280; Open Tues-Thurs 2pm-11pm, Sat-Sun 1pm-5pm, Mon & Fri 6:30pm-11pm; Archeryny.com)*

Houdini's Secret Museum

Inside an anonymous Midtown office building, there's a place to inspire the child in all of us, a hidden gem of a museum celebrating the most famous magician of them all: Harry Houdini. The small but magical **Houdini Museum** exhibits how the "King of Cards" became the world's greatest escape artist. Escape coffins, punishment suits, mystifying props and original posters are on display among hundreds of other authentic Houdini memorabilia to explore in this impressive collection. The museum is also housed inside an actual working magic shop, Fantasma, a must-visit for any aspiring young magician.
(213 West 35th Street, Suite 401, New York, NY; +1 212-244-3633; Mon-Sat 10am-6pm, Sun 10am-5pm; Houdinimuseumny.com)

Aladdin's Confectionary Cave

Indulge your inner Willy Wonka with a visit to **Economy Candy**, open since 1937 and still packed to its 20 foot-high pressed tin tiled rafters with sweets and treats. Chocolate covered apricots, halvah, wax lips, five-pound bags of toffee, long strands of strawberry shoelaces and everything in between. Economy Candy actually started life as a shoe shop, until the Great Depression, when Morris Cohen realized that the candy he had on the counter was selling faster than his shoes. This wondrous sweet shop survived the immigrant exodus from the Lower East Side, through the urban decay that followed in the 1980s and 90s, and thrives as a family business in the midst of the widespread gentrification that has seen almost all the old, traditional shops disappear amidst rising rents. "It's a changing neighborhood," says Mitchell Cohen, Morris' grandson, "but one thing always remains the same: people love candy." If there's a special sweet you remember from your childhood and thought it no longer exists, chances are Economy Candy has it – a giant bag full of it.
(108 Rivington St, Lower East Side, NY 10002; +1 212-254-1531; open everyday 9am-6pm, from 10am on Sat & Mon; EconomyCandy.com)

Honey, I Shrunk Manhattan

If you ever find yourself stuck with the kids in Times Square in need of a quick exit from the chaos, remember this name: **Gulliver's Gate**, a suprisingly good museum amidst a riot of tourist traps and garish entertainment. This 50,000-square-foot ode to miniatures was partly funded by a Kickstarter campaign, but no expense has been spared in creating this giant experience in a miniature world. There's a 1:87 scale model of Manhattan, but the exhibits also cover entire continents. The miniature artists have their workshops on site, with viewing windows to watch them at work. Visitors are also challenged to find the museum's hidden "Easter Eggs" throughout the exhibits in a real-life game of *Where's Waldo?* Even cooler, you can shrink the entire family and have yourselves 3D printed into miniature models to take home. Tickets start at $22

for kids and $31 for adults – arguably a justified price for finding the perfect little respite hiding behind the bright lights of Times Square.
(216 W 44th St, Midtown, NY 10036; everyday 10am-8pm; Book online to save on tickets at Gulliversgate.com)

Ghosts of Coney Island's Past

Look at vintage photos of old Coney Island, and you'll see a riotous show of electric lights, thrilling (but dangerous) rides and other amusements that were simultaneously enchanting, completely bizarre and ahead of their time. Up until the mid 20th century, Luna Park, Dreamland and Steeplechase Park each sought to outdo each other, creating ever more elaborate entertainment to attract the millions that flocked to Coney Island every summer. One sideshow even exhibited premature babies inside glass incubators, a technology previously unknown to the medical community at the time. Doctors generally considered premature babies to be genetically inferior "weaklings" that they could do little for, but for 25 cents, the public could gawk at them from behind the glass. What might seem like ghastly entertainment was, in fact, pioneering science and often, the only hope for desperate parents. Neonatal care was expensive and the boardwalk boasted the latest high-tech incubators, imported straight from Europe. The miniature Coney Island hospitals at Luna Park and Dreamland were financed by the public's fascination and would go on to advance neonatal medicine and save countless more lives to come.
As Coney Island fell into decades of neglect and abandonment starting in the 1950s,

Wonder Wheel
at Coney Island

many of the old rides and fun fairs were torn down and forgotten, but for nostalgic thrill-seekers, there are still some surviving giants to be conquered. Loop de loop into the past on **The Cyclone**, a nearly 100-year-old wooden roller coaster still running to this day. The fact that it's wooden is terrifying enough, and then there are the tiny carriage cars which make you feel as though you could be thrown out at any moment. It's loud, clunky and it's wonderful. Another true Coney Island classic is the iconic **Wonder Wheel**, built in 1920. Stick to the outer cars for a less stomach-wrenching ride and the highest views, or test your tolerance in one of the middle cars which slide around on rails as the wheel rotates.
(The Cyclone, 801 Riegelmann Boardwalk, Brooklyn, NY 11224; open 11am-10pm during season; Check the calendar at Lunaparknyc.com/ Deno's Wonder Wheel, April-October, Check hours at Denoswonderwheel.com)

Coney Island Museum

Right in the heart of the seaside resort is the **Coney Island Museum**, where you can truly immerse yourself in the heyday of America's playground. Funhouse mirrors, original bumper cars and vintage amusement park ephemera all wonderfully capture the lost decades of crowds that thronged the famous Boardwalk. But this is much more than a just a museum – the nonprofit is keeping the old Coney Island traditions of the dime museums and vaudeville alive. The museum hosts the annual colorful Mermaid Parade as well as modern-day sideshows of "wonders and human curiosities." The more adventurous can even try their hand at the Circus Sideshow School and learn ancient skills from fire breathing to sword swallowing.

Coney Island amusement parks are seasonal, with most attractions open only in the summer. During the offseason, the museum is open Saturday & Sunday only (12pm-5pm) and Wednesday to Saturday (12pm-6pm) and Sunday (2pm-6pm) during the summer. *(1208 Surf Avenue, Brooklyn, NY, 11224; +1-718-372-5159; Coneyisland.com)*

Raised on a Farm for the Day

No need to apply for summer camp in Oklahoma to ride around on the back of a tractor, feed the livestock, learn how to make fresh butter or see first-hand where fresh food comes from. The **Queens County Farm Museum** is the only historic working farm left in New York City and it's open to the public seven days a week, all year round, free of charge. Roam 47 acres of farmland, home to dairy cows, sheep, pigs and chickens. Visitors can purchase goat feed from the welcome center, and freshly-picked tomatoes, eggplant, asparagus, berries and more are available to buy from the farmstand between mid-May to early November. (You can also volunteer at the farm on Tuesdays & Sundays, see pg 197). The museum works hard to preserve its historic buildings and greenhouses that date back to the 1700s, including a charming red farmhouse which was built by Dutch settlers. Powered by a windmill, the picturesque old home looks as if it could have been dropped here by a cyclone straight from Kansas with Dorothy in tow. Hayrides with the farmer are a popular weekend highlight (weather permitting) as well as guided tours of the Dutch farmhouse. *(73-50 Little Neck Pkwy, Queens, NY 11004; +1-718-347-3276; Open everyday 10am-5pm; Queensfarm.org)*

"Life is more fun if you play games"– Roald Dahl

Pass on the simple joys of *Scrabble, Monopoly* and *Clue* to generation Z at **The Uncommons**, Manhattan's only board game café. For $10 per person ($5 for students from Mon-Thurs), enjoy rediscovering your childhood favorites over pizza and smoothies while challenging your children to get off their smartphones and play a real game. The cozy Greenwich Village café has one of the largest game libraries on the East Coast, including ones you've never heard of, or missed out on as a kid. When your firstborn child has destroyed you in a game of *Battleship*, take them across the road and see if they take to playing chess at one of the last old-fashioned gaming parlors in the city, see pg 108. *(230 Thompson St, New York, NY 10012; Greenwich Village; +1 646-543-9215; Mon-Thurs 8.30am-12pm, Fri & Sat 8.30am-1pm, Sun 8.30am-11pm; Uncommonsnyc.com)*

A Tropical Jungle Railway

If you have a thing for miniature models and the kids love trains, then the **New York Botanical Garden's Holiday Train Show** should be firmly marked in your calendar. Set inside a sprawling 19th-century greenhouse in the Bronx, an elaborate model train whizzes around the New York City jungle, stopping at hundreds of city landmarks crafted out of bark, leaves, pine cones and other natural materials. Nearing its third decade, held every year from the end of November to late January, the artistry gets more impressive every year.

Psst! Send the kids home with the babysitter and stick around for the "Bar Car Nights": an after-dark viewing of the train show with cocktails and roving a cappella groups to serenade Mom & Dad's date night.
(2900 Southern Blvd, Bronx, NY 10458; open Tues-Sun 10am-6pm + out of hours events; Check Nybg.org/event/holiday-train-show)

New York Botanical Garden's Holiday Train Show

© Terry Robinson

Halloween at the Headless Horseman's City of Jack O'Lanterns

From early October to mid-November, about an hour's drive or train ride from Manhattan, the woods of Sleepy Hollow transform into **The Great Jack O'Lantern Blaze**. Thousands of hand-carved pumpkins form a whirling carousel, a herd of dinosaurs, a pumpkin planetarium and a very orange Statue of Liberty – pretty much any way you can imagine carving and compiling pumpkins, this incredibly talented team of artisans has done it. It all takes place on the spooky, 353-year-old Van Cortlandt Manor grounds, where you can warm up with locally-made apple cider and donuts as you meander through the estate after dark, ooh-ing and ahh-ing at the electrifying displays. It's a Halloween they'll never forget.
(Van Cortlandt Manor, 525 S Riverside, Croton-on-Hudson, NY 10520; book at hudsonvalley.org/events/blaze)

The Great Jack O'Lantern Blaze
at Van Cortlandt Manor

The Story of New York's Bravest

If nothing lights up their faces more than the sight of a shiny red fire truck, a trip to the **New York City Fire Museum** will definitely go down well with the kids. Housed inside an actual historic fire station, this century-old *Beaux-Arts* building was once home to Engine Company No. 30, today filled with everything related to the history of New York's bravest. Early horse-drawn wagons and beautifully preserved engines, lanterns, buckets and uniforms– they all tell the story of how the city was protected, from the early volunteer days of the "bucket

brigade'" and dueling rival fire gangs of the *Gangs of New York* era, to a memorial for the first responders on 9/11.
(278 Spring Street, New York, NY, 10013; +1 212-691-1303; Mon-Sun 10am-5pm; Nycfiremuseum.org)

New York City Fire Museum

A Triple Scoop of Chocolate Chunk from the Old Fireboat House
Getting ice cream from the white 1920s clapboard building that sits quaintly beside the monumental Brooklyn Bridge, is the kind of moment that sticks in your childhood memories forever. The converted fireboat house was once used for practice by firefighters from the nearby marine station. Today, it's the **Brooklyn Ice Cream Factory**, serving old-fashioned, freshly made ice cream, hot fudge banana splits, sundaes and shakes. A rewarding spot to grab a cone after wandering the streets of Dumbo or, better yet, Vinegar Hill (pg 45). Note: cash only. *(Fulton Landing Pier, Brooklyn, 11201, NY; +1 718-246-3963; open daily 12pm-10pm)*

For more family adventures, see how to escape the city without really trying on pg 197.

Too Tired to Cook for the Team

When Mommy needs a Bloody Mary and the kids are bouncing off the walls, what are your best options?

1 Swing open the bright red door of **Tavern on Jane** and make yourselves at home in this West Village cottage on the corner, that looks like the sort of place you might stumble upon while road tripping through the mountains. The Bloody Marys come loaded with crudité and hand cut chips while the tables are equipped with kids crayons to keep them busy doodling all over the tablecloths. There's something for everyone on the menu of this cozy, no-fuss local's joint where the fireplaces are going in winter. Expect a reliably warm welcome for your family all year round.
(31 8th Ave, West Village, NY 10014; +1 212-675-2526; open everyday 12pm-4am; Tavernonjane.com)

2 Order straight from the pantry at **Court Street Grocers**, a rustic American kitchen in the heart of Carroll Gardens, arguably Brooklyn's most idyllic and well-equipped neighborhood for raising young families. Pick the kids up from one of the karate schools down the street and treat the team to "Ultimate Warrior" pork rolls or "Macho Man/ Woman" garlic bread sandwiches. Stock up on essential groceries from the pantry while the little warriors wind down in the dining area.
(485 Court St, Brooklyn, NY 11231; +1 718-722-7229; Mon-Thurs 7am-7pm, Fri 8am-7pm, Sat 7am-6pm, Sun 9am-6pm; Courtstreetgrocers.com)

3 Biscuits, pies and pancakes, oh my! **Bubby's** is the shabby chic restaurant of TriBeCa that willed itself into being when owner Ron Silver realized just how much his neighbors enjoyed his home-cooked American fare. Trendy without feeling trite or up-tight, here, buttermilk is its own food group. Ron Silver also happens to be a major Folk Art collector, and numerous original works hang on the walls by African-American outsider artist, Mose Tolliver. Make use of the vintage photo booth downstairs and snag free recipe postcards by the entry.
(120 Hudson St, Tribeca, NY 10013; +1 212 219-0666; Open daily from 8am-10pm, til 11pm on weekends; Bubbys.com)

Tavern on Jane

Just the Girls

A few itinerary ideas for your Mother/ daughter/ sister trip...

You're invited to a Secret Tea Salon of the Belle Epoque

New York's Gilded Age was an era of gracious living, and little else was more important in a lady's social standing than her appearances at high afternoon tea. To rediscover this old-fashioned delight, look for the engraving of a small teacup on the facade of an 1834 brownstone in the heart of Gramercy Park. From the moment you enter the elegant Georgian rooms of **Lady Mendl's Tea Salon**, you'll be whisked away and transported to the high society drawing rooms of Edith Wharton's Manhattan, described so eloquently by the Pulitzer Prize-winning American novelist who drew upon her own insider's knowledge of the old New York "aristocracy." Champagnes, teas, sandwiches and cakes, each course is as sumptuous as the surroundings. Reservations are a must, the *prix-fixe* menu is currently $59 and little ones under 12 have to sit this one out. Dress elegantly, as if you'd been summoned to tea by Miss Wharton herself. The historic brownstone is also home to the Inn at Irving Place (pg 352), a boutique hotel with 8 cozy rooms, and an intimate martini bar below the tea salon, serving light bites and opening onto a bamboo garden at the back. *(56 Irving Place, New York, NY, 10003; +1 212-533-4600; Wed-Fri 1pm-4pm, Sat-Sun 12pm-5pm; Ladymendlsteasalon.com)*

A Wise Woman's Secret to Feeling Fabulous

It's what's underneath that counts, right? There's a reason founder Rebecca Aspan is known as "the Lingerie Evangelist." Her Greenwich village store, **La Petite Coquette**, est. 1979, is heaven on earth for those seeking glamorous intimates with a side of expert advice. Head in for a free bra-fitting (no appointment necessary) in a space that feels like a French boudoir, where scarlet walls and fringed lamps set the *coquette* tone. *(51 University Pl # 4, Noho, New York, NY 10003; Mon-Sat 11am-7pm, Sun 12am-6pm; Thelittleflirt.com; Instagram: @lapetitecoquttenyc)*

Banana Splits with Alice in Wonderland

Andy Warhol called it his favorite sweet shop, and *Vogue* editors planned their next issues at this enchanting New York icon just down the block from Bloomingdale's. Dreamt up in 1954 by three friends with a passion for sweets who (serendipitously) met at a dance class in the city, **Serendipity 3** quickly became a favorite amongst stars like Marilyn Monroe, Cary Grant, and Jackie O. Surrounded by gorgeous Tiffany lamps, giant clocks, kitsch and bric-a-brac, toss a coin to choose between their outrageous Banana Splits and devilish butterscotch sundaes. The Art Nouveau-inspired menu is also packed with savory options for lunch, from the breaded "Chicken Diva" to the "Monet Salad."

Pop into the restaurant's general store next door to pick up everything you might need for your own Mad Hatter's tea party.
(225 E 60th St, Upper East Side, NY 10022; +1 212-838-3531; open daily 10am-1am)

Passing on Mama's Recipes
If Mother Goose was a real person, she'd be Bonnie Slotnick. Her cookbooks are so lovingly curated and cozily presented, they'll take you back to memories of your mother's kitchen shelves. Take Mom along to **Bonnie Slotnick Cookbooks** for one of her tasting parties (see pg 106) where chefs offer recipe samples alongside a cookbook signing.
(28 E 2nd St, Greenwich Village, NY 10003; +1 212 989-8962; open daily 1pm-7pm, closed on Thurs)

A Little Shop of Miniature Dreams
This is the kind of place that you imagine comes alive when the shopkeeper closes up and leaves for the night. For three decades, Leslie Edelman has been creating a magical miniature world inside **Tiny Doll House**, an Upper East Side jewel box of childhood memories and exquisite craftsmanship. It's New York's only dedicated dollhouse and miniatures shop, and while it might be a small boutique by any standards, you could spend well over an hour in here and still not have looked at every item. If you can't have your dream Victorian townhouse, how about a miniature one? No room in your life for a collection

Tiny Doll House

of antique birdcages? Start small with a display of teeny tiny ones along your window sill. You don't have to be into dolls to fall for this little shop in a big way. *(314 E 78th St, New York, NY 10075; +1 212-744-3719; Open hours may vary so call ahead, Mon-Fri 11am-5pm, Sat 11am-4pm; Instagram: @tinydollhousenewyorkcity)*

 Also with the girls, try the New York shopping guide on pg 165, Drag Queen Bingo at the Stonewall Inn, pg 101, Barbetta, pg 189, for Mother's Day and the off-Broadway theatres and live shows in the West Village on pg 23-30.

Serendipity 3

Brooklyn Army Terminal

08
Down the Rabbit Hole

"It is ridiculous to set a detective story in New York City. New York City is itself a detective story".

– Agatha Christie

Abandoned and Underground Adventures

Some adventures hold more risk than others, so be careful what you ask for. From the risk-free to the risqué to the "at your own risk," enjoy responsibly.

Brooklyn's Orwellian Ghost Terminal

In 1958, Private Elvis Presley was deployed from the **Brooklyn Army Terminal** to serve his country in West Germany. Even the most well-known name in the entertainment world couldn't escape the draft. The magnificent, neglected building that was once the port of arrival and departure for 200,000 soldiers a year, is today an empty shell; built for war, forgotten after peace. Under the glass atrium, a mossy grass grows on the old train tracks where troops and military supplies came and left. Bulky concrete balconies jut out over the tracks (pictured on pg 242), designed for loading materials in and out of the warehouse space. The whole thing feels like a super-industrialized train station with a dystopian 1984 overtone, which in many ways, is exactly what it was. Strangely beautiful in its decay, with an abundance of natural light and space, today it houses a handful of industrial and commercial tenants, but it's mostly closed off to the public – unless you sign up for a private visit offered by Turnstile tours (turnstiletours.com). But there is another way to gain access to the Brooklyn Army Terminal without having to share it with a group tour. We checked out the current list of "tenants" in the building, which presumably use the empty terminal for its ample storage space. Notable names include the American Museum of Natural History and the Solomon R. Guggenheim Museum, as well as the NYPD Intelligence Division, but most interestingly, a nonprofit arts organization called Chashama (Chashama.org), which nurtures artists by transforming unused property into affordable workspace. They have over 90 visual artist studios within the Brooklyn Army Terminal and host open days, offer volunteer programs, internships and of course, the opportunity to apply for your own studio or gallery space. We like where this is going. *(140 58th St, Brooklyn, NY 11220; Bklynarmyterminal.com)*

Staten Island's Boogeyman

In the backwoods of Staten Island lies the largest collection of abandoned buildings in New York: the **Staten Island Farm Colony**. Originally, the old farm colony started life with good intentions back in 1829, as a working "poor farm" for the homeless, who could grow their own crops in return for housing and learn to become self-sufficient. At one point nearly 1,700 people lived and worked at the farm colony until the Social Security system was adopted on the federal level and the program eventually closed in 1975. For decades, the colony fell into decline, its complex of abandoned hospital wards and dormitories gradually being reclaimed by nature. Eeriness surrounds the old colony, and it takes a brave soul

to enter its pitch black warren of basements and tunnels. Nearby is the infamous Willowbrook State School for disabled children, which closed in 1987 after public outcry over decades of institutional abuse. Both Willowbrook and the Farm Colony were the rumored hunting grounds of the Cropsey Killer. Part urban legend, part true crime story, former attendant at Willowbrook, Andre Rand, was Staten Island's original "boogeyman" with a hooked hand. Locals called him "Cropsey," the Staten Island kidnapper who would drag misbehaving children into the woods. Five children actually disappeared between 1972 and 1987, only two of their bodies were ever discovered, all were thought to be victims of the Cropsey Killer. Today, the future of the Farm Colony is in the balance; recent plans are afoot to turn the abandoned Colony into affordable housing, whilst preserving parts of the historic site. But for now, the haunting ruins lie silent, awaiting the intrepid explorer.
(Brielle Avenue, Staten Island, NY, 10314)

Staten Island Farm Colony

Time Travelling on the Subway

Located in a decommissioned subway station in downtown Brooklyn, you'll enter **The New York Transit Museum** as if you were entering the actual subway, down the steps of the old Court Street entrance. You'll first learn the incredible and important story of the sandhogs, the term given to urban miners that built the New York City subway lines, sewers and tunnels. But the real magic begins when you head down onto the decommissioned Court Street train platforms, last used in 1946. Today the platform is filled with vintage and antique subway cars, which you can wander in and out of imagining yourself commuting through the past. The oldest cars date from the early 1900s, built beautifully out of wood, with etched glass doors, ceiling fans and wicker seats. Step inside one of the striking teal cars used to ferry passengers to the 1964 World's Fair and notice the authentic vintage advertising that pops out at you above the windows, promoting Jane Fonda's latest movie *Barbarella* or warning passengers to keep an eye out for the Soviet menace. For those who enjoy all things retro, the Transit Museum is the ideal place to don your best vintage attire for an impromptu photo shoot, transporting yourself back to those bygone days when riding the subway was still elegant.

Keep an eye out for the museum's special events, which can include 'nostalgia rides' on working vintage subway cars and antique buses, and jazz swing parties on the trains. Become a member and you'll be able to join one of their exclusive tours of Manhattan's fabulous 'lost' City Hall station (see pg 252).
(99 Schermerhorn Street, Brooklyn, NY, 11201; +1 718-694-1600; Tues-Fri 10am-4pm, Sat-Sun 11am-5pm; Nytransitmuseum.org)

MTA Transit Museum

Exploring the Ruins Of Rockaway Beach

"It's not hard, not far to reach, we can hitch a ride to Rockaway Beach," sang *The Ramones* in their 1977 punk rock classic. The largest urban beach in the United States, stretching for miles, and facing the Atlantic Ocean, **Rockaway Beach** was once known as New York's Playground.

The Wise and Son clock on the Riis Park boardwalk

© NPS/Noble

Jacob Riis Park

As early as the 1900s, it had amusement parks, bars and resorts, and the beach itself became a hotbed of prudish controversy for the early seaside fashions and taboo swimwear sported on its sands. In the 1960s, Robert Moses, "master builder" of the 20th century, had a hand in changing the landscape of this neighborhood in Queens forever, when his plans for a grand, seafront highway connecting Brooklyn to the Hamptons, saw many of the amusements demolished. The highway was never completed and a small section remains intact, known locally as the "road from nowhere to nowhere."

Today Rockaway Beach is slowly recovering from the devastation of Hurricane Sandy, with new art installations and beachside bars popping up, and a small, nonprofit community theater. Combined with its surprisingly large collection of abandoned buildings to explore, Rockaway Beach makes a rather fascinating day out in New York City.

Start with the ruins of **Fort Tilden**, New York City's abandoned first line of defense. The imposing complex of concrete pillboxes, bunkers and munitions rail lines were built in 1917 to defend the city from a German naval attack during

Fort Tilden
© Bob (Contort Yourself)

World War I. A "Nike" surface-to-air missile base was added when the enemy became Soviet Russia, but with the advent of long-range ballistic missiles, the military outpost eventually became obsolete and Fort Tilden was abandoned to the elements in the 1970s. Explore the concrete monoliths that once pointed giant guns out to sea and climb into half buried pillboxes. Wander along the deserted beach and into houses filled with sand – the former army barracks and living quarters of those who once guarded New York against attack. Today some of these buildings host summer art shows, presented by the Rockaway Artist Alliance (RockawayArtistAlliance.org). **Studio 6 & 7 Galleries** invite artists to create works and installations inspired by the environment and history of the fort.

Standing sentinel over the surf of Rockaway Beach is the beautiful Art Deco **Jason Riis Park Bathhouse**. Eye-catching in red brick, decorated with fabulous fonts and tiles and capped with two soaring towers, it has been sadly neglected for many years. Along with the neighboring park and beach, it was named in honor of Jacob Riis, the pioneering photojournalist whose 1890 publication, *How The Other Half Lives*, did much to highlight and reform the shocking conditions of those living in New York's tenement slums. Fittingly, this part of the Rockaway Peninsula became known as "the People's Beach," and its grand, luxurious bath house was open to all. It once had a balcony restaurant overlooking the sea and plans for the world's largest solarium. It never quite managed to draw the same crowds as nearby Coney Island, however, and increasingly scarce funds led to the bathhouse losing its luster. The windows were eventually boarded up, and Hurricane Sandy saw to the rest.

In recent years, Brooklyn Bazaar has taken over parts of the beach surrounding the bathhouse, holding regular events and food markets during the summer (*Riisparkbeachbazaar.com*). Hopefully one day this grand Art Deco building will be fully restored back to its original purpose, but until then (and during the off-season), you can wander through its empty Art Deco pavilions and courtyards, trying to picture a glamorous day at the beach during the Jazz Age. (*Jacob Riis Park, 157 Rockaway Beach Blvd, Queens, New York, 11694*)

Continue a few minutes east and you'll find an abandoned hospital right on the beach. **The Neponsit Health Care Centre** opened in 1918 as a children's tuberculosis hospital before becoming a care home for the elderly. The hospital was hurriedly closed down virtually overnight amidst controversy in 1998 and has been abandoned ever since. With a crumbling sanatorium in your shadow and the Atlantic Ocean at your feet, it's probably one of the most surreal places you'll ever sunbathe. Fuel up on a good chili dog, fresh burgers and $3 beers from **Rippers**, one of the few restaurants right on the boardwalk, with picnic tables, live music and carefree summer vibes.

Like *The Ramones* said, Rockaway Beach is not hard to reach. Take the 2 train to Flatbush Avenue, and then the Q35 bus to Riis Park. In the summer,

American Princess Cruises run a ferry from Pier 11 at Wall Street to Riis Landing, on weekends and holidays.*(Rockaway Beach, Queens, 11693, NY; For info about the Gateway National Recreation Area: Nyharborparks.org)*

Like the High Line (if it was still Abandoned)

Time travel back from Rockaway Beach towards Manhattan on the **QueensWay**, an abandoned railway that once ferried holiday makers from the affluent Rego Park suburb in northern Queens down to Ozone Park and onto the beaches. The elevated railroad over in Queens has been in steady decay since it closed in 1962. The tracks, embankments, stations and trestles have become an urban wilderness, making it the ideal stomping ground for an urban explorer. A fire in the 1950s saw the Long Island Railroad eventually close down this section of the line, but there are proposals underway to transform the 3.5 mile Rockaway Beach Line into a family friendly 'cultural greenway' similar to the High Line. The transformation of a neglected elevated railroad that ran up Manhattan's West Side into an urban park proved a great success, and the High Line has swiftly become one of the city's most popular attractions. But for now, it's still possible to walk up onto the old tracks of the QueensWay to explore this overgrown, forgotten train line that passes silently through the back gardens of Queens. Adventurous souls can find a good access point to the railway at the children's park on Fleet Street.
(TheQueensway.org regular runs events such as walking tours on the railroad).

Courtesy of Queensway

The Grandest of Ghost Stations

City Hall Station is the most beautiful stop on the subway system, but no one ever gets to use it. Built in 1904, it featured grand, vaulted tiled ceilings by master craftsman Rafael Guastavino, leaded skylights and chandeliers, but its small, curved platform proved unable to accommodate the ever-growing subway cars and it was eventually closed in 1945. Today you can still catch a ghostly glimpse of the platforms by staying aboard a Downtown 6 train after its last scheduled stop at Brooklyn Bridge. The train loops around to go back uptown, passing through the abandoned station. The middle cars of the Downtown 6 are usually the best viewpoints, as the train slows down to pass through the curve of the platform. Everyone still on the train will most likely get off the stop before at Brooklyn Bridge but stay onboard to hack one of the best secrets of the New York City subway. The excellent New York Transit Museum (pg 247) offers occasional walking tours, but you'll need to be a member to join.

City Hall Station

The Secret Subway Portal to the Gilded Age

Hidden away in the corner of busy Times Square subway station, is an old, unused door that says 'Knickerbocker' on the lintel. At the far end of the Grand Central shuttle platform, this doorway was once a discrete way to enter (or exit) one of the grandest hotels in New York, a *Beaux-Arts* masterpiece owned by John Jacob Astor. A jewel in the crown of the Gilded Age, the Knickerbocker Hotel recently reopened, but **the secret Knickerbocker entrance** remains closed ... for now. *(Track 1 platform, Grand Central Terminal-42nd Street Shuttle, New York, NY, 10036)*

New York's Abandoned Submarine Yard

Behind the famous Coney Island boardwalk is **Coney Island Creek**, a largely forgotten backwater that was once cut off entirely from Brooklyn, back when Coney was truly an island. Today, however, this Creek is rarely visited, home to salvage yards, auto repair shops and a waste recycling plant. A far cry from the thrills of the nearby funfair, it's also home to the most captivating of abandoned delights – a graveyard of ghost ships. You'll have to poke through the brush off the path of Calvert Vaux Park Greenway Rd, where you'll discover about two dozen shipwrecks in the creek. No one is quite sure when they arrived, or where they came from. It's thought some were old whaling ships, ancient US Navy vessels, or forsaken barges which were scuttled and left to rot. But in the midst of the decaying shipwrecks is one that's not like the others: a mysterious and forgotten yellow submarine that could well have sprung straight from the pages of Jules Verne. Before the rust and seawater had its way with the vessel, it was once at the center of a doomed expedition to search for treasure. For years, rumors circulated around its true origins. Urban legends suggested it dated back to the Civil War and the era of the first submarines such as the Monitor, built in the nearby Brooklyn Navy Yards. Eventually, it was identified as the hand-made sub of Brooklyn shipyard worker Jerry Bianco, who planned to hunt for the treasure of the ill-fated luxury ocean liner, SS Andrea Doria, which sank off the coast of Massachusetts in 1956 along with 52 souls and a million dollars. Bianco christened his submarine the Quester I and launched her with high hopes in 1970 with the traditional bottle of champagne. Unfortunately, the Quester I immediately tilted sideways, and got stuck in the Creek where she remains, half submerged, with her Steampunk-looking hull and conning tower visible, as though preparing for one last dive into the ocean. *(Co-ordinates: N 40.5813118, W 73.9959665, Access from the Calvert Vaux Park Greenway Rd, NY 11214)*

The Abandoned Half of Ellis Island

It's estimated that a staggering 40% of all Americans can trace at least one ancestor who passed through the famous immigration halls of Ellis Island, and before it was abandoned in the 1950s, around 12 million immigrants had come through its gates. Forty years later, the main registry hall was restored and turned into a pristine New York City attraction, where a never-ending stream of tourists follow in the footsteps of their ancestors as they first stepped foot in America. But that's only half the story of Ellis Island, literally. The more curious visitors to Ellis Island will spot a strange collection of forlorn buildings on the south side of the island when they disembark the ferries. These old, crumbling buildings were once the **Ellis Island Hospital Complex**. If you were an immigrant arriving on American shores and sent to this half of the island, it was probably the last place you wanted to be. Being sent here meant further medical examinations awaited, or worse, quarantine for infectious and contagious disease, and it was quite possible that you might never leave. Upon arrival at Ellis Island, immigrants would form a winding line into the main Registry Room. Armed with sticks of chalk, teams of doctors managed to whittle down an initial medical exam to just six seconds. Anyone with a suspected illness or medical condition was marked

on their clothes: 'C' meant conjunctivitis, 'PG' for pregnancy, 'S' for signs of being senile. Perhaps more alarming were the evaluations of immigrants based on eugenics and mental health. Given that some immigrants couldn't speak English, or had lived their whole lives in remote villages, judging what constituted mental impairments was a grey area. An 'X,' signified a suspected mental disorder, and a circled 'X', meant insanity. Immigrants marked with chalk were quickly separated from their families, and sent to the now abandoned hospital. Today, donning a hard hat and stepping behind the locked gate to the south side is a particularly moving experience. You can almost sense the human anguish that unfolded here; the upheaval of leaving home and making a trans-Atlantic voyage in steerage class to a foreign country, only to be suddenly separated from your family. Some stayed just days, others weeks, while those deemed incurable were sent back to their ports of origin. During the Great Depression, more people left the United States than arrived, and with new government restrictions on who could enter the country, Ellis Island began its inevitable decline. Neglected and barely used, buildings steadily fell into disrepair and some parts of the hospital complex are in such decay today that they are unsafe to enter. That's where *Save Ellis Island* comes in: a tireless organization largely staffed by volunteers who've made it possible for small groups to take a hard hat tour of the old hospital. Part of their mission is not just to spread awareness of what happened here, but to shore up some of these buildings. Many have already been saved, at least temporarily. Walking through the weed-covered forecourts, old autopsy rooms and quarantine areas will raise the hairs on the back of your neck. Prefer your history with some grit? Skip the crowds and take the unique opportunity to explore this largely-ignored half of an island that looms large in American history.
(Book your hard hat tour of Ellis Island at Saveellisisland.org)

Ellis Island

A Not-so-Fairytale Castle

Bannerman's Castle might look like a medieval European storybook setting, but these American ruins have seen their fair share of disaster. The only real occupants of the castle were weapons of war and temperamental explosives housed in this elaborate military surplus warehouse built in 1901. Just 50 miles north from New York City, located on the Hudson River's Pollepel Island, the arsenal that wouldn't look out of place in a *Game of Thrones* episode was built and designed by Francis Bannerman VI, a Scottish-American who made a name for himself buying and selling surplus military equipment at the close of the American Civil War. The castle finds itself in its current state of abandonment following an incident in the 1950s which saw one of Bannerman's only ferryboats smash into the island during a storm, causing an explosion on impact. Prior to that, in 1920, 200 tons of shells and powder exploded in a major

Bannerman Castle

accident, which sent Bannerman's business into a slow and steady decline. In 1967, the mysterious island was purchased by the State of New York and opened to the public for tours. But in 1969, further disaster wreaked havoc on the arsenal when a fire devastated the roof and flooring, rendering the island off-limits once again. After decades of trespassing, vandalism, neglect and decay, by 2009, nearly half of the structure's front and east walls had collapsed.

Lately, things finally seem to be looking up for Bannerman's Castle, with its very own trust working to permanently stabilize the remaining structure. Bannerman's is once again open to the public, and every third Sunday from May through October, you can hop aboard the Estuary Steward, ride over to the island and wander around on a self-guided tour while being serenaded by classical musicians. You can even bring a picnic and enjoy a live music concert with Bannerman's ghostly castle as your backdrop (just watch out for wobbly walls). Historians are on hand to answer questions about the island, and kayak tours around its shores are also available.

(Pollepel Island, NY; Island Walking Tours are Sat-Sun at 11am and 12pm, May-Oct. Cruise info available at +1-855-256-4007; Bannermancastle.org)

Reach a Haunted Hospital via Cable Car

New York City has many islands along the East River, several of which were used as dumping grounds for the cities "undesirables": the sick, the poor and the criminal. At the southern tip of Roosevelt Island, formerly known as Blackwell's Island, are the ruins of the **Renwick Smallpox Hospital**. The deadly disease ran rife through the city's crowded immigrant tenements, and the afflicted were first sent here to be quarantined in 1854. Falling into disrepair a century later, recent efforts have been made to stabilize the haunting ruins. A night-time visit is recommended, when the spooky Gothic ruins are illuminated. The island was at different times home to a prison, an asylum, a distinctive Octagon-shaped building at the opposite end (recently converted into apartments), and has been the proposed site of numerous ambitious architectural projects that were never completed. With several architecturally significant buildings to check out, it's well worth the novelty cable car ride. The most fun you can have with your Metrocard is to escape the subway and soar over New York in a bright red gondola with the Roosevelt Island Tramway, the first commuter tramway in America.

(E Rd, New York, NY, 10044; take either the F train to Roosevelt Island, or the Tramway, and head to the southernmost tip of the Island; Theruin.org)

The Forbidden Island of the East River

Oozing mystery, **North Brother Island** has been abandoned and off-limits for over fifty years. The buildings, silently swallowed by nature over the years, were once the home and final resting place of Typhoid Mary, the infamous Typhoid-carrying cook who traveled from household to household in New York City, infecting over 50 people with the disease until she was forcibly isolated. Most of the decaying architecture, some of which can be glimpsed from the Bronx, belonged to the Riverside Hospital, founded in the 1850s to treat and isolate victims of the disease. No stranger to tragedy, in 1904 over 1000 souls perished on the deserted island when a pleasure steamer caught fire just off its shores. Last used as a refuge home for heroin addicts in the 1960s, the island was eventually turned into a closed-off wildlife sanctuary in the early 2000s, and has been left mostly undisturbed ever since. Plans might be afoot for small, organized public trips to this most elusive of abandoned destinations, but for now, only if you have "compelling academic and scientific purposes" to visit should you apply for permission from the Parks Department. Or Plan B: apply for a job with the NYC Audubon, which monitors the island and the New York harbor for Heron nesting activity.
(Nycgovparks.org/park-features/north-brother-island/visit)

Renwick
Smallpox Hospital

The City's Forgotten Art Deco Airport

Long before LaGuardia and JFK, there was **Floyd Bennett Field** in Brooklyn, the city's first municipal airport, built in beautiful Art Deco style in 1928. When Howard Hughes became the fastest man to fly around the world in 1938, 25,000 people gathered at the Brooklyn airport in Jamaica Bay to welcome his Lockheed Electra home. Aviation legends Amelia Earhart, Charles Lindbergh and Wiley Post all broke aviation records at Floyd Bennett Field too, during an age when air travel was still seen as a glamorous adventure, reserved for the wealthy elite. American Airlines operated regular flights from Bennett Field in the 1930s, but situated at the very southern tip of Brooklyn, it failed to attract enough commercial airlines. Today, the forgotten airport lies mostly empty and neglected. While the ground floor of the terminal has been restored and houses a small museum, upstairs, the air traffic control tower and old crew sleeping quarters are steadily declining. Some of the old hangars were converted into modern recreational centers, but the others lie in ruins. Winds howl through the cavernous hangars where you can still make out faded ghost signs of vintage fuel advertisements. The vast runways are covered in weeds. At the far edge of the empty airfield by the water is Hangar B, built during World War II and filled with old airplanes. This aviation graveyard is home to the Historic Air Restoration Project, a small group of dedicated volunteers, mostly old veteran air force mechanics and aviation enthusiasts, who dedicate their time to restoring beautiful old World War II fighters, seaplanes and DC3s. You can find the HARP volunteers in Hangar B on Tuesdays, Thursdays and Saturdays. Floyd Bennett Field's heyday may be long gone, but the pioneering spirit of the golden age of aviation lives on through the work of these volunteers, in this forgotten airfield in a small corner of Brooklyn.

(3159 Flatbush Avenue, Brooklyn, NY, 11234; +1 718-338-3799; The Ryan Visitor Centre in the old terminal is open daily 9am-5pm in the summer, Wed-Sun, 9am-4:30pm in the Winter. You can also camp at Floyd Bennett Field; Nps.gov/gate)

◀ Floyd Bennett Field
▼

Digging for Treasure (and Love) in NYC

Theirs is a love of strange and beautiful proportion; the kind measured in porcelain, preserved animal bones and antique household artefacts excavated from the city. Belle Costes is a hunter of treasures primarily in the New York City area, and her partner in crime and in life is Scott Jordan, otherwise known as the "Bottle Man": a seasoned treasure hunter in his own right with all the charisma of a Mark Twain character. When these two dig around the city (and sometimes in some pretty down and dirty locations), they find ornate antique bottles, pocket watches, clay pipes, powder compacts, toys, dentures, oyster shells as big as your face and keys to doors that no longer exist. "It is an endless array of old trash," shares Belle, "mapping the history of New York as one of the busiest cities for the Industrial Revolution".

There's no formula for becoming a treasure hunter like Scott and Belle, but in the latter's case, a childhood growing up amongst the forgotten treasures of Governor's Island (see pg 298) sure helped. "Sometimes we'll spend weeks digging, and come up dry. Other times, these things seem to roll right out of the earth." Landfills, privies, shorelines and construction sites are all fair-game for a dig (this is also the part where we note that the two always ask for permission when necessary). "Williamsburg is an area we'd like to explore more," says Scott. "It's hard to imagine a time when we'd stop digging," adds Belle, back-lit by a wall of technicolour glass bottles at their home in Queens, "I mean it's addictive. And when you have someone who gets it? Well..." You can usually find Scott and Belle selling their excavated bottles and most recently found treasure at the Grand Bazaar NYC flea market (see pg 118) on Sundays during the warmer months. Find Belle on instagram *@girlfindstreasure* and Scott *@greybeardboy*.

Our favorite rabbit hole is called a "privy vault or a cistern well" where much older artifacts are found dating as far back as 1820s to 1860s. We have found an intact Colonial shoe with its buckle circa 1780s when we dug in a South Street Seaport construction site a few years ago. That is as close to being in the past as you can get, to hold someone's shoe who walked the streets of New York during The Revolutionary War. When we dig, we dig to find layers of history.

– *Scott Jordan & Belle Costes, New York treasure hunters*

Colonial shoe with its buckle circa
1780s found by Scott and Belle

Courtesy of Scott and Belle,
pictured here, digging in New York City

Treasure Hunting at Dead Horse Bay

It might sound like somewhere found on an old pirate's map, but **Dead Horse Bay** gets its name from a very real and grisly past: for this stretch of shoreline at the far reaches of Brooklyn was once home to several horse processing plants (which is exactly what you think it is). The remnants of the carcasses were discarded here, littering the beach with horse bones. Thankfully, those skeletons are long gone (but don't be too alarmed if you find a hunk of bone poking out from the sand) and the beach is now home to a rather less macabre, albeit equally peculiar sight. Walking up to the beach, it looks like the sand is covered with bright pebbles, glinting in the sun. Upon closer inspection, however, you'll find the beach to be completely covered in glass washed up on the sand. Old medicine and soda bottles, jugs of liquor and porcelain cosmetic jars can be found, some over a hundred years old. A few years ago it was common to find Victorian porcelain dolls heads and other such curiosities, that were once used as landfill. Dead Horse Bay feels like a wild, remote place, with the occasional shipwrecked pleasure boat floundering. Even a hulking, rusted safe has made its way there. Stout shoes are essential to enjoy pouring over these washed up remnants of New York's past. Make sure to check online when it's low tide for the best scavenging.
(Located next to Floyd Bennett Field, paths lead to Dead Horse Bay from Flatbush Avenue, opposite where it meets Aviation Road; make sure to check online when it is low tide for best scavenging)

Brooklyn's Underground Railroad Church

Hidden in the tunnels and crypts of **Plymouth Church** on Orange Street awaits one of the city's most remarkable secrets. Behind the organ, hidden at the bottom of the stairway, lies what must have been one of the most dangerous and secret places in all of New York: a key stop on the legendary Underground Railroad. The clandestine 19th-century tunnel system helped slaves across America escape the plantations of the South. "I will both shelter them *[fugitive slaves]*, conceal them or speed their flight," once said the church's fiery preacher Henry Ward Beecher, an ardent abolitionist. "While under my shelter, or under my convoy, they shall be to me as my own flesh and blood." True to his word, escaping slaves who landed in Brooklyn Heights on the East River, were hidden in tunnels and crypts underneath Plymouth Church, before they could be moved on northwards to safety. Those caught risked certain death. Incredibly, their hiding places are still there and the church offers a fascinating tour of them after most services on Sundays. You can also sit in the same pew as Abraham Lincoln, for Plymouth was the only church he visited in New York, and near the entrance, you'll find a 40-pound piece of Plymouth Rock from the landing site of the Mayflower on display. *(57 Orange Street, Brooklyn, NY, 11201; +1 718-624-4743; Services are Sundays at 11am; Info on tunnel visits at Plymouthchurch.org)*

Secrets of Grand Central Terminal

Thronging with 750,000 daily visitors and 250,000 daily commuters, more than just a place to catch a train, Grand Central Terminal is filled with secrets. One of New York's most loved landmarks speaks to a time when public buildings were built with beauty in mind. Take your position on one of the balconies of the main concourse, ideal for people-watching from above, and catch glimpses into strangers' lives as they pass through the beating heart of New York City. The eye is soon drawn to the ceiling, a majestic depiction of the Zodiac constellations. Only the eagle-eyed commuters have noticed that the constellations are in fact painted backward, a rather monumental mistake that was spotted several months after the grand opening in 1913. In the far corner of the ceiling near the claw of Cancer, you can spot a small black rectangle in the brickwork. It was left over from Grand Central's massive restoration in the 1990s and shows the state of the ceiling before years of soot and cigarette smoke was cleaned. Next, turn your attention to the information booth right in the middle of the hall. The countless passengers seeking information on train times and platform numbers probably don't realize that the stunning four-faced clock atop the booth is one of the most valuable items in the city, thought to be valued at around $20 million.

Cocktails at the Railway Mogul's Secret Man Cave

Tell your date to meet you under that $20 million clock in the middle of Grand Central, only to then whisk them away through the building to a cocktail bar hidden inside the inner and outer walls of the busiest train terminal in America. **The Campbell** was once the former apartment and office of Jazz Age railway financier John Campbell. It was a place to entertain millionaire clients from out of town (pictured on pg 265), and where he often spent the night at Grand Central. But after his death in 1957, the space was used as the signalman's office, before transit police eventually took it over to store their guns and equipment. They even had a small jail in the area where the present-day bar stands. The apartment was lovingly restored in 1999 and today, the space once again has the air of a 19th-century mogul's stately home, with high-beamed ceilings, sumptuous stained glass and a vast fireplace dominating the far end complete with Campbell's original safe underneath. If you have to bid a romantic farewell to someone, the Campbell is by far the grandest place to have a cocktail while waiting for a departing train. *(15 Vanderbilt Avenue, New York, NY, 10017; +1 212-297-1781; open daily 12pm–2am; Thecampbellnyc.com)*

Grand Central's Rooftop Tennis Club

Venture downstairs to the lower track level of Grand Central, and you will find the sumptuous Oyster Bar (pg 305) which opened its illustrious doors back when the Terminal did in 1913. With your back to the Oyster Bar, turn left up the

ramp, and halfway along you'll find a rarely-used elevator that will take you to one of the station's best-kept secret – a public tennis court. Open to everyone, the **Vanderbilt Tennis Club** is housed in what used to be a CBS television studio. Every day from 6 am until 1 am, players in the know enjoy a match or two in secret confines, high on the roof of Grand Central Terminal. *(4th Floor, 15 Vanderbilt Avenue, Midtown, NY 10017; +1 212-599-6500; open everyday 6am-1am; Vanderbilttennisclub.com)*

No racket? No problem. Grand Central is filled with shops as you'd expect to find in any major train terminal, but has some slightly peculiar surprises all of its own. Head down the 45th Street Passage, and tucked out of the way, you'll find **Grand Central Racquet** offering equipment and apparel for tennis. You can even get your old rackets restrung *(40 E 45th St, NY 10017; +1 212-856-9647; Mon-Fri 7.30am-6.30am)*. Just next door is the charming **Central Watch**. For three generations this family-owned business has been fixing watches with unparalleled service in the city, as well as selling a fantastic collection of vintage, high-end watches. *(Between Track 38 & 39, +1 212-685-1689 Mon-Fri-8am-5pm; CentralWatch.com)*

John Campbell's apartment inside Grand Central Station circa 1923

A Top Secret Underworld

Two of Grand Central's greatest secrets will require some resourceful sleuthing. Buried deep underground is a place known cryptically as **M42**. The sub-basement contains a hidden power station that powered the New York railroad during World War II. It was thought to be a prime target for German saboteurs, so much so that armed guards had orders to shoot interlopers on sight. The terminal occupies 49 acres of land below ground, occupying the space beneath most buildings that surround 15 Vanderbilt Avenue. One of the holy grails of New York urban exploration is **Track 61**, a secret platform that ran underneath the Waldorf-Astoria. The hotel's VIP guests could use it to pass in and out of New York City without ever having to go outside. Local lore has it that a freight elevator was built big to carry Franklin D. Roosevelt's limousine from a train carriage to the hotel parking garage, hiding his wheelchair use from the public eye after he became a paraplegic at age 39. The secret platform is no longer in use, but the old train carriage that once transported the President is still there gathering dust in the depths of Grand Central Terminal.

Both *UntappedCities.com* and *NYAdventureclub.com* have been known to organize special tours of the M42 power station and Track 61.
(89 East 42nd Street, New York, NY, 10017; open daily 5am-2am; Grandcentralterminal.com)

M42 power station
under Grand Central Station

Grand Central Station © John Collier, 1941

Hiding in Plain Sight

Mysterious buildings of note and urban secrets hiding right under our noses

The Fake Townhouse Hiding a Mystery Underground Portal

On a street in Brooklyn that takes you towards the river where the cobblestones begin paving the road, there's a townhouse that deserves a second look. Despite its impeccable brickwork, number **58 Joralemon Street** is not like the other houses. Behind its blacked out windows, no one is home – and no one has been for more than 100 years. In fact, number 58 is not a home at all, but a secret subway exit and ventilation point disguised as a Greek Revival brownstone. The house stands directly nine stories above the New York City subway tracks for lines 4 and 5. If you approach the front door and peek through the crack, you'll eyeball a bleakly-lit, windowless room with concrete flooring and a metal bunker-style door that would lead to a bat cave if this was Hollywood. Every so often, neighbors have reported seeing men dressed in special work suits in the middle of the night hanging around the stoop at number 58. The property was once a private residence dating back to 1847, but as the first underwater subway tunnel connecting Manhattan and Brooklyn was being constructed, the Metropolitan Transportation Authority acquired the house and converted it into a giant subway ventilator. For decades, vented air simply poured out from the windows, but in the 1990s, the MTA decided to be a little more neighborly and fully restore the historic facade.

58 Joralemon Street

The industrial steel shutter vents, now situated on the building's roof, were permanently shut and replaced with sleek opaque window panes. One neighbor who was lucky enough to be shown inside by MTA officials said it was reminiscent of "something out of *A Clockwork Orange* ... open and cavernous" with a nine-storey staircase that plunges down to the train tunnel below. At some point, number 58 Joralemon Street also became a designated emergency exit, and during an evacuation, subway passengers would have to climb up a grim metal staircase to reach a windowless room with a door. If they opened that door, it would lead them to this New York City townhouse stoop, as if they'd exited through a surreal portal from the underworld.
(58 Joralemon Street, Brooklyn, New York, NY)

Dr. Evil's Big City Lair

The most ominous looking skyscraper in NYC, it could easily be the lair of a rich supervillain with its brutalist and windowless design – a hunch that isn't far off. **The Long Lines Building** at 33 Thomas Street is a 550-foot-tall windowless skyscraper, which has also been called 'the tallest blank wall in the world'. Completed in 1974, it's one of the most secure buildings in America, designed to withstand nuclear fallout, built to house telephone switching equipment – or so they say. In recent years, journalists identified 33 Thomas St as the likely location of a covert NSA mass surveillance hub which monitors our phone calls and internet data. Not the kind of place you want to sneak in and snoop around, but certainly a fascinating building to keep an eye out for in lower Manhattan and inspire your next conspiracy theory.
(33 Thomas St, New York, NY, 10007)

The Long Lines Building

The Hess Triangle: New York's Tiniest Real Estate Hold Out

Look through old photographs of the city, and chances are you'll come across one of **Village Cigars**. This small tobacconist, with its distinctive red shopfront and slightly peculiar triangular shape, has been a long-standing staple of Greenwich Village. Just outside the shop, where Christopher Street meets 7th Avenue, is a well-worn, small triangle mosaic set into the pavement. It reads "Property of the Hess Estate, Which Has Never Been Dedicated For Public Purposes." The story behind the unusual mosaic lies in a dispute between David Hess, who owned an apartment building on the site, and the City of New York. Working to widen the subway system in 1910, the City seized and demolished buildings along 7th Avenue, also seizing the Hess apartment. But the family noticed that they'd missed a tiny triangle-shaped plot of land. Refusing to sell it, the Hess family instead installed the tiny mosaic, a fascinating remnant of a holdout against the City of New York. The mosaic is still there, sold to Village Cigars in 1938. *(110 7th Avenue S, New York, NY, 10014; +1 212-242-3872; open 24 hours; The Hess Triangle is in the pavement just outside the entrance)*

Wall Street's Hidden Clues to the Golden Age of Steamships

There is a Citibank branch in Lower Manhattan with a peculiar secret. Occupying the prestigious address of **Number One, Broadway**, it looks like a normal enough bank branch, until you look closely at the two entrances. One doorway, leading to the ATM, has an ornately carved stone frame that reads "First Class." The other, leading to the bank lobby itself, is marked with "Cabin Class," for this building was once the ticketing office of J.P. Morgan's vast shipping empire, the very same empire behind the *RMS Titanic*. If the Titanic had ever made a return voyage to England, this is where you would have come to buy your ticket. These bank doors are mostly overlooked by the tens of thousands of visitors who flock to Lower Manhattan every day to sail to the Statue of Liberty or get a photo in front of Di Modica's *Charging*

Number One, Broadway, formerly the White Star Line offices

Bull. But throughout the modern Financial District, clues are everywhere, reminding us that New York was first a port before anything else. "A city of hurried and sparkling waters, city of spires and masts", wrote Walt Whitman. The bank building at Number One Broadway was just the start of what was once known as "Steamship Row" during a glamorous era of ocean travel. This suitably grand street of imposing skyscrapers housed the offices and ticketing halls of the juggernauts of ocean liner companies that sent floating palaces across the seas, bedecked with ballrooms above, while thousands of immigrants awaited passage to the New World in steerage below. Next door to the Citibank is a Subway sandwich shop, today looking rather forlorn, but look again, and you'll notice a fine, stone staircase leading into numbers **9-11**, **Broadway**. It was here, on the morning of April 15th, 1912, that crowds began to gather as newspapers reported that the impossible had happened: the unsinkable Titanic had sunk. Relatives and friends of passengers flocked to these very steps, desperate to find out news of their loved ones. The discerning eye will notice that the old iron fence around the Subway sandwich shop is adorned with rows of stars, representing the White Star shipping company that once operated here. A few doors down at **Number 25, Broadway**, the ground floor is occupied and owned by the Italian luxury restaurant chain, Cipriani, but carved into stone above the entrance, and emblazoned on its gleaming bronze doors, you can clearly see that this once was home to a giant of ocean travel, the Cunard Line. Decorated as opulently as its vessels, the great hall of Cunard's New York HQ was adorned with elaborate Renaissance-revival murals depicting ocean voyage. The last ticket was sold here in 1968, and Cunard sold the building three years later, but the company still exists and is the only remaining cruise line still offering a regularly scheduled passenger service between Europe and New York. Today, it's still possible to come to America the old fashioned way, traveling from Southampton to New York, a voyage that Cunard has run ever since 1848. The Queen Mary 2 takes seven nights to cross the Atlantic, evenings that can be spent dancing in the largest ballroom at sea. But for every luxury liner, there were dozens of pedestrian steamship companies operating out of Lower Manhattan, and traces of their existence can be found all around Wall Street. Just remember to look above doorways and up at the ceilings of imposing *Beaux-Arts* buildings. These hidden and mostly overlooked fragments of New York tell of a time when the most delightful way to travel the world, was by sea.

Canoe Your Way Through New York History

Forget double-decker bus tours, join the fleet of 25 canoes at the **North Brooklyn Boat Club** for free "Public Paddle" tours down the East River. You'll learn about the geography and history of the city in a way that just doesn't occur to landlubbers, sharpening your knowledge of various creeks and inlets

for future exploring. Check their site for paddle dates, and other activities, such as "Nautical Knitting & Live Jazz," believe it or not.
(51 Ash St, Brooklyn, NY 11222; +1 347-915-6222; Northbrooklynboatclub.org)

The Long Lost World of the Luxury Flying Boat

While ocean steam liners and plush sleeper train cars have their charms, surely no other travel vessel could match the grandeur of the Pan Am Clipper Class. Those sleek, hulking seaplanes were the ultimate luxury – flying and floating five-star hotels, roughly the size of a modern commercial jet plane, complete with deluxe sleeper cabins, honeymoon suites, a dining salon and cocktail lounge. Relive the golden age of aviation by heading to a little-known part of LaGuardia airport, located just a few miles away from the bustling main terminals in Queens. **Marine Air Terminal** is a small, beautiful Art Deco gem, currently being used by Jet Blue, but for a brief window of time before WWII, was the First Class-only terminal for passengers embarking on one of Pan Am's majestic, giant flying boats. Today, the Marine Terminal looks much like it did in 1940 when the first scheduled Clipper left here bound for Lisbon. Gleaming chrome doors and delightful Art Deco signs point the way to the restaurant, arrivals and departure lounges, while a central small rotunda is home to one of the largest WPA murals ever commissioned, portraying the history of aviation. Even if you're not taking a flight, it's still possible to wander in and enjoy the elegance and quiet of the terminal – a taste of how air travel used to be. You'll also notice a curious sculpture on the entry's left with a telephone number on its side, beckoning you to call for "more information." Most unexpectedly, at the other end of the line is the artist's widow – a soft-spoken lady who'll shoot the breeze with you about her late husband's impressive life's work, what outfit she's wearing to dinner and why you're not on your damn plane yet. It's perhaps the strangest conversation you'll ever have in an airport but we like to think of her as the secret fairy godmother of LaGuardia Airport.
(Terminal A can be reached by the Q47 bus, although a taxi is probably easier. After exploring the terminal, head around the back to the waterfront, where the giant flying boats would have docked)

Secrets of Central Park

Every year, tens of millions of visitors come to enjoy Central Park: America's first major landscaped public park that's almost six times larger than the country of Monaco. With over 800 acres to explore and its own dedicated NYPD precinct, you'd better believe Central Park is hiding more than just a few secrets...

Central Park's Secret Cave

You won't find it on any official maps or find signposts to show you the way. Hidden away in the middle of the park is a mysterious cave so ancient, it predates Central Park itself. Expect to hop over some fences and tread through thick undergrowth to find Central Park's legendary "Native American Cave", a mysterious place that earned its moniker after evidence was allegedly discovered inside of early Native American inhabitants. While much of Central Park was sculpted into picturesque lawns, tree-lined avenues and lakes, its architects, Frederick Law Olmstead and Calvert Vaux, deliberately created some wilder, more overgrown places. They created a maze of hills, winding step paths, and lush, thick undergrowth they called "The Ramble." Over 150 years later, not much has changed here, and it's easy to forget that you're surrounded by one of the world's busiest cities. Lurking in the midst of this idyllic reverie is the hidden cave. To find it requires keen eyes once you're at the northern end of The Lake, near where the Ramble Arch meets Oak Bridge. At a high point overlooking the water, look down and to your left, you'll see some crude, rocky steps, mostly hidden by plants. A quick hop over the fence and the stairway will lead down to the cave, " an Eldorado of pleasures," wrote James Miller in 1866. At the foot of the stone stairway is a sheltered inlet leading out to The Lake, where intrepid boaters can row right up to the cave's mouth. The *New York Times* ran a peculiar story in 1897 with a headline that read, "Lived A Month In A Cave." It told the sad tale of one Susie Grunelt, a 15-year-old girl from Bohemia who ran away from her parents' house on East 71st. In the 1970s, the Parks Department sealed up the cave for good and it fell off the city's radar. But if you can manage to find its steps and hidden inlet, you'll be in one of the quietest, most secluded spots in the city. *(The Cave is located by the Ramble in Central Park, 79th St Transverse, New York, NY 10024; +1 212 310-6600; Open daily from 6am-1am)*

For the Groovy Shroom Hunter in You

Somehow, it makes perfectly groovy sense that the New York Mycological Society was founded by the experimental artist and composer, John Cage, in the 1960s. Consider **Mushroom Hunting in Central Park** your "in" with some legitimate fungi fanatics. You're advised to "bring lunch, water, a knife, a whistle and a basket" for an unforgettable way of experiencing the city's most famous park. Just please, don't eat the little buggers, as there are quite a few toxic ones in Central Park. Nonmembers attendance: $5..
(Visit newyorkmyc.org/walks for info)

Fishing in Central Park Lake

Did you know you can fish in New York City? Carp, Bass, Catfish, Black Crappie, Pumpkinseed Sunfish, Chain Pickerel, Bluegill Sunfish, and Crayfish – all of these species can be legally fished on a catch-and-release basis, right in the

Wagner Cove

middle of Manhattan. There are certain rules governing acceptable bait, fishing seasons, hours, locations etc., so before casting your rod, it's best to inform yourself over at the Charles A. Dana Discovery Center at the Harlem Meer, where you can also rent rods and buy the right bait. Once you're ready to catch some fish, set yourself up at the secluded wooden gazebo on **Wagner Cove**, one of the park's loveliest hidden spots by the water. And if you're lucky, you might just catch yourself a 15lb carp.

Psst! Did you know you can camp overnight in Central Park? Technically, it's illegal, but every so often, the city's park rangers will escort some lucky folks into the park after dark for a night under the stars. To be one of those campers, you need to enter a secret lottery via Nycgovparks.org/reg/rangers.
(Wagner Cove coordinates: N 40.7747857, W 73.9733505)

A Hidden Hiking Sanctuary

How do you make the city magically disappear? Located just north of the Pond in Central Park, is the **Hallett Nature Sanctuary**. In the 1930s, city planner Robert Moses closed off four acres on a peninsula inside the park with a view to create a bird sanctuary. Nature intervened and rapidly took over the sealed off parkland, and the peninsula was eventually closed off to the public, becoming a semi-secret part of Central Park. Recent sterling work by the Central Park Conservancy saw the Hallett Sanctuary reopened in 2016 with limited hours. To limit the human impact, only 20 people at a time are allowed in. You'll enter through a charming, rustic gate, and soon you will find yourself in the calm of the woods where gray squirrels, raccoons, rabbits and woodchucks take refuge from the city. In May, hundreds of azaleas are in full bloom throughout the trail. And don't miss the waterfall flowing down thousand-year-old rocks on your way out.
(Directions: Enter the park at the entrance at Central Park South and Sixth Avenue. Head down a set of stairs in between an information kiosk and a statue of Jose Marti on a horse. When you approach the Pond turn left, walking up a hill until you get to an intersection, where you turn right. Continue until you see the distinctive gate. The Hallett Nature Sanctuary is generally open daily, from 10am until half an hour before sunset)

Central Park's Ruined Fort

The northwest of Central Park is a wild, wooded place, in fact, Central Park was designed to be a microcosm of New York State– more rugged and wild in the north like the Catskills while the south is less rustic to evoke the city and its suburbs. Noticeably few visitors venture as far north into the famous park, where you're surrounded by waterfalls and dense forest. On top of a secluded hill in the North Woods are the ruins of a fort, known as **Blockhouse No.1**. It was built to protect northern Manhattan from attack following the war with Britain in 1812, and aside from Cleopatra's Needle, it is actually the oldest structure in Central Park. The fort was hurriedly built in 1814 by local Columbia students, firemen, masons and tradesmen, who all pitched in to build their own defenses, which might explain its somewhat ramshackle appearance. It was already a ruin by the time Olmstead & Vaux decided to design the park around it. There were originally two other forts in this part of the city, but today the one hiding in Central Park is the only one left, you just have to find it, which is a little tricky. The nearest street entrance is West 108th Street, but we recommend hiking through the North Woods from the south first to build up suspense. (*W.108th Street, New York, NY, 10026; +1 212-310-6600; Centralpark.org*)

 Also don't miss: Survival training in Central Park, miniature yachting in Central Park and a marionette show in a 143-yr-old Swedish cottage (pg 228-230).

Stranger Things
Enter the NYC twilight zone...

The Real-Life Doc Brown

The Holographic Studio, now in its 4th decade, is the oldest holographic studio in the world (apparently there are others). The gallery was founded by one of the pioneers of holography, Jason Sapan, who prefers to go by the name Dr. Laser — rest assured he is as fun as he sounds and his enthusiasm for holography is so contagious, you'll find yourself wanting one of those laser thingies of your own. Even if you have no prior interest in the medium, Dr. Laser is a true storyteller and unique New York character worth meeting (he did the lights at Studio 54). You'll find over 200 of his holographic artworks here, including some jaw-dropping portraits of Andy Warhol and Isaac Asimov. As the Doctor shows you around his zany museum, you get this strange feeling that he could be a real-life time-traveler, showing you a possible future that never really happened. A mad scientist's New York laboratory reminiscent of Doc Brown's from *Back to the Future*, it won't be long before you'll be back to show a friend. (*240 E 26th St, New York, NY, 10010; open Mon-Fri 2pm-6pm; Holographer.com*)

America's Egyptian UFO Cult

Are you just a little bit curious about Brooklyn's answer to Scientology? With its towering sculptures of Anubis, Osiris and other Egyptian deities, the temple façade of the controversial "Nuwaubian" cult is one of the more mysterious buildings in Brooklyn. Just next door you'll find its bookstore, **All Eyes on Egipt**, but suffice to say, a stroll past the temple will do for most. The Nuwaubian Nation cult was founded in the 1970s by Dwight York, a self-declared prophet who manipulated thousands into believing they were cosmic purveyors of a hodge podge extraterrestrial truth. It may sound harmlessly confusing, but the cult spiraled out of control. The rise and fall of York's reign is a story worth digging into, as it speaks to the degree to which the African American community was disenfranchised and hounded by the NYPD in the 1970s. Where the city was failing, Dwight York stepped in to offer a fresh, self-sufficient community (and spaceships) but today, he's serving a 135-year sentence for child abuse and racketeering. Despite his absence, the Nuwaubian Nation lives on in Bushwick. If you step inside the adjacent bookshop, which is packed full of Nuwaubian brochures and merch, keep in mind that many present-day members don't defend York. In fact, they may be willing to talk to you about what went wrong, their community building plans for the future, and maybe, just maybe, give you a peek inside that mysterious temple. *(717 Bushwick Ave, Brooklyn, NY 11221; +1 718-452-9329; Open daily from 10am-8pm, and noon to 8pm Tuesdays)*

All Eyes on Egipt, Bushwick

The Art of Fake News

Remember when the Staten Island Ferry fought a giant squid just like the one described in Jules Verne's *20,000 Leagues Under the Sea*? Or that one time a UFO hovered over a NY harbor? **Joe Reginella's memorial sculptures** invite you to pay your respects to a bevy of invented historical tragedies with utterly ridiculous twists. Local renegade sculptor with a sense of humor, Joseph Reginella, has left countless tourists doing a double take at his sculptures, wondering if they should Google the "1929 Brooklyn Bridge Elephant Stampede." Keep an eye out for them around Battery Park and Staten Island. *(Facebook.com/joseph.reginella)*

A Magician's Secret Library

Hidden inside a midtown office building is a strange and magical library holding over 15,000 books, some dating back to the 1400s. The **Conjuring Arts Research Center** is a place filled with ancient texts, some so rare they can't be found anywhere else in the world. They contain such centuries-old secrets as the origins of card magic, mentalism and sleights of hand. But far from being a dusty repository, the center is a practical resource open to the public, a library for magic 'scholars' and researchers that has done sterling work in collecting and preserving this most secretive of subjects. *(11 West 30th Street, New York, NY, 1001; +1 212-594-1003; Conjuringarts.org)*

A Masked Theatrical Adventure inside a 1930s Time Capsule Hotel

Approach the mysterious-looking building at 530 West 27th Street, unmarked save for a brass plaque on the door, where upon entering you're given a playing card, and shown to a dimly lit, smokey jazz club. When your playing card is called by the band leader, you are given a mask, whisked away from your companions, and plunged into an immersive, anonymous adventure called **Sleep No More**, which is equal parts *Macbeth* and Hitchcock's *Vertigo*. To give anything more away would be to divulge the secrets of one of New York's most memorable ways to spend an evening. It all takes place inside The McKittrick Hotel, built in 1939 and intended to be New York City's finest luxury hotel. But when suddenly World War II broke out just days after its grand opening, the hotel was "condemned and left locked, permanently sealed from the public... until now." It's all part of the drama invented by your theatrical hosts. In the same building, there's a bar and restaurant, dressed up as an authentic 1930s Scottish railway station, complete with full-sized train and platform (pg 163) amongst other secretive delights waiting to be explored.

(The McKittrick Hotel & Sleep No More can be found at 530 West 27th Street, New York, NY, 10001; The Heath, Gallow Green and the Manderley Bar can be found and Numbers 542 & 532 respectively; Mckittrickhotel.com)

 Also, see the McKittrick Hotel's rooftop garden on pg 163.

Cabinets of Morbid Curiosity

Beginners Taxidermy Class

Those Victorians had some pretty interesting hobbies to pass the time. Case in point: the peculiar practice of anthropomorphic taxidermy, which transforms pets and domestic vermin into tap-dancing, top-hat-wearing shelf companions. **Brooklyn Taxidermy** is a Greenpoint taxidermist and entomology art studio founded by taxidermy artist Amber Maykut, who'll guide you through the

beginner and advanced steps to completing your own taxidermied mouse. You could also choose to start with a chipmunk class or butterfly pinning, but let's just be clear, no specimens are killed for the sake of taxidermy. You'll learn how to skin and mount your specimen and then choose from miniature props to give your furry friend some human characteristics. To get over your squeamishness, interestingly, all classes are BYOB. Gift certificates are also available to purchase online and Amber sells her own anthropomorphic work on Etsy.
(681 Morgan Ave, Brooklyn, NY 11222; +1 646-481-0871; Brooklyntaxidermy.com)

Anthropomorphic taxidermy

© Courtesy of Brooklyn Taxidermy

Gift Shopping for the Addams Family

Obscura Antiques and Oddities is perhaps the only place in New York where you can buy a mummified cat, a child-sized straight jacket or a human gallstone the size of a softball. Having trouble finding a unique gift for that hard-to-buy-for friend? Venture into the shop that's part macabre museum and part gallery of the grotesque. This delightfully morbid East Village emporium evokes the old cabinets of curiosities or the literal skeletons you might find in an old dusty closet. The likes of Chloë Sevigny and Dita Von Teese have been known to drop into the delightfully ghoulish store – the perfect place to find peculiar medical, masonic or circus sideshow antiquities, and probably the only place to find art made of human nail clippings.
(207 Avenue A, New York, NY, 10009; +1 212-505-9251; Obscuraantiques.com)

A Cinematic Sideshow

The first thing you should do when walking into downtown Brooklyn's **Alamo Drafthouse** cinema is take a look at the carpet. If the orange, red and brown hexagonal pattern looks familiar, its because it's the very same carpet from the Overlook Hotel in *The Shining*. The Alamo Drafthouses started out in Austin, Texas with the tremendous idea of not only showing thoughtfully curated films but serving you handmade cocktails, beers and food directly to your roomy seats. Simply fill out a slip, wave it in the air, and you'll soon be enjoying your movie with an Old Fashioned in hand. But what makes Brooklyn's branch of the Alamo Drafthouse especially unique, is its collaboration with **The House of Wax** cocktail bar on the 4th floor across from the cinema. The bar is home to the surviving exhibits from a peculiar 19th-century Berlin waxwork collection known as Castan's Panopticum, a strange mix of cabinets of curiosities and forgotten sideshow museums that shocked and intrigued visitors from 1869 until 1922. Here you will discover a delightfully morbid cabinet of horrors wonderfully curated and preserved by Ryan Matthew Cohn from Obscura Antiquities and Oddities (the strange gift shop we mentioned on pg 279). Order a "Napoleon Death Mask" for a peculiar nightcap following an evening at the pictures. *(445 Albee Square West, Brooklyn, NY, 11201; +1 718-513-2547; Thehouseofwax.com; head to the 4th floor for both the bar and the Alamo Drafthouse; Drafthouse.com/theater/downtown-brooklyn)*

The Brooklyn Catacombs

The second most popular tourist attraction in 19th-century America after Niagara Falls was a cemetery in Brooklyn. Before Central Park was built, **Green-Wood** was founded in 1838 as one of the first "rural" garden cemeteries in the country; visitors would picnic, promenade and take carriage rides through 478 acres of beautiful rolling hills and miniature valleys, past lakes and ponds, and ornate, beautiful mausoleums. Today, Green-Wood is still an exceptional place to visit and explore. You can take a Twilight Tour and weave through its fascinating graves, ending with a visit to the catacombs, normally closed to the public. If you become a volunteer, you can help organize the vast archives and undertaker's ledgers and even attend the occasional private cocktail party in the catacombs. Green-Wood is still a working, active cemetery, and asks you to visit respectfully. Check Green-wood.com for details on upcoming events and tours, or download the self-guided mobile app and find your own way around. *(Main entrance is on Fifth Avenue and 25th Street in Brooklyn, NY. Open everyday 8am-5pm October-March, 7am-7pm April-September)*

Greetings from Rabbi Shaul's Spiritual Taxidermy Museum

It's hard to recall any other place on earth that's dedicated to collecting every animal mentioned in the Torah but **Torah Animal World** in Brooklyn has done exactly that, making it the largest (and perhaps only) Hasidic taxidermy museum in the world. Rabbi Shaul Shimon Deutsch is the man behind this unique cabinet of curiosities, which he runs out of his home in the Orthodox Jewish neighborhood of Borough Park. The Rabbi single-handedly curated this unusual biblical collection, and unlike most museums, encourages visitors to reach out and touch all his furry friends to truly feel history coming alive. In case you were looking for the Noah's Ark of taxidermy, it's here, waiting to blow your mind. The collection had to be relocated from its larger previous location to survive tough economic times, so pop by and help one of America's most unusual taxidermy museums stay afloat.

(1603 41st St, Brooklyn, NY 11218; +1 877-752-6286; open every day from 9am-9pm, until 2pm on Fridays, Torah Animal World is open to all but appointments are necessary)

Torah Animal World

Where to Plan the Perfect Murder

"Nobody shoplifts from a store that knows 3,214 ways to murder someone!" says a sign at **The Mysterious Bookshop**. A treasure trove of crime, thriller, espionage and suspense books line the shelves of the oldest specialist mystery bookshop in America. Rare first editions, obscure titles, and their own publishing wing, combined with fantastic "meet the author" events make this shop in Tribeca the perfect place to come in and sleuth around.

(58 Warren Street, New York, NY; +1 212-587-1011; MysteriousBookshop.com)

Prospect Park's Hidden Quaker Cemetery

What most visitors to Olmstead & Vaux's beautiful, sculpted Prospect Park
don't know, is that there's a secret working cemetery hidden inside it. The
old cemetery actually pre-dates Prospect Park by some twenty years, the
park having been built around it in 1867, so that today, it remains fenced
off and hidden from sight by dense forest. Nearly 2,000 people lie at rest
in the sequestered **Quaker Cemetery**, including, quite unexpectedly, actor
Montgomery Clift. Once inside Prospect Park, follow the inner loop until West
Drive turns into Center Drive. Venture into the forest and after less than a
minute you will come across a fence. The Quaker Cemetery lies within.
(Check prospectpark.org for further information about visiting Prospect Park)

Naughty New York

To the easily-offended: avert your eyes now.

Burlesque in Bushwick

There are no rules, no genders and no beauty stereotypes when it comes to the
burlesque bars of Bushwick. Somewhere in between the Ziegfeld Follies and
a surreal fetish show, the world of Marquis de Sade lives on at **Company XIV**,
where a dazzling troupe of performers at the top of their game invite you to
fall down their "baroque burlesque rabbit hole". Catch an erotic adaptation of
Alice in Wonderland or *The Nutcracker* while sipping on absinthe cocktails in a
decadent but intimate theatre. Perfect for spicing up date night or celebrating
with friends, it's a spectacular evening you won't forget.
(Book tickets at Companyxiv.com)

There's MoMa and then there's MoSex

You have to be 18 years or older to visit the **Museum of Sex**. Once you get past
the front of house sex shop, the rest of the museum offers a blend of low and
high-brow art from eras past and present through provocative and powerful
exhibitions. Learn about the earliest sex pioneers, have a giggle over some
historical pornography and don't miss the boobie bounce house.
*(233 5th Ave, Manhattan, NY 10016; +1 212-520-7600; Open daily from morning to
near midnight; Museumofsex.com)*

Manhattan's Last Sex Hotel

Valentine's Day is the busiest day of the year for **Liberty Inn**, offering pay-by-
the-hour rooms in the meatpacking district since 1977. The vibe is David-Lynch-
meets-retro-porn set, thanks to glittering headboards, neon lights, pop art decor
and a vending machine selling lube and condoms. "Impeccably clean," said *The
New York Times*. Cash only.
(51 10th Ave, Meatpacking District, NY 10014; +1 212-741-2333; Llibertyinnyc.com)

New York's Erotic Masseur for Women

"Close your eyes. Turn off your mind. And open yourself up to full-body bliss" are the guiding words of "Dr. M", the erotic masseur who's been unwinding New York women with his personal practice, **Her Private Pleasures**, for 15 years. With an extensive list of media coverage and glowing testimonials, he might just be one of America's greatest sex-positive treasures: for 1-hour, the 40-something-yr-old Dr. M"(not his real name, not a real doctor, but just roll with it) uses his hands to massage female clients with "a melange of rhythms" until, ideally, they hit that happy ending. "He listens to how your body responds to his touch," a loyal client told New York Magazine's *The Cut* in 2018. There's no Tantra, no chanting, no inkling of reciprocation. You just cut the bullsh*t and get down with your sensual self in a luxury doorman building in Uptown Manhattan, with the utmost discretion, comfort, and safety. "You don't have to make anyone else feel good," said another woman, "There are few good things that happen to you in life that are quite so selfish." Clients are all ages and all professions, and simply put, all kinds of happy. Sessions are complimentary but donations are appreciated, that is, only if you feel the service you received warrants it.

(Located in Upper Manhattan. Learn more on his website, herprivatepleasures. strikingly.com)

Burlesque in Brooklyn
Courtesy of
Company XIV

43 Willow Place, Brooklyn Heigh
pg 29

09

New York Time Traveller

NAME: _____

BORN: in the wrong era _____

DRINK OF CHOICE: Old Fashioned _____

PERSONAL HEROES: None living _____

PREFERRED MODE OF TRANSPORT: Time machine

IF THIS FITS YOUR DESCRIPTION. YOU'VE COME TO THE RIGHT CHAPTER.

The First American Century

From the first settlers of New Amsterdam to the birth of a new nation, let's set our time machine back just a few hundred years and see what the OG New Yorkers were up to...

Manhattan's Last Farmhouse

In the midst of Inwood's towering apartments and neon-lit bodegas, you'll find the **Dyckman Farmhouse**, central Manhattan's oldest abode, and only farmhouse. The Dyckman family arrived here in 1661 and snatched up 250 acres. The white clapboard cottage has been perched on its hilltop for over 200 years. Legend has it that Dutch immigrants purchased the entire area from the Lenape tribe for $24 and some glass beads. Stepping inside the Dyckman family's surviving house today, at the center of what was once prime farmland, feels a bit like walking with friendly colonial ghosts, who've left behind their old buckled shoes by the fire, quilts folded neatly on their beds and personal possessions casually strewn around the living room. Life was far from easy when they set up house here, and the Dyckmans had an admirable track-record of letting weary travelers recuperate at their home, becoming the unofficial inn of the area. The home remained in the family, maintained by descendants, until 1916, when ownership was handed over to the city of New York. They brought back in some of the family's original furnishings, turned the abode into a museum about Dutch colonialists, and even recruited a group of New York "relic hunters" to unearth everything from fossilized pig teeth to dice made out of bullets from the yard. Bring a pack lunch to eat in the quaint front yard, or on one of the two classically Dutch porches. Visiting is free and donation based.
(4881 Broadway, New York, NY 10034; Thurs-Sat 11am-4pm; +1 212-304-9422)

Dyckman Farmhouse

© Beyond My Ken

There's something about that fence...

While tourists are lining up for a photograph with the Charging Bull of Wall Street, just behind the crowds is one of the more obscure relics in the city, hardly noticed by anyone – the **oldest fence in New York City**. It was erected in 1771 to surround Bowling Green, itself the oldest public park in New York. Used as a cattle market before it became a park, this small downtown green is also believed to be the spot where Peter Minuit bought Manhattan Island from the Native Americans. There was once a statue of King George III here, but it was torn down by Patriots after the Declaration of Independence was read out at nearby City Hall. This wrought iron fence surrounding it is all that remains. On closer inspection, you'll notice something quite remarkable; for the tops of the fence posts are rather rough looking. They were once decorated with the British royal crowns which were sawn off by the rampaging Sons of Liberty. *(Bowling Green, Broadway and Whitehall Street, New York, NY, 10004; +1 212-639-9675; Nycgovparks.org)*

George Washington's Dinner Table is Still Set in This Manhattan Tavern

Fraunces Tavern was *the* go-to spot for all Revolutionary festivities, from the farewell dinner that a certain George Washington held for his officers in 1783, to the "Evacuation Day," party thrown by the governor once the British split. Whether it was being pummeled by a cannonball or safeguarding plans of Revolution, the most remarkable thing about the 300-year-old watering hole is the fact that it's still standing amongst Manhattan's skyscrapers – and still serving the thirsty. You can trace the tavern's history as far back as 1719, proudly perched on the tip of a sparsely-populated Manhattan, when the site had a view of the entire bay. Situated at 54 Pearl Street at the corner of Broad Street, it is officially the city's oldest building. Head upstairs to the tiny but important museum to bask in some seriously weird U.S. treasures. Washington's table and dinner party settings have been perfectly preserved in one room, while encased strands of his red hair (and his tooth) sit in the next. Entry is $7. Head back downstairs after visiting the museum for dinner in the 18th century oak-paneled Tallmadge Room, whose kitchen claims to serve the president's favorite pot pie. Finally, head to the whiskey bar for a nightcap before stepping out of its doors, and back into the 21st century. Or not quite! Across the street, under the colonnade, you'll find the preserved remnants of 17th century New York, discovered in an archaeological dig, now displayed beneath a glass sidewalk.

(54 Pearl St, Financial District, NY 10004; +1 212-425-1778;
Open daily from noon to 5pm; Frauncestavern.com)

An Appetite for History

Turn the clock back to 1799 at the **Mount Vernon Hotel Museum**, which offers a 19th century culinary tour for a taste of the past with your Antebellum dinner date. Wander the orchards and bake a pie fit for the house's original Mistress, Abigail Adams Smith (John Adams' daughter), and indulge in the sweetest treat of all: candied flowers. *Ye olde swoon.*
(421 E 61st St, Upper East Side, NY 10065; Call +1 212 838-6878 to book a tour, Tues-Sun 11am-4pm; Mvhm.org/group-tours)

Bespoke Letterpress at a 19th-Century Era Print Shop

Down in the historic South Street Seaport district, **Bowne & Co. Stationers** originally opened in 1775 as a small batch maritime and financial printers. Today, you can literally step back in time on the original wooden floorboards, past shelves and drawers full of inks, and metal letter blocks in the most beautiful fonts at this wonderfully charming letterpress and printers. Part store and part living museum, Bowne & Co. is home to over half a dozen working old presses. Reopened in the 1970s as part of the South Street Seaport Museum, the shop is filled with delightful hand-printed goods, and still takes orders for all your bespoke, old-time printing needs. But best of all is the opportunity to join in on regular workshops where you learn the traditional way to handset type. Our favorite class is where you learn about and get to make a "broadside" poster. Using wooden block type, these eye-catching posters were historically used to advertise political rallies, shipping lines, vaudeville acts and the like. It's easy to forget that New York was once a bustling harbor filled with masts, fish markets, maritime merchants and a teeming waterfront. The whole neighborhood is fantastic to explore, with a museum, preserved ships, cobbled streets and warehouses that capture the bygone days when New York was one of the world's most thriving port cities. The South Street Seaport does excellent work preserving and evoking this era of old New York, and nowhere more so than the enchanting Bowne & Co. Stationers and Print Shop.
(209 Water Street, New York, NY, 10038; +1 646-628-2707; Southstreetseaportmuseum.org/water-street/bowne-printers)

A Stroll between Centuries in Brooklyn Heights

For all of Brooklyn's ever-growing popularity, you've not discovered its true virtues until you've taken a stroll around Brooklyn Heights. Packed with picturesque cobbled streets, Victorian townhouses, over 600 pre-Civil War era houses and a few mansions that look like they've come straight off the set of *Gone with the Wind,* if we could just take all the cars away, it would be as if we'd stepped back in time to the 19th century. Despite its name, there are very few high-rise buildings in Brooklyn Heights and very few modern eyesores to spoil the view of a perfect promenade in what is often called America's first suburb...

Begin your Brooklyn Heights stroll along the iconic promenade where the East River meets the Hudson, a pedestrian walkway offering the finest views of the Manhattan skyline. Take a left inland towards the end of Pier 5 onto **Joralemon Street** and enter the two-hundred-year-old enclave of Brooklyn Heights...

Begin your zig-zagging discovery of its beautiful tree-lined streets, first with **Columbia Place**, then **Willow Place** and **Hicks Street** after that. Don't miss number **43 Willow Place**, a mansion set slightly back from the pavement, frozen in time (pictured on pg 284). With its weathered white columns, worn shutters, peeling paint and overgrown ivy, it could almost be a ruined plantation home from the Antebellum South. One of these days, we plan to pluck up the courage to knock on the door and find out what's inside. Spot its identical twin across the street, kept in pristine condition. Back on **Joralemon Street, at number 58**, you'll find our favorite fake townhouse (see pg 268): *Behind its blacked out windows, no one is at home – no one has been for more than 100 years. In fact, number 58 is not a home at all, but a secret subway exit and ventilation point disguised as a Greek Revival brownstone.*

Further up Joralemon, take a left onto Henry Street and disappear down an alley called **Hunts Lane** on your right, lined exclusively with carriage houses where horses were once kept. These stables, that once catered to the homes of

Hunts Lane

Joralemon Street, have now been converted into multi-million dollar residences themselves. There are plenty more photogenic alleys just like this one to be explored if time is on your side.

At the corner of Henry Street and Remsen Street, take a moment to notice the doors of **Our Lady of Lebanon Maronite Cathedral**, for they were once the opulent doors of the dining hall from the doomed luxury liner, the SS Normandie. In 1935, she was the fastest ship afloat. The dining room was longer than the Hall of Mirrors at Versailles, and every inch as grandiose. She caught fire in 1942, capsizing in New York Harbour. Many of the Art Deco treasures which decorated the stricken ship were sold off, and the doors which graced the dining room found their way to this church in Brooklyn Heights.

Long before it was home to anyone else, the native Lenape people called this area *Ihpetonga*, meaning "the high sandy bank"; hence the "Heights" In the early 1800s, the rocky outcrop was already home to several farms and half-a-dozen families of early settlers. When the Brooklyn Steam Ferry Boat Company began offering regularly scheduled crossings in 1814 to and from Lower Manhattan, many affluent New Yorkers moved across the East River. Over six hundred new homes had sprung up by the Civil War and much of Brooklyn Heights' charm lies in the fact that almost all of them are still family homes. Over on Pierrepont Street, you can get your historical bearings with a stop at the **Brooklyn Historical Society** (see pg 108, 143), a beautiful library open to the public, along with its museum, Wednesdays to Saturdays from 1– 5 pm.

Turn back up Pierrepont Street towards the river and find **Willow Street**. At number 151, you'll find one of Arthur Miller's beautifully-preserved old carriage houses. He lived here in the 1950s until he left to marry Marilyn Monroe, and wrote *Death of a Salesman* at 31, Grace Court, before moving over to Willow Street. Famous Brooklyn Heights residents over the years have included Truman Capote, Bob Dylan, W.H. Auden, Mary Tyler Moore, Walt Whitman, Thomas Wolfe and plenty others. At number 70 Willow Street, you'll see an eye-catching pale yellow Greek Revival house. That's where Truman Capote wrote *Breakfast at Tiffany's* and *In Cold Blood.*

It makes our brow a little moist to think this historic district narrowly escaped destruction in the 1960s when city planner Robert Moses plotted to tear much of it down and replace it with modern concrete buildings. In the mid-1950s, a new generation of property owners had already begun moving into the Heights, pioneering the Brownstone Revival by buying and renovating pre-Civil War period houses. The consolidated opposition against Robert Moses's clearance plan for luxury rental housing led to a veritable middle-income movement, and the entire neighborhood became the first protected historic district in New York in 1965. The movement created an especially neighborly atmosphere in Brooklyn Heights that remains palpable even today.

Tumbleweed Saloons of New York

▶

When your time machine breaks down somewhere in the mid-19th century
and there's no room at the inn, just keep on rollin' from one New York saloon
to the next...

An East Village Dinosaur

The floors of the venerable **McSorley's Old Ale House** are strewn with sawdust.
A cast iron stove provides warmth in the cold New York winters, and the walls
are covered with framed newspaper clippings, old photographs and artifacts,
most of which haven't been disturbed for at least a century. Not for nothing
did this coziest of saloons once be called "The Old House At Home." Rivaling
Pete's Tavern as one of the bars which claim to be New York's oldest, McSorley's
would appear to take the honors, having opened its weathered doors in 1854,
though some records show the old saloon closed for a spell in 1860. What is
indisputable, however, is the sense of history and old-timey feel the moment
you step inside. Only one drink is served here, the house beer, coming in two
small glasses, and in "light" or "dark" variety. The dinner menu consists of boxes
of crackers, blocks of cheese and raw onions. McSorley's is the bar room of "old
New York," or as the bar's motto puts it, "we were here before you were born."
The bar drew many writers to its friendly confines, including E.E.Cummings, who
wrote his poem, "I was sitting in McSorleys" in 1923. But it is with writer Joseph
Mitchell that McSorley's is most associated. Writing often about the street
characters who lived on the fringes of New York society, Mitchell published
McSorley's Wonderful Saloon in 1943. He chronicled the motley clientele of the bar
– the mechanics, booksellers, waterfront workers, bar room scroungers and old
men who he met there. Although best avoided at the weekends when it resembles
a loud fraternity house, during the week, McSorley's Old Ale House retains the
air of an older, forgotten New York. Hardly anything has changed since Joseph
Mitchell wrote, "it is equipped with electricity, but the bar is stubbornly lit with a
pair of gas lamps, which flicker fitfully and throw shadows on the low cobwebby
ceiling each time someone opens the street door."
(15 E 7th St, East Village, NY10003; +1 212-473-9148; Mon-Sat 11am-1am,
Sun 1pm-1am; Mcsorleysoldalehouse.nyc)

A Cozy Storyteller's Tavern

When **Pete's Tavern** pulled its first pint in 1864, Abraham Lincoln was still
president, the American Civil War was at its boiling point, and even Manhattan itself
was under attack by the Confederate Secret Service who attempted to burn down
the entire city, setting fire to 13 major hotels, a theater and P. T Barnum's American
Museum. Fast forward one century to Prohibition when Pete's Tavern disguised
itself as a flower shop, catering to thirsty New Yorkers while so many other bars in

the city closed up shop. This dark, wood-paneled old bar is also steeped in literary history. Ludwig Bemelman created his much-loved children's character *Madeline* right here. The prolific short story writer, O. Henry, was also a regular and the tavern's second booth from the doorway has a small, hand-written sign, saying, "In this booth, O.Henry wrote *Gift of the Magi* in the year 1905." Many of O.Henry's stories, known for their surprise twist endings, featured common New Yorkers. *The Gift of the Magi* told the story of a poor, married couple wanting to give each other Christmas presents. Delia, the penniless wife, sells her most treasured possession; her long and beautiful hair; to buy a watch chain for her husband. At the same time, her husband sells his grandfather's pocket watch to buy bejeweled combs for Delia's hair. Bar legend has it, he wrote this story on the back of a menu. *(129 E 18th St, Gramercy Park, New York, NY 10003; +1 212-473-7676; open everyday 11am-2.30am, til 4am on weekends; PetesTavern.com)*

McSorley's Old Ale House in 1937

Cozy Up Cowboy

Saloons aren't complete without a set of swinging doors and Greenpoint's **The Black Rabbit** has many. A series of snug, wooden booths line one wall of this 19th-century bar, each with their own swinging portals, secluding drinkers in romantic private compartments. Add a fireplace and a lush garden at the back and the Black Rabbit can easily be called one of the most charming bars in Brooklyn. If that's not enough, it's also home to a fantastic weekly trivia nights, as well as tarot readings on Wednesdays and Bingo on Sundays. *(91 Greenpoint Avenue, Brooklyn, NY; +1 718-349-1595; Mon-Thurs 4pm-2am, Fri 4pm-4am, Sat 2pm-4am, Sun 2pm-2am, trivia nights are Tuesday at 8pm; Blackrabbitbar.com)*

After Work with Walt Whitman

Before becoming one of America's most influential poets, a young Walt Whitman came to New York City as an aspiring newspaperman. A few years before writing *Leaves of Grass*, Whitman was the editor of the *Brooklyn Daily Eagle* in the 1840s, and his pre-Civil War Brooklyn has been dutifully recreated at **Henry Public** in historic Cobble Hill. It might be a relatively new addition, but this feels like a step back in time to a friendly saloon where the young Walt could unwind after a hard day at the paper. Their turkey leg sandwich will, in Whitman's words, make you sound your "barbaric yawp over the roofs of the world." On Sundays, a jazz & blues band usually sets the mood in the afternoon. Afterwards, head up to 28 Old Fulton Street by the Brooklyn Bridge to check out the Eagle Warehouse, once the home of Whitman's old newspaper. *(329 Henry Street, Brooklyn, NY, 11201; +1 718-852-8630; Henrypublic.com)*

Henry Public

Brooklyn's No-Frills Watering Hole since 1885

Despite having gone by series of different names over the last century **The Brooklyn Inn** still has the same 19th-century bar, untouched antique woodwork and a welcoming neighborhood atmosphere that offers small talk with a bartender or the choice to be left in peace with a book. No frills here, just an old jukebox and a pool table where you could imagine hanging out with Paul Newman in his role as *The Hustler*.
(148 Hoyt Street, Brooklyn, NY, 11217; +1 718-522-2525)

Happy Hour at the oldest continually-operated bar in all of Brooklyn

There's been a bar on the corner of Berry Street since 1887, first an Irish tavern and then a tasting room for the Doelger Brewery in the early 1910s. Its curved copper and wood exterior still bears the name of that brewery in its ornate stained glass windows. In the 1950s it became **Teddy's Bar & Grill**, a family bar run by husband and wife team, Teddy and Mary Prusik, and although they've since moved on, the current owners are very careful about preserving the ornate Victorian interiors. As a result, Teddy's can be spotted in several period television shows, including *Boardwalk Empire*. And fun fact: in 1988, the bar took a chance on a then-unknown microbrewery by serving the company's first ever case of what is now Brooklyn Brewery's signature lager, known the world over. Happy Hour starts at 4 pm on weekdays, but on Mondays, you can order $5 Margaritas from 5 pm to closing. On Tuesdays, it's two for one burgers from 5 pm and on Wednesdays, wine bottles are half the price, also from 5 pm until closing. *(96 Berry St, Brooklyn, NY 11249, +1 718-384-9787; Mon-Thurs 11.30am-12pm, Fri & Sat 11am-2am, Sun 11am-12am)*

Greetings from the Gilded Age

Brooklyn's Victorian Wonderland

Wander a few blocks south of Brooklyn's Prospect Park and you'll suddenly find you've stumbled into an enchanting enclave like nowhere else in the borough: **Historic Ditmas Park**. Occupying just over half a dozen streets, you are now in one of the largest concentrations of preserved Victorian homes in America. Ornate turrets, sweeping wrap-around porches and brightly colored homes all line the wide, leafy streets, so that (for a few blocks at least) you might imagine yourself in 19th century America. The boundaries are easy to spot: stone columns elaborately engraved with PPS, back when the small, swish neighborhood was known as Prospect Park South. The street names were given suitably regal-sounding English names such as Marlborough and Westminster. Start at the B/Q Church Avenue Station, and heading down Church Avenue, take the first left on Buckingham Road, where you'll find one of the most breathtaking buildings in all of Brooklyn: a whimsical, beautiful Japanese home. The origins of this special neighborhood lie in the expansion of the subway system which led to the creation of this plush, residential district as a viable alternative to Manhattan. Thankfully protected as a historic district today, it remains one of the most charming but little-known sites of Brooklyn. *(Albermarle is the main street to walk down, but make sure to wander down the side streets. The historic district's boundaries are Church down to Beverley, running north to south, and Coney Island Avenue to the subway line, running west to east.)*

An Abandoned New York City Palace Revived

How did an entire palace, smack in the middle of Manhattan, go untended to for over 70 years? For so long, Temple Court was a hidden jewel of the Gilded Age, closed off to the public thanks to an endless succession of failed development plans. Only the occasional curious explorer gained access to document its steady decline. It's the grandfather of all the surrounding modern high-rises, the first in Manhattan, boasting nine floors crowned by a large pyramidal skylight. After four years of highly secretive restoration work, in 2016 Temple Court was finally revived and became **The Beekman Hotel**, unveiling the old-school glamour of the original structure. A front-desk ornate with Persian rug design welcomes guests at the entrance and leather couches, fresh-cut flowers and wooden cabinets of curiosities set the scene for endless lounging. Imagine Truman Capote and his entire 5th Avenue posse of swans, politicians and artists all mingling on the plaza level, blowing away cigar smoke and recounting their stories from summers in Europe. Nibble on French delicacies at the restaurant, Augustine, wash it gently down with a Negroni and crane your neck up at the sky of New York. And by good old New York tradition, there is, of course, a rooftop terrace.

(123 Nassau St, Lower Manhattan, New York, NY 10038; +1 212-233-2300; TheBeekman.com)

The Beekman

Impatient Husband Daycare

The "Ladies Mile" was a popular shopping district in the early 1900s and conveniently located at the heart of it was the **Old Town Bar**, where weary husbands could hide out sipping on Jameson's at the 55-foot-long mahogany and marble bar, while the wives shopped til they dropped. Many famed Manhattan bars have come and gone. This one, however, has not only survived but remained virtually untouched – the legendary men's bathroom included. Tucked at the back of the bar, a museum-worthy old Manhattan urinal installed in 1910 remains frozen in time, and the Old Town also claims to have the oldest working dumbwaiter in New York. Just as welcoming as it was over a century ago, with its snug booths, distressed mirrors, well worn tiled floors and tin ceilings, the Old Town is a classic New York saloon, home to possibly the finest men's urinals in America.

(45 East 18th Street, New York, NY, 10003; +1 212-529-6732; Oldtownbar.com)

Old Town Bar men's room

The Great American Gothic Mansion

Perched upon the Hudson River is the **Lyndhurst Mansion**, the Gothic estate that could double as Count Dracula's summer home. Designed in 1838, this is the stuff medieval fairytales are made of; vaulted ceilings, a four-story tower, and an onion-domed glass conservatory made it one of America's finest Gothic Revival mansions, as well as the guardian of a dreamy decorative arts collection. Don't miss the special visit to the 1894 bowling alley or take a "Backstairs Tour" which highlights the servants quarters à la *Downton Abbey*. During the holidays, they don't skimp on decking its halls in glittering Christmas decorations so check their website for special festive events. *(635 S Broadway, Tarrytown, NY 1059; +1 914-631-448; Thurs-Tues 10am-4pm; Visit Lyndhurst.org)*

The Safest Place to Drink in the City

One of the more unusual places to enjoy your evening cocktail in New York, could also be one of its most secure, for **Trinity Place** is a bar and restaurant located inside a giant basement bank vault built in 1904. Pass through the enormous circular door and marvel at the intricate locks of what was once billed as the largest and strongest bank vault in America. Sidle up to the sumptuous basement bar and choose from the stock of wine bottles kept in an antique caged elevator. Make sure to look up on your way out, as the bar is housed inside one of a pair of beautiful neo-Gothic buildings, connected by a steel footbridge. Sneak into one of the two lobbies after dinner at number 111 and 115, to get a peek at the most dramatic office buildings in all of New York, dripping in gold and gothic splendour. You can imagine a man like Jay Gatsby waiting for the elevator to take him to a lunch meeting at the old Lawyers Club, which onced catered to Wall Street's elite on the 20th floor.
(115 Broadway, New York, NY, 10006; +1 212-964-0939; Mon-Fri 11am-12am, Sat-Sun 10.30am-12am; Trinityplacenyc.com)

Gatsby's New York

Put your glad rags on the for Roaring 20s

A Lawn Party with the Ghosts of Gatsby

Mingle with the ghosts of Nick Carraway and Daisy Buchanan, sip elegant cocktails and dance the afternoon away under the summer sun. One weekend a year in New York, such a fanciful afternoon is entirely possible. **The Jazz Age Lawn Party** has been the swinging, well-dressed highlight of the summer calendar since 2005. Set sail from Manhattan dressed in white linens, headed across the New York harbor for the uninhabited Governors Island, marked by the ghostly remnants of a deserted army base. A world unto itself, the island had once guarded entry into New York harbor, but for many decades, the old army base lay silent and abandoned; empty Colonial Revival houses that were once home to officer's quarters lay alongside unused churches, silent parade grounds, an old theatre and a castle fort. For most of the year, the island was inaccessible to the public, but recent summers have seen this tranquil sentinel turned into an increasingly used recreational space. One of its most popular events, of course, is the world's largest prohibition era-inspired, swinging lawn party. One of Manhattan's most glittering events in the summer diary, it draws thousands of well-heeled revelers to the island. At the heart of all this 1920s splendor, is the event's creator, Michael Arenella (see pg 218) who you might mistake for Gatsby himself as he glides across the stage in a handsome three-piece suit with his live brass swing orchestra. Dust off your finest white linens and beaded flapper dress, because F. Scott Fitzgerald himself said it best in his iconic novel: "Can't repeat the past?...Why of course you can!"

(This event is usually held on the last weekend of August; check Jazzagelawnparty. com for dates, details and tickets)

The Jazz Age Lawn Party

Afternoon tea (and gin) with F. Scott Fitzgerald

Ernest Hemingway once joked that when Fitzgerald died, his liver should go to Princeton and his heart to the Plaza. Find the ghosts of Scott and his beloved Zelda in the hotel's cinematic **Palm Court**, where the couple once drank orange blossom cocktails spiked with bootleg gin. Still the preserve of Manhattan's grandest afternoon tea tradition, the breathtaking Palm Court bar serves cocktails late into the evening under that beautiful stained glass atrium. In the 1940s, Conrad Hilton did away with the domed ceiling so he could add air-conditioning (but also because it was starting to fall down into the guests' teacups). Decades later in 2005, after studying old photographs of the atrium and three small chips of glass that survived from the original, a team of architects finally gave the Plaza back its stained-glass ceiling. Situated adjacent to the sumptuous lobby is the Champagne Bar, with its stunning wall of vintage bottles, which has been serving the finest bubbles since 1907. If you have something to celebrate, there is nowhere grander to sip fine champagne.

(768 5th Avenue, New York, NY, 10019; +1 212-759-3000; Theplazany.com)

Art Deco Dream Den

An off-grid subterranean speakeasy straight out of Gatsby's Jazz Age New York, **Slowly Shirley** is a sophisticated late-night cocktail lounge in the West Village

NEW YORK TIME TRAVELLER

with talented bartenders serving retro-dressing regulars and couples on second dates. Dress to match the beautiful Art Deco setting that looks a little like you've been invited aboard what could be Gatsby's private yacht.

(121 W 10th St, West Village, NY 10011; +1 212-243-2827; Tues-Sat 6pm til late; Slowlyshirley.com)

The Real Prohibition Speakeasies

The secret is out on the faux speakeasy, and the biggest nightlife trend of the last decade looks like it might be going out of favor faster than you can say "craft cocktails." To their credit, there are some great copycat Prohibition bars that we hope will stick around for the long run, but then there are the real ones that actually survived Prohibition and still serve thirsty New Yorkers today. There aren't many, but these are the real-deal historical speakeasies of New York City...

Where the Wine in still served in Tea Cups

Make your way down a dark back alley using the same hidden entrance that famous gangsters like Bugsy Siegel, Lucky Luciano and Meyer Lansky used 85 years ago. **The Back Room** is one of only two speakeasies in New York City that operated during Prohibition and still exists today. An authentic example of the underbelly of New York's past, this original 1920s speakeasy was often used for "business meetings" between the city's most notorious characters, and more recently, HBO borrowed the underground den for the set of *Boardwalk Empire*. We highly recommend you visit on a quiet Sunday or Monday night to really drink in the cinematic atmosphere without the weekend crowd. Prohibition never ended at the Back Room bar where wine is served in teacups and the stronger stuff in brown paper bags.

(102 Norfolk St, Lower East Side, New York, NY 10002; +1 212-228-5098; open every day from 7:30pm to 3am; Backroomnyc.com)

Scott & Zelda's Place

Manhattan folklore has it that the term to "86" someone (to throw someone out), is derived from **Chumley's** secret door at 86, Bedford Street in Greenwich Village. This small, former blacksmith's shop was turned into a speakeasy during Prohibition by owner Leland Chumley. With sawdust covering the floor which had a trapdoor, the bar was unique in that it had two unmarked entrances on separate streets. The main Barrow Street entrance was accessed through an anonymous courtyard, while the secret back door on Bedford provided a speedy escape route during police raids. Chumley's made the ideal swigging spot for many a famous writer to hang up their dust jackets. A plaque in the bar recalls, "a celebrated haven frequented by poets, novelists and playwrights who helped define twentieth-century American literature." Chumley's suffered a disastrous collapse in 2007, which saw it shuttered for years before the venerable drinking den of many a hard-boiled writer finally reopened after a decade of darkness. The sawdust has gone, but the literary charm remains, not least at one quiet secluded table underneath twin portraits of F. Scott & Zelda Fitzgerald, who once sat there side by side.

(86 Bedford St, Greenwich Village, New York, NY10014; +1 212-675-2081; open Mon-Sat 5.30pm-12am; Chumleysnewyork.com)

A Most EarRegular Bar

Once you've settled in with a drink at this historic Manhattan watering hole on Spring Street, take a moment to locate the old wooden phone booth near the entrance. Venture inside, turn the "On Air" switch on, close the door and be seated. Pick up the red phone receiver, wait for the dial tone, and after the beep, introduce yourself and tell your tale. Your story will be recorded for broadcast on the in-house radio station and become part of the bar's 200-year history. In another two hundred years, maybe someone will be listening to your tipsy 21st-century tale from the venerable **Ear Inn**. The grandfather of New York's grand old saloons, Ear Inn is still in much the same condition as it was back when it was a dockside drinking den for sailors at the end of the 18th century. Continuously serving alcohol since 1817, make sure to check the pavement by the door where you'll spy a plaque set in the sidewalk explaining how the Hudson River used to be just steps away, before landfill and urban development moved the shoreline several blocks. The house is so old, the original owner, African-American tobacco merchant James Brown, can allegedly be spotted in Leutze's famous painting," Washington Crossing the Delaware." For most of its history, the bar didn't have a name (which came in handy during Prohibition), but patrons nicknamed it the "Green door," quite simply because the building's front door was green. It was finally given a name when the current owners took over in the 1970s. To avoid the lengthy Landmark Commission's red tape review

Ear Inn

of new signage, they simply covered up part of the old neon "BAR" sign, turning the *B* into an *E*, giving the New York tavern a legendary new name: the Ear Inn.

Serving top quality pub food to its loyal regulars, the Ear Inn is also blessed with live swing music three nights a week (Sun, Mon & Wed) provided by the cleverly-named house band, The EarRegulars. The upstairs apartment once served as a smuggler's den, boarding house, brothel, doctor's office, and today, it's occasionally available to rent for the weary traveller who doesn't mind the rowdy sailors downstairs.

(326 Spring Street, Manhattan, New York, NY, 10013; +1 212-226-9060; earinn.com; Mon-Sun 11.30am-4am)

In a Mid-Century Mood

Predominantly stuck in the 1950s, sometimes jumping back to the 1930s & 40s, let's binge on vintage New York, when the internet age was still a few decades away...

What a Wonderful World in Queens

If New York ever feels too big, complicated and impersonal, take a break and head out to Corona in Queens, for the refreshing taste of a quaint, family-friendly old neighborhood– starting with ice in a paper cup. For over 60 years, the Benfaremo family has made Italian ices for local kids and their parents before them, served from the window of an unchanged Mom & Pop shop. **The Lemon Ice King of Corona** keeps it simple and does not mix their ices (so says the old-fashioned signs with big red letters). You can go with the classic $2 lemon ice, but we'd recommend trying the peanut butter too (with chunks of peanut) or cotton candy or rum raisin for a little extra kick. *(52-02 108th St, Corona, NY 11368, +1 718-699-5133; everyday 10am-11pm).*

Louis Armstrong, resident of Queens, NY

In summer, walk your ice cups over the road to what the locals call "Spaghetti Park" (aka. William F. Moore Memorial Park) to watch bocce games being played by members of the tight-knit Italian community. Stop in at **Leo's Lattacini**, a Met's-friendly Italian deli established in 1935 boasting the freshest handmade mozzarella this side of the Atlantic. Its patio is the perfect place to put your feet up with a six-foot pastrami and enjoy a kitsch trompe l'oeil view of Tuscany, but its nostalgic interiors also tug on our heartstrings. *(46-02 104th St, Queens, NY 11368; +1 718-898-6069; Tues-Sat 10am-4pm.)* Then wander over to **Louis Armstrong's House**, a delightful time capsule of mid-century design, today an intimate museum preserving Satchmo's legacy. It'll have you whistling "What a Wonderful World" on your way home, having forgotten all about your New York blues.

(34-56 107th St, Corona, NY 11368; +1 718-478-8274; Tues-Fri 10am-5pm, Sat & Sun 12pm-5pm; Louisarmstronghouse.org)

 Also not to miss nearby: The Queens Museum (pg 127) where the 1939 New York World's Fair lives on.

Long Island Bar

Downtown "Nighthawks" Time-Warp

Nurse a gimlet at **The Long Island Bar** on a rainy night à la Edward Hopper. This corner diner was run by Brooklyn lovebirds Emma and Buddy Sullivan for over 50 years, and Emma and her family still own it and live locally. The young team running it today have preserved it down to the very last detail, from the cursive neon signs and chrome flanking its exterior to Buddy's cigarette burns on the wooden bar inside. Buddy has since passed, but his memory as bartender endures. Stop in for an evening drink and a side of deviled eggs and a dozen clams. *(110 Atlantic Ave, Brooklyn, NY 1120; +1 718 625-8908; Open Mon-Thurs 5pm-12am, Fri-Sat 5pm-12am; Thelongislandbar.com)*

Italian Nostalgia served with Red Sauce

Five years before America got its first pizzeria in 1905 there was **Bamonte's**, which came along at the very start of the century in 1900. A real-deal 4th generation Italian family-run restaurant, these old walls are covered in photos of the who's who of Italian-American royalty going generations back. The waiters/ extended family members with Italian-tinged Brooklyn accents are always in their tuxedos, and the classic signature Neapolitan menu has not changed since the 50s. They even still have working wooden telephone booths as well as an antique cash register behind the old bar. The gigantic handmade cheese ravioli is a mandatory choice.
(32 Withers St, Brooklyn, NY 11211; +1 718-384-8831; open Wed-Mon for lunch & dinner)

Hey Sailor

Back when New York was a thriving port city, the waterfront was a bustling, working class neighborhood, home to longshoremen, stevedores and sailors. Think Gene Kelly, Frank Sinatra and Jules Munshin in *On the Town* circa 1949, as they launched their shore leave singing Comden & Green's "*New York, New York.*" The working piers at Brooklyn's downtown waterfront may be long gone, replaced with manicured parks and swish shops and restaurants, but a few steps from the river, one remnant has survived: **Montero Bar & Grill**. When the docks were still working, Montero's would open early in the morning for those coming off the night shift. It's still run by the children of the original owner and the old bar is covered with weathered nautical memorabilia. The days of the longshoremen have sadly gone, but one of their old watering holes remains a friendly, local bar. Find it under the flickering light of one of New York's most beautiful old neon signs, across from The Long Island bar (previous page)..
(73 Atlantic Avenue, Brooklyn, NY, 12201; +1 646-729-4129; Mon-Tue 3pm-3am, Wed-Thurs 12pm-3am, Fri-Sun 12pm-4am)

Don Draper's Manhattan

Mad Men may have departed our screens a few years ago now, but it remains beloved in the hearts of those who love all things vintage and Manhattan. For seven seasons, the employees of Sterling Cooper spent a large part of their time knocking back cocktails all over the city and a large part of *Mad Men*'s charm was its authentic portrayal of 1960's Manhattan. While three martinis at lunch and three packs of Old Gold a day have fallen out of favor, it's still possible to

Sardi's

drop in on many of the favored spots of the Madison Avenue ad man.
Follow Don Draper to Grand Central Terminal, evoking the timeless romance
of train travel, where if you venture downstairs to the lower track level you'll
find his seafood joint of choice, the **Grand Central Oyster Bar**. The vaulted,
beautifully tiled ceilings have provided the perfect setting for a power lunch
since 1913 when the terminal itself first opened. Just be careful not to whisper
too many insider secrets! The archway in front of the restaurant has a famous
acoustical quirk, making it a whispering gallery. Someone standing in one
corner can hear someone in the opposite corner perfectly, no matter how
quietly they're scheming. This underground architectural jewel is one of the
landmarks of the New York culinary scene. Ask for a seat at the bar and order a
dozen Blue Points...and a Gibson or two to wash them down.
(89 E 42nd St, Manhattan, New York, NY 10017; +1 212-490-6650;
Mon-Sat 11.30am-9.30pm; Oysterbarny.com)

Over at the corner of Third Avenue, you'll find a venerable red brick saloon
amidst gleaming skyscrapers that's been holding its ground since 1884. A regular
drinking spot for the more rank-and-file employees of *Mad Men*'s Sterling
Cooper, **P.J. Clarke's** was the first port of call when Peggy Olson wanted to
celebrate her initial success as a copywriter and ended up dancing to the Twist
on the jukebox. Truly a taste of old New York, Nat King Cole christened their
bacon burger the "Cadillac of hamburgers."
(915 Third Avenue, Manhattan, New York, NY 10022; +1 212-317-1616;
Mon-Fri 11.30am-2am, Sat-Sun open from 10am; Pjclarkes.com)

But of course, we can't talk *Mad Men* without an Old Fashioned – the cocktail
perhaps most synonymous with the show and the mystery man at its center,
Don Draper. The Old Fashioned at **Sardi's** is one of the best in the city. And not
for nothing is Sardi's restaurant known as the toast of Broadway – almost every

famous actor who ever starred on Broadway is immortalized in the distinctive caricatures that grace the crimson walls of this iconic New York nightspot. Don Draper himself was knee deep in nefarious activities here; out on the town at Sardi's with one mistress when he bumps into another. He gets the heart of palm salad and orders a steak tartare for the lady. Sardi's is a New York rite of passage, best experienced later in the evening when the Broadway actors come in for their post-show meals.

(234 W 44th St #3, Manhattan, New York, NY 10036; +1 212-221-8440; Tues-Sat 11.30am-11pm; Sun 12-7pm)

After swanning around Midtown, we're heading down to Greenwich Village's delightful **Minetta Tavern.** Today it's somewhat more of a swanky affair, thanks in part to its Michelin star, but when it opened in 1937 it was more New York saloon than high-end Parisian bistro. Favored amongst such hard-drinking writers as Hemingway, Eugene O'Neill and Dylan Thomas, Minetta Tavern has been revamped, but still retains much of its period charm, and is a very suitable last stop on our *Mad Men* journey.

(113 Macdougal St, Greenwich Village, NY 10012; +1 212-475-3850; open Wed-Sun for lunch dinner, Mon & Tues dinner only; Minettatavernny.com)

And as you soak in the timeless New York of Don Draper, remember his words during an ad pitch for the Kodak carousel: *"Nostalgia: it's delicate but potent ... it takes us to a place where we ache to go again ... It lets us travel the way a child travels – around and around, and back home again, to a place where we know we are loved."*

Last of the Luncheonettes

Walking inside **The Lexington Candy Shop** is like stepping into an Edward Hopper scene. It's one of the last original New York lunch counters that could once be found all over the city offering affordable snack food such as sandwiches, pie, egg salads and ice cream sodas. Opened in 1925 and still family-owned, the Upper East Side luncheonette has made numerous cameos in movies and television over the years. A perfectly cozy stop-off after visiting the nearby The Met, it may be slightly overpriced for diner food, but you come for the novelty and the milkshakes made by an original 1940s Hamilton Beach milkshake mixer.

(1226 Lexington Avenue, Upper East Side, New York, NY, 10028; +1 212-288-0057; Mon-Fri 7am-7pm, Sat 8am-7pm, Sun 8am-6pm; Lexingtoncandyshop.net)

 Other luncheonettes of note: Eddie's Sweet Shop (pg 225), Hildebrandt's (pg 50), Anapoli Ice Cream Parlor (pg 179).

70s & 80s NYC

The fascinating aesthetics of New York's grittiest era...

No Frills, All '80s Thrills

Who wouldn't love a diner that makes you feel like you're on a lunch break with Melanie Griffith in *Working Girl*? The **Floridian Diner** is dripping in uber '80s chrome fittings, mirrors and turquoise bar-stools. After a beach day at Rockaway or Coney Island, make a pit-stop at the Floridian Diner. Grab a booth with a retro tech jukebox, pick your favorite track from the '80s and dig into a homemade pie.

(*2301 Flatbush Ave, Brooklyn, NY 11234; +1 718-377-1895; Open 24/7*)

Floridian Diner

A 1970s American Time Capsule of Fast Food

If you've ever had one of those debates about which are the best fast food chains, it's time you discovered the fast food icon you've probably never heard of: **Roll n Roaster**. Take a little road trip to the other side of Brooklyn with the kind of food buddies who swear by Wendy's and In-N-Out to sample the famous thinly-sliced, juicy hot roast beef sandwich with onions and cheese sauce on a gravy-dipped bun. Everything about this place screams the seventies, from the old wood paneling and orange, brown & yellow color palette to the vintage food packaging that doesn't look like it's ever been updated. The prices are unbeatable and their excellent motto is: "You can have cheez on anything you pleez." Hangover food at its absolute best.

(2901 Emmons Ave, Brooklyn, NY 11235; +1 718-769-6000; everyday 11am-1pm, until 3pm on Sat & Sun; Rollnroaster.com)

Blondie and the Ramones live on at Punk Alley

The legendary *CBGBs* club will go down in history for defining American punk rock culture in the 1970s and 80s. The downtown Manhattan dive that fostered the best new talent the NYC music scene had to offer sadly closed its doors after 30 years in 2006 and has since been replaced by just another designer clothing store – a far cry from its Debbie Harry and Iggy Pop days. But if you want to scope out the real soul of the scene today, the good news is that it's still alive and well (for now) at a flea market over in Bushwick. **Punk Alley** is where you'll find the heartbeat of a real, enduring punk scene in New York City. Home and hangout to a new wave of punk rock musicians, it's very much their space and they like it exactly as it is. Picture a narrow alleyway with shipping containers on either side converted into shops, which contain everything you might need to pass off as a punk. Your visit wouldn't be complete, however, without a stop into one of the best record shops in the city. At **Rebel Rouser**, you can be sure to find the kind of vinyl that would gain you respect from serious record collectors and also pick up rare books, vintage clothing, patches and buttons. Here, punk is most certainly not dead.

(867 Broadway, Brooklyn, NY 11206; open Thurs-Sun 12pm-7pm)

If Twin Peaks Had a Bowling Alley

Take a trip from Brooklyn's Sunset Park to suburban Milwaukee, Wisconsin, via the well-worn but much-loved portal of **Melody Lanes NY** bowling alley. This joint is the real deal, a place where pot-bellied "Leaguers" come to compete with one another in a place happily stuck in the 1980s. Of course, locals know the real draw is behind the bar, in the form of local legend Peter Napolitano, ex-merchant marine turned bowling alley bartender. His brain is a twilight zone of homespun philosophies, from the "Theory of the 3 Selves," to "Heminzietsche" (where Nietzsche and Hemingway collide). "This whole place could go down like the Titanic," he tells us over a beer, his red bow-tie perfectly in place as always, "but my bar here would be just fine. We'd be floating, 'cause we've got an understanding with the universe."

(461 37th Street, Brooklyn, NY, 11232; +1 718-832-2695; Sun-Thurs 9am-12am, Fri-Sat 9am-3am; Melodylanesny.com)

Desperately Seeking Tiki

Otto's Shrunken Head is what happens when a dive bar dresses up in a
Tiki grass skirt and then throws on a leather jacket from Madonna's punk
rock wardrobe of *Desperately Seeking Susan*. Take yourself back to the gritty
downtown scene of 1980s New York and sip on a rum cocktail served with a
tiny paper umbrella, half-expecting Madonna herself (circa 1985) to swan in
and take over the open mic night. As well as serving amazing drinks, Otto's is
a fixture in the East Village music scene, regularly hosting a diverse group of
bands playing everything from rockabilly to metal to country. And naturally, Mai
Tais taste better under the light of puffer-fish lamps while you're seated on a
zebra print bar stool.
(538 E 14th St, East Village, NY 10009; +1 212 228-2240; Open daily 2pm-4am)

I'm a constant time traveller...
travelling between my different
selves, between the inner and
the outer, between past and
present. And yeah, also the
boroughs. My favourite place
to feel the past? Coney Island.
Especially the boardwalk.

– Peter Napolitano, longtime bartender at
Melody Lanes

In the Shadows with NYC's Self-Styled Guardian Angels

People forget that in 1979, New York was burning. To relive it today would almost be like entering an unrecognisable dystopian society where street gangs ruled the city after the sun went down. Times Square's Disney stores were occupied by peep shows and drug dens. Some neighbourhoods half-resembled war zones, marred by urban decay. The subway? It was the scariest place you could think of. But in 1979, if someone boarded your train car or came towards you on a dark street corner dressed in the red and white **Guardian Angels** uniform, it meant you were going to be safe.

It all started with just one guy at the boiling point of a historic crime epidemic. In 1977, Curtis Sliwa was the 23 year-old night manager of a McDonald's in the Bronx, overwhelmed by the violence that was unfolding all too regularly in his restaurant and decided to take matters into his own hands. He formed a group dedicated to combating crime primarily on the subway and within two years, the Guardian Angels had nearly 500 volunteers. With Curtis at the helm, they trained in basic martial arts, learned first aid and devised a special subway patrol system. They would ride the worst trains in the city, each member to a car. At every stop they would all pop their heads out of the open subway doors and if an Angel didn't step out, it meant that someone needed backup and they would all converge on that car.

They put themselves in places where the police wouldn't go and put their

The Guardian Angels on duty

lives on the line in a way most people wouldn't, which is where the organisation ran into its fair share of controversy over the years. For most New Yorkers however, The Guardian Angels were a very welcome sight, and still are, particularly if you'd almost forgotten they existed after Rudy Guiliani's crime cleanup saw them fade from public consciousness in the early 90s. When crime rates dropped, it seemed like they were no longer needed by the public, but the Guardian Angels are still very much in operation today, tackling crime not just in New York City, but internationally, through its various chapters around the world. They're still taking on the bad guys of Gotham's underworld too, with a new female-driven division on patrol called the "Perv Busters", tackling sexual harassment on the subway in the era of the #TimesUp movement.

Silwa, who was born in Brooklyn to Polish and Italian parents, recruited his Angels from all walks of life; black, white, hispanic, male, female; many of them reformed gang members who wanted to put an end to the wave of crime that plagued their communities. Curtis outfitted his diverse team of crime fighting citizens in military-style red berets and gave them jackets and t-shirts embroidered with their logo. It was forbidden to carry weapons, but they would break up fights where knives and firearms were involved, talk down gang members and protect vulnerable kids from gang-related violence. The Guardian Angels quickly became NYC's coolest crime-fighting squad, stepping in as the city's real-life superheroes.

While they were championed by the public, historically their relationship with the New York City police was very different. Where did one draw the line between a good samaritan and vigilante? "Back in the 70s and 80s, we had a very bad relationship with the police," an Angel told us one afternoon as we shadowed them while on patrol. "They despised the Guardian Angels 'cause they believed we shouldn't be on the subway doing their job. But they weren't doing *their* job." Ask most people who visited NYC as a tourist for the first time in the early 1980's and they'll almost always have a harrowing story to tell. Hotel managers were known to provide guests with fake wallets, so they could hand something over to the inevitable mugger instead of their real wallets.

"Crime has gone down overall," says Curtis today about the state of the city, "especially violent crime. A lot of it is good policing, but a lot of it is technology. There are cameras everywhere." The Guardian Angels founder wasn't always so diplomatic about the NYPD mind you, and in the 1980s, he was particularly vocal about the shortcomings of the local police with the media. But the more Curtis courted the press to raise awareness for the Angels, the more it backfired on him. At the height of the organisation's notoriety, he pulled some rather questionable and outlandish stunts, which included staging several of the Angels' sensational crime busts and even fabricating his own kidnapping at the hands of the NYPD. At the time, such outlandish claims weren't so far-fetched in a city driven to the brink of chaos by drugs, crime and corruption.

From very early on, Curtis Silwa and his group of "vigilantes" had been vilified publicly by city officials, as well as by the police and the media looking for someone to blame. Silwa admitted that his falsified kidnapping claims were intended "to make himself seem more valuable to the public". With crime through the roof in the early 1980s, New York City was at the centre of a nationwide debate on race, crime and the legal limits of self-defence. And the Guardian Angels were right in the thick of it. While the organisation set out with noble intentions to protect New Yorkers first and foremost, there were also reports of bullying, racial profiling and harassment at the hands of some members on the subway during the peak of their patrols in the 80s.

Riding the subway with the Guardian Angels today however, it's clear that those kind of members aren't around anymore. New members – who are heavily vetted – go through a 6 month, team-based training period in martial arts at the GA headquarters in Brooklyn to learn how to defend themselves, others, and detain criminals while police are being called. Absolutely no weapons, Curtis says, are ever carried by Angels and members are physically searched by each other, before patrolling the city for a minimum of 4 hours a week, both in the subways and on the streets.

Curtis is no doubt the golden orator of the crew, which isn't to say the other members aren't articulate, but there is a fanfare with his language that shows why the Angels have become so legendary – and controversial – with his voice as their megaphone. His opinions ring out hard and clear, and earned him a second career as a radio host on a local conservative station for the past two decades. But his opinions also nearly got him killed in 1992, when Silwa was allegedly kidnapped (this time for real) by crime family boss John Gotti after publicly offending the mobster on the radio. As the story goes, Curtis was picked up by two gunmen in a yellow taxi who shot the Guardian Angels founder twice before he was able to leap from the front window of the moving cab and escape. John Gotti was charged with attempted murder but never convicted. If one thing is certain, Curtis Silwa deserves his own movie biopic.

Today, the Guardian Angels have chapters around the world as far as Japan, as well as involvement in anti cyber-bullying and pro-animal rights work. There is new energy in the group, particularly with "The Perv Busters", the all-female task-force that comes with its own catchy tagline: *who you gonna call?* (when you see a perv).

Modern-day vigilantes or forgotten Knights in red? If you do cross paths with a Guardian Angel, just remember it takes a certain kind of person to put on a uniform and go looking for trouble ... and no hero is perfect.

55. Jewish garment worker, New York Ci?
- 1920.

26. A SYRIAN ARAB AT
1926

Tattoo marks on
hands, (a sign of ma?
not show in the phot?

Photo-study

26. ITALIAN CHILD FINDS HER FIRST
PENNY 1926 ELLIS ISLAND

This little girl finds the
wonders of Ellis Island and the New
World far more fascinating than the
first penny clasped in her hand.

Photo-study by Lewis W. Hine

11. SLAVIC MOTHER AND CHILD AT
ELLIS ISLAND - 1905

The woman in the background
carries her baggage in typical peasant
fashion. The identification tag on
her chest is the first touch of
American civilization.

Photo-study by Lewis W. Hine

22. A FINNISH STOWAWAY AT ELLIS ISLAND
1926

The desire to come to America must
ve been very strong for this young man
face all sorts of uncertainties.

Photo-study by Lewis W. Hine

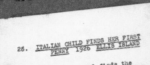

10
Around the World in a New York Minute

It should go without saying that New York is so much more than shopping sprees on Fifth Avenue, cosmopolitans at the Plaza and strolls through Central Park. Beyond and beneath the postcard New York, this city has a whole different layer of beauty in its diversity, and if you don't ditch the clichés, you'll be missing out on some of the most vibrant and delicious neighbourhoods NYC has to offer. These are places where you don't need a passport to discover a feast of culture from all around the world, so let's take a journey...

"Ed Koch once said that New York City is where immigrants come to audition for America. That's what happened to my parents; that's what happened to me."

— Lin-Manuel Miranda (creator and star of *Hamilton*)

Making it in America

All Aboard the International Express

You can go to Colombia for breakfast and the Philippines for lunch. You can find Little India at one stop and then discover the real Chinatown of Flushing at the next. The glory of New York has always been its diversity, but nowhere is it as dizzyingly, colorfully concentrated as it is beneath the belly of the aptly crowned **"International Express" Line 7 Train** which runs on elevated tracks through Queens, offering panoramic views of the urban landscape. It'll take you from Grand Central to just about anywhere in the world, in a manner of speaking.

Line 7 Train © MTA

Officially recognized by the White House Millennium Council in 1999 as a "National Millennium Trail," to surf the Line 7 is to dive into New York's immigrant story and better acquaint yourself with the city's diverse ethnic cultures that have thrived here since the early 1900s. As the train leaves the Manhattan skyline behind and enters Sunnyside, Queens, you'll notice that the scale of things here is a little different. The houses are low-slung and 100-year-old clapboard cottages are sandwiched between Thai eateries, bail bond stores and Turkish beauty salons. Your first stop could be **Woodside-61 St**, formerly known as "Irishtown," for a pint and a solid Shepherd's Pie at **Donovan's Pub**, the former gin mill turned family restaurant in 1966 *(57-24 Roosevelt Ave, open every day)*. The quaint and kitschy watering hole represents Woodside's proud Irish community, which once accounted for up to 80% of local residents in the 1930s but has since yielded to a smattering of Korean, Thai, Chinese and South American communities which began moving into Woodside during the 1990s...

One stop over at **69th St and Fisk Avenue Station** we found **Deum Bar**, a most unique and secret place where restaurant workers unwind after their shifts, listening to live bands perform Thai folk songs, pop, jazz – you name it, until 4 am. Incredibly easy to miss, its unassuming doors, wedged between a Chinese restaurant and a bicycle repair shop, don't open until 11:30pm. Head down a staircase to find a small narrow bar serving cheap drinks and offering a full program of Thai music concerts and karaoke. This little Southeast Asian dive is a real trip; one of those improbable places in New York City that you should make a note of coming back to one evening just to do something completely unexpected. (*71-26 Roosevelt Ave, Jackson Heights, +1 917-691-4855; NY 11372, Open every day 11.30pm-4 am; Facebook.com/deumnyc*).

Between the Woodside and 69th St station, you can decide between sampling some fried fish, Filipino style, at **Ihawan** (*4006 70th St*) or getting your fill of Salvadoran *pupusas, tamales* and plantain at **Izalco** (*64-05 Roosevelt Ave*), a charming little restaurant that looks as if it's been transported straight from the town its named after. For dessert, put your feet up for a second in Colombia with a little help from **La Dulce Bakery** (*67-10 Roosevelt Ave*). It's a hole-in-the-wall treasure with checkered walls, and all the *pan fruta* you could ask for – and for pennies, of course.

Butala Emporium, Little India

Continue your ride on Line 7 to **Roosevelt Ave–Jackson Heights Station** and discover the street vendors of **Little India**. For everything from Bollywood movies, books, vitamins, herbs to floral garlands as long as a jungle python, you'll want to head to **Butala Emporium** (*132 E 28th St*). This place is two floors of anything you might need to throw your own Bollywood-themed party or redecorate with the festival colors of India. For shopping in general, there are two overwhelmingly present options: those that sell gold jewelry and those that sell Diwali dresses to wow during wedding season. Pop into **Jackson Diner** *(37-47 74th St.)*, practically at the foot of the train, for arguably the best Indian buffet in all of New York City. And check out those technicolor desserts at **Al Neimat** *(37-03 74th St)*. In the words of patron Andrew Kahn, "If I could marry someone besides my wife, I'd marry the food from Al Naimat."

Next stop, **90th St-Elmhurst Ave** in Corona, for a lesson in Pan-Latino cultures, an endless supply of cowboy boots and food truck city. Make a beeline for the **Torta Neza** truck *(usually at Roosevelt Avenue & 111th St.)* and try one of their famous La Torta Pumas sandwiches. Find your dream, cherry red cowboy boots at **Zapateria Mexico NY Inc** *(88-07 Roosevelt Ave)*, one of the rare stores that's authorized to sell Stetson gear, where the staff is incredibly friendly. Just like Little India, this area is buzzing with its own breed of sounds and smells. Mariachi music crackles out of barber shops and into the streets, while trolleys of freshly fried churros seem to follow you everywhere. Now then, our last stop on the Express? China. Hop back on Line 7 until you reach the **Flushing Main St. station**...

The Real Chinatown

New York City has the largest Chinese population of any city outside of Asia. Did you really think those measly two square miles on the Lower East Side could contain all that culture? In the 1970s, the borough of Queens spawned its own Chinatown, eventually surpassing the original Manhattan Chinatown in size. Parts of Flushing became known as "Little Taiwan," newly populated by exiled families of Chinese Nationalists who had lost the war against the Communist Party. There are now multiple satellites of Chinatowns across the borough of Queens, but Main Street, Flushing is a sure way to discover some of New York's best and most authentic Asian cuisine...

The Golden Shopping Mall in Flushing is absolutely not gilded, in fact, half of the lettering is falling off the sign above the entrance, but don't be deterred – this is heaven on earth for those in search of authentic Chinese food. The street-level vendors of this food hall are one thing, but head back outside, through the double doors under the green awning and creep down into a steamy underground Hong Kong-style emporium of no-frills canteen restaurants, many of which received the Anthony Bourdain stamp of approval. Yes, it's dingy and cramped, but this is the cheapest ticket you'll ever get to China. Try foods you'll never find in Manhattan's so-called Chinatown: pork bone soup, which comes with a straw for sipping out the bone marrow, chive pocket pancakes and Arabic-Chinese hybrid lamb burgers. Save room for the Lan Zhou Handmade Noodle stall, where thick but light noodles are stretched by hand, plopped into

a savory broth, and sipped in silence. When you've finished devouring your $5 dinner, make your way past the $1 bootleg Chinese blockbuster movies and come up for air with a stroll at the nearby Queens Botanical Garden.
(41-28 Main St, Queens, NY 11355; +1 917-478-4536; Hours vary by vendor)

The Golden Shopping Mall, Queens

Inspired to cook up your own Chinese feast? Head to the always-bustling **Sparkling Supermarket**. You'll find live crab, sea cucumber and salted deep sea fish, buckets of tofu, green tea candies and a million other things you never knew you needed.
(41-22 Main St, Queens, NY 11355; +1 718-888-9665; Open daily 8am-10pm)

The Notorious Tenements

At the turn of the century, New York started to swell with immigrants and tenement housing was built in direct response. An estimated 2.3 million people (two-thirds of New York City's population at the time) were living in tenement housing, mainly on the Lower East Side. Up to seven people could live within a shoebox space of about 30 square meters, squeezing up to 120 people into houses that had been built as single-family homes by a previous wave of German immigrants. One of New York's most fascinating museums, the **Tenement Museum** is situated inside an actual preserved tenement that had been closed up and abandoned for decades. "It was as though people had just picked up and left," says the museum founders, "it was a little time capsule." The museum now runs a first-rate walking tour through the building, telling the stories of some of the people who actually lived and worked here, for the tenement homes were also a place of business. Many of the tenement parlor rooms also served as cottage garment industries, where whole families would stitch, press and sew clothing in cramped, hot conditions that gave rise to the term "sweatshop." The founders of the museum wanted to create an experience that honored the thousands of immigrants that lived at 97 Orchard Street. Designed as if the occupants of the building might have disappeared only moments ago, with everything just as they left it, a visit to the Tenement Museum is an incredible insight into the living conditions that both characterized the old neighborhood and cried out for social reform.
(103 Orchard St, Lower East Side, New York, NY 10002;
open everyday 10am-6.30pm, until 8.30pm on Thurs; Tenement.org)

Little Syria, NYC

There was once a vibrant neighborhood in Manhattan known for its store signs and local newspapers written in Arabic, and the smell of fresh Baklava wafting out of cafés. Little Syria existed just south of the current location of the World Trade Center, roughly in present-day TriBeCa: the cultural hub of America's first middle eastern immigrant community. From the 1880s until the 1940s, Arab-Americans arrived from Greater Syria, which then included present-day Lebanon, Syria, Jordan and Israel, escaping religious persecution and poverty in their homelands. The area became home to thousands of Syrians, as well as Armenians, Greeks and other communities from the Middle East and the Mediterranean. The Christian Syrians established several churches, one of which was St. Joseph's Maronite Church. Amazingly, a cornerstone of this church was discovered in the debris following the September 11 attacks, more than sixty years after the neighborhood's dissipation.

A *New York Times* article from 1899 on the Syrian Quarter described how the newly-arrived immigrants made a home for themselves in this "tousled unwashed section of New York," while holding onto their roots...

"Turks, Armenians, Syrians, when they ship for America, do not leave all their quaint customs, garments, ways of thinking at home. Nor do they become ordinary American citizens directly after landing. Just enough of their traits, dress, ideas remain, no matter how long they have been here, to give the colonies they form spice and a touch of novelty."

Little Syria slowly disappeared from the heart of Manhattan as the Arab population became affluent enough to leave the tenements and move to other areas such as Brooklyn. In the 1940s, the remaining community was displaced by the construction of the Brooklyn-Battery Tunnel. You'll be hard pressed to find any authentic Middle Eastern restaurants in TriBeCa these days, but head north a few stops on the subway to the West Village where you'll find **Mamoun's**, a family-run falafel joint since 1971, making it the city's oldest, continually running establishment of its kind. When *The Village Voice* first reviewed it in 1976, they noted, "Kissinger could take a lesson in diplomacy here – he's got Arabs and Jews eating at the same table." Indeed, you'll find people from all walks of life here, wolfing down their lunches on-the-go or indulging in an early morning snack after the nightclubs close. Mamoun's is open every day until 5 am serving a fantastic Lamb Shawarma and Falafel the way it should be (it's vegan-friendly too). Just go easy on that hot sauce tempting you at the counter. It's fire in a bottle. *(119 Macdougal St, New York, NY 10012; open every day 11am-5pm; Mamouns.com)*

Little Syria, Manhattan circa 1910

The Chosen Bagels and the Sacred Knish

In a small corner of Manhattan was once a world where Yiddish was spoken more than English and pushcart peddlers ruled the sidewalks. Jewish dietary laws don't allow for meat and dairy products to be sold or eaten together, so throughout the Lower East Side two particular types of Jewish food shops were common: those selling cured meats became "delicatessens," while those offering fish and dairy became "appetizers." At one point, there were over 30 appetizers thriving in the Lower East Side which sold mainly smoked and cured fish, cream cheeses and salads made from potatoes, fish and chopped liver – all to be enjoyed in a perfect bagel.

Joel Russ began his career in America selling food on the streets of the Lower East Side. The enterprising immigrant from Poland started selling pickled herring from a pushcart, and his trade became so popular, he opened a brick & mortar in 1914. The common practice of most small businesses at the time was to take on the family's name, followed by "& Sons." But with no sons, Joel Russ made his three daughters partners, and **Russ & Daughters** is still family owned today. The smoked salmon is sliced so thin that one *New Yorker* food critic claimed he could read a newspaper through it. Care to test that out? There's also smoked sable and whitefish to choose from, the hand-whipped cream cheeses laced with sturgeon, lox and caviar, and hand rolled, water boiled bagels. "Russ & Daughters occupies that rare and tiny place on the mountain top," wrote the late Anthony Bourdain, "reserved for those who are not just the eldest and the last – but the best." Take a ticket, prepare to wait a little, and order a toasted onion bagel with scallion cream cheese and the traditional salt-cured belly lox. *(179 E Houston St, Lower East Side, New York, NY; +1 212-475-4880; open everyday 8am-6pm)*

No 19th-century eating tour of the Lower East side would be complete without a Knish. This particular Jewish comfort food originated in Eastern Europe, but at East Houston and Eldridge Street you'll find the oldest knishery in the United States – the **Yonah Schimmel's Knish Bakery.** Made of mashed potatoes, cabbage and onions, then covered in dough and baked but never fried, and always round and never square, this staple food was simple to make, hearty and cheap. Yonah Schimmel was a Jewish immigrant from Romania, who arrived in New York in 1890, and like many of the food vendors in the Lower East Side, he began by selling his knishes from a hand drawn cart. These push carts packed the narrow streets of the Lower East Side and sold everything from fruit, pots and pans, carpets, clothing, eyeglasses and inexpensive street food. Schimmel's knishes proved so popular, he was able to open a small bakery on East Houston, moving across the street in 1910, where it has remained ever since. Still family-owned, with low tin tiled ceilings and wooden display cases of knishes under glass, Yonah Schimmel's offers one of the last genuine tastes of a part of New York history that has all but disappeared. Order the standard potato knish, heated and served with mustard and black coffee. *(137 E Houston St, Lower East Side, New York, NY 10002; +1 212-477-2858; everyday 9.30am-7pm)*

 Psst! Find a guide to the best bagel spots in New York on pg 89.

Where Harry Met Sally

Meg Ryan famously faked an orgasm for Billy Crystal at one of the **Katz Deli** booths, but two decades on, there's still plenty of entertainment at this iconic Lower East Side institution. A visit to Katz's deli is unlike anything else in the city and that starts with the ticket you're handed when you walk in, which looks like a vintage fairground stub from the 1930s. The first rule of Katz's is: *don't lose that ticket!* It's your deli passport, where meat slicers, cooks and waiters will mark down what you have as you carry it from station to station. Losing the ticket carries a $50 flat fine. Family-owned since 1888, their specialty is hot pastrami, corned beef and brisket, piled high on traditional rye bread (don't even think about asking for white bread or you'll be publicly scorned). Owner Jake Dell never takes a day off, walking the aisles of the vast hall, talking with customers, whether first-time tourists or long-time regulars. Follow his advice and order a hot dog, half a pastrami sandwich with matzo ball soup and a side of Latkes– traditional Jewish chopped & shallow fried potato pancakes. *(205 E Houston St, Lower East Side, NY 10002; +1 212-254-2246; open every day for breakfast, lunch and dinner & in between; Katzsdelicatessen.com)*

Night at the Fish Market

 Katz Deli

© *Ercwttmn*

If you're eating seafood somewhere in New York, chances are that it came from the famed **Fulton Fish Market**. While you're sleeping, so much commerce passes through what is one of the oldest fish markets in America, that its known as the true stock exchange of the city. There are actually two places to explore here, starting with the ruins of the original market down in Lower Manhattan's waterfront district. From 1822, chefs, store owners and restaurateurs would come to the bustling market in the early hours of the morning to buy fish fresh from the boats pulling up the East River from the Atlantic. The historic, bustling market moved to a modern facility up in the Bronx in 2005. Still opening at 1 am, co-op vendors set up inside the 400,000-square-foot market (it's the world's second largest fish market after Tokyo's) and get to work heckling the freshest seafood on the East Coast. But it doesn't all come from the Atlantic coast – Fulton has long handled seafood from all over the world – lobsters from South Africa, salmon from Norway, catch of the day from Alaska, all flown in nightly by jumbo jet. Visitors are as welcome to the New Fulton Fish Market as professional chefs. Just $5 gets you inside but wear something warm and get there at the start because the freshest stuff sells out quickly. If you have a big enough freezer you can come home with a bag of 100 oysters for $40.

As for the original fish market, it seems likely that the redevelopment of the South Street Seaport will see it either demolished or repurposed, but for now, it's an abandoned reminder of when Lower Manhattan was one of the busiest ports in the world.

(800 Food Center Dr, Unit 65B, Bronx, NY, 10474; +1 718-378-2356; Mon-Fri 1am-7am; Newfultonfishmarket.com)

Nueva New York

Over 2.4 million Hispanics reside in New York City, more than any other city in the United States. Let's take a page out of their address book...

Dancing & Dominoes at Toñita's

Swing open the nondescript door of the **Caribbean Social Club** on a night out in Brooklyn and you'll be transported to a San Juan watering hole circa 1960-something, where the conga rhythm is gonna getcha and the Puerto Rican grandmother you never knew you had is waiting with open arms (and $3 Coronas). They call her Toñita: the boss lady and unofficial patron saint of this *"Mi casa es su casa"* joint that's been going for over 40 years. Wearing giant sparkling cocktail rings and a warm, knowing smile, you can't miss her; playing Dominoes at one of the tables with her neighborhood veterans or serving shots at the bar to the young night owls of Brooklyn. That Toñita's still exists in the heart of gentrified Williamsburg is a miracle – a proud, final hold out for the area's Latino community to still call home. Prior to hipsterdom, this neighborhood was known as *Los Sures* (Spanish for "Southside"), the pulse of Brooklyn's working-class Puerto Rican community. Toñita moved to New York from Puerto Rico in the '60s, bought several buildings on the block for peanuts and opened up this social club to host the neighborhood baseball teams after their games. You'll notice posters of bygone sports teams, family members and

friends. In the decades that followed, she fiercely held her ground amidst an ever-changing city. The bar operates on a bit of an honor system – you'll fetch drinks yourself from one of several coolers, perhaps grab a plate of rice, beans and chicken that simmer by the stove. And that's when it's clear: you don't just hang at Toñita's, you *marinate* in it. In the warm glow of color we'll just call, "Yellow, 1979," exists a world apart from the modern and fast-paced New York City we know. The Caribbean Social Club doesn't have formal business hours or a very active phone line, but try your luck midweek around 9 pm for a nostalgic game of pool or on a Saturday evening, close to midnight, to dance the night away surrounded by local history and good vibes.
(244 Grand St, Brooklyn, NY 11211; +1 718-388-1455)

Tonita at her
Caribbean Social Club

The Little Dominican Cigar Factory of Manhattan

Drop in on the guys at **Martinez Cigars** where the merchandise is hand-rolled right there in the shop by some real New York characters. For forty-something years, this well-worn Midtown location has proudly maintained the tradition of making cigars the old-fashioned way, just as you would find it done in a Cuban or Dominican factory. For the talented and specially-trained rollers, known as *torcedores,* the art of cigar-making is in their blood, passed on from

their parents or grandparents who did it before them. Working with bags of raw tobacco leaves delivered straight from South America, they'll make you a fresh one on site, stogie in mouth, puffing, slicing and rolling away as they debate the latest baseball game and make bets on the next one. Merengue and Bachata play on the stereo, old baseball memorabilia covers the walls and of course, there's that powerful, mysterious smell of the finest tobaccos that wraps around you. Martinez is the only cigar company that produces directly in Manhattan. And this family-run business, built in the heart of New York by a Dominican immigrant (just two years after arriving in America in 1974), is a rare and unexpected reminder of the real American dream.
(171 West 29th Street, New York, NY, 10001; +1 212-239-4049; visit the factory Mon-Fri 7am-7pm, Sat 10am-6pm, Sun 10am-5pm; Martinezcigars.com)

Martinez Cigars

Hispanic Soul Food from a Midtown Freight Elevator

There's a "hole in the wall" and then there's **El Sabroso**, a secret lunch counter hiding inside a loading dock next to a freight elevator in the garment district. $7 will get you a seriously delicious no-frills feast served on a styrofoam plate. Choose from baked chicken, steak and fried onions, pork chops and other lunch specials, all served with Spanish rice and red beans and salad. Owner Tony Molina is Ecuadorian but got most of his Pan-Latin recipes from a Dominican woman who worked at the previous incarnation of this freight elevator restaurant before he took it over in 1998. Molina warmly greets all his guests like friends and invites you to sit with him at the counter (if there's room) to enjoy your *comida hispana*. True to its name, El Sabroso (the tasty one), is simply that and more.

(265 W 37th St, New York, NY 10018; *+1 212-284-1118; Mon-Fri* 7am-5pm; cash only)

El Sabroso

The Unofficial Buena Vista Social Club of Queens

Live Latin Jazz, coconut mojitos, and music lovers dancing under the papel picado like there's no tomorrow? Just another day at **Terraza 7**, a Colombian party in Jackson Heights making enough noise for all of Latin America. Catch a mambo big band, flamenco concert or Sunday jazz jam at this bohemian Latino club tucked away behind Roosevelt Avenue on Line 7, where musicians fill the venue with the sounds of Bogotá from a mezzanine stage above the bar. Get your "buena vista" and sit up close with the musicians on the upper level (tickets range from $7-$15) or work on your cumbia moves on the dance floor downstairs. In addition to the world-class music, Terraza 7 is host to a diverse range of events from film screenings to poetry slams, so remember to check in on their website before your next visit. Expect to feel right at home with the welcomoing local Latino community of Queens and leave feeling more in love with New York City than ever before.

(40-19 Gleane St, Queens, NY 11373; +1 347-808-0518; Open daily 5pm-4am; Terraza7.com)

A Mexican Treasure Chest

Every inch of **La Sirena Mexican Folk Art** is covered in paper flowers, sugar skulls and the *Virgen de Guadalupe*. The tiny boutique is a cultural kaleidoscope of Latin American countries, and the best crafts they have to offer. What's more, "the pieces are bought directly from the artists, whenever possible," says owner Dina. Come to soak up a bit of the magic from her little slice of paradise and take a little silver *Milagros* (good luck charm) home with you. *(27 E 3rd St, East Village, NY 10003; +1 212 780-9113; Open daily from 12pm-7pm; Lasirenanyc.com)*

The Italian Forefathers

Pietro Cesare Alberti was a Venetian seaman, who in 1635, became the first Italian to reside in the Dutch colony of New Amsterdam, soon to be known as New York City. In the 19th century, a wave of Sicilian and Neapolitan immigrants settled in East Harlem and the Lower East Side. World War II played a role in breaking up the tight-knit communities by introducing young Italian GI's to a new world outside of the traditional Italian microcosms and by the 1970s, New York was already starting to mourn the loss of Little Italy...

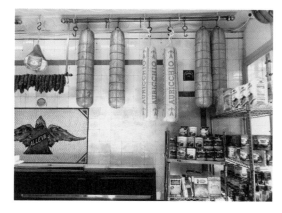

Alleva Dairy

Navigating Little Italy

Much of the Lower East Side's authentic Little Italy has sadly disappeared along with the Italian families who once lived in this pocket of Lower Manhattan, but there are a few gems left, starting with **Alleva Dairy**. Resisting the rising rents, this charming cheese shop has been here on the corner of Mulberry and Grand streets since 1892. Stock up on fresh mozzarella, the best olive oil and paper-thin prosciutto (ask them to wrap it around a slice of mozzarella to taste). If co-owner and actor Tony Danza is working behind the register, you're in for a treat. *(188 Grand Street, New York, NY, 10013; +1 212-226-7990; Mon-Sun 9am-7pm)*

One of the best places in Little Italy to slurp some spaghetti (that's the way the real Italians eat it), is in the courtyard of **Il Cortile**. Since the 70s, they've been serving the perfect Spaghetti Pomodoro and Linguine Vongole. Pro tip: Italians never ask for parmesan on the linguine, it ruins the flavor *(4603, 125 Mulberry St, NY 10013; +1 212-226-6060; everyday 12am-10pm; ilcortile.com)*. Last but not least, there's **Ferrara Bakery & Café**, a house of secret recipes since 1892. They have a Cannoli you can't refuse and the ricotta cheesecake is out of this world. Don't forget the Limoncello.
(195 Grand St, New York, NY 10013; +1 212-226-6150; everyday 9am-11pm; Ferraranyc.com)

An Italian Summer Street Party

A glittering, 80-foot-tall, three-ton shrine towers over a crowd on a hot summer's day in New York City. At its base sits a brass band, and below them, over a hundred men who've been entrusted with one seemingly impossible task: to lift that shrine, and its musicians, with their bare hands into the heart of the madness of the **Giglio Feast**. It's New York's biggest little summer festival, and for over 100 years it's been turning a handful of the city's streets across the boroughs into a glittering fairground of American Italia. You'll start to notice tinsel decorations appearing in the trees and on fire-escapes around mid-July, which is the first tell-tale sign that "Giglio" is under way. Once it's arrived, locals have 12 days to make merry. *Bambini* run around eating shaved ices, funnel cake and zeppole. Leathery, Italian-American grandpas smoke cigars on the steps of local churches and ladies sell official Giglio merchandise beside Virgin Mary statues. Paying homage to the patron saints, this is a big celebration for the Italian-American community. It's celebrated not once, but twice during the summer months on opposite sides of the East River. Since 1903, the "Dancing of the Giglio" has been performed for thousands of visitors in East Harlem on the second Sunday in August, keeping the neighbourhood's old Italian heritage alive thanks to the Giglio Society of East Harlem. Meanwhile over in Williamsburg, Brooklyn, the festivities kick off in July over 12 days, and when the sun goes down, Giglio really becomes a feast for the eyes.
(Find more information at olmcfeast.com and eastharlemgiglio.org)

Little Italy circa 1900

Cannoli with the Real-Life Corleone Family

You'll hear thick Sicilian accents and Italian spoken in the kitchen at **Ferdinando's Foccaceria**, which has been serving authentic specialties from the city of Palermo since 1904. Customers have been coming to this time capsule in Carroll Gardens since they were children. The lingering joke is that Ferdinando's looks so much like a mob café from old New York, that the framed pictures on the wall might just be concealing bullet holes. Leonardo DiCaprio and Martin Scorsese have given it their stamp of approval as evidenced by their photographs proudly hanging on the 100-year-old front door. You'll want to try the *arancini* and the famous Panelle sandwiches (filled with chickpea flour fritters, ricotta cheese and mozzarella) and don't skip out on the *cannoli*. Bonus: there's a garden and grotto in the back that you can have all to yourself even on a sunny day.

(151 Union St, Brooklyn, NY 11231; +1 718-855-1545; Mon-Thurs 11am-8pm, Fri, Sat 11am-10pm)

Slavic Secrets

▶

New York City is home to the largest Russian-speaking population in the Western Hemisphere. The biggest communities today are "Little Ukraine" on the Lower East Side, a Polish neighborhood in Greenpoint and the Russian-Jewish community of Brighton Beach.

Behind Manhattan's Red Curtain

Denis Woychuk's Ukrainian grandfather was a successful bootlegger in the 1920s, but that was pretty much all he knew about running a bar. In the 1980s, he began renting gallery space inside an old Ukrainian social club in an East Village tenement building. "The old men kept the bar. It was still their club," remembers Denis, who was first introduced to the Ukrainian Labor Home as a boy. He sat with his father's friends, gulping down his first shots of vodka on the third floor, which prior to becoming a socialist drinking den, had operated as one of Lucky Luciano's speakeasy bars during Prohibition, called the Palm Casino. "The bar had a little kitchen belonging to the old men's wives, and I dined Friday nights with my artist friends on perogies and three bean salad, maybe a little pot roast or some kapusniak, served by these little old Ukrainian ladies who made everything by hand. All told, a four-course meal with a shot of vodka cost $5. Even artists could afford that."

The Soviet posters, the propaganda, the photographs of communist revolutionaries; all that was locked away on the fourth floor in secret after the McCarthy era. Today, it's all on display, hanging in Denis Woychuk's own drinking den tucked away on the second floor at **KGB Bar**. The dimly-lit, red-hued counter-culture venue with a history of left-wing radicalism, looks every inch the bar where KGB agents might have sought refuge decades ago. The communist theme isn't overly gimmicky, although there is that big red hammer and sickle flag above the bar, but the Soviet relics here are the real thing. Much of what you see hanging on the walls, from the old photographs to the propaganda, came from the labor club's attic. And the old propaganda makes an interesting conversation point over a cocktail.

Beatnik literary readings take place here frequently, but otherwise, it's a place where you can have a conversation without shouting over the crowd. Unlike other bars in the East Village, noise levels here are more or less in keeping with the KGB theme. Below the bar, you'll find Kraine Theatre, host to **The Cabaret Showdown** (see pg 23), but what became of that third-floor drinking den, formerly operated by Italian mobster Lucky Luciano? One flight up from KGB is now **The Red Room**, another hidden bar that serves Green Fairy absinthe and hosts nightly live jazz, blues and burlesque shows.

(KGB Bar/ Red Room; 85 East 4th street, East Village, NY 10003; everyday 7pm-4am; Kgbbar.com)

But if you're still thirsty for more KGB secrets, you can geek out to the max over Cold War espionage at Manhattan's **KGB Spy Museum**. Exhibiting over 3,500 original objects collected over 30 years by the museum's designer, you'll find lipstick guns, cameras concealed in shoe brushes, cipher machines and a reconstructed KGB office. Why is there a Soviet spy museum in the middle of Manhattan? It's not entirely clear. The collector and designer behind it all is Julius Urbaitis, who actually runs another KGB museum out of a Cold War bunker over in Lithuania. But when an American entrepreneur (who prefers to remain anonymous) visited the bunker and decided they liked the concept, money was invested and sure enough, in early 2019, Manhattan's KGB Spy Museum was born. Who could our mystery American investor be? Let the political conspiracy theories commence...

(245 West 14th Street, Chelsea, NY 10011; +1 917-388-2332; open everyday 10am-8pm)

Soviet Spa Day

Many a New Yorker has heard tales of the **Russian and Turkish Baths**, a Manhattan health club reminiscent of a Soviet-era sanatorium, where unwinding entails slapping some mud on your thighs, gnawing a sausage and getting expertly beaten with oiled down switches into a new set of skin. Founded in 1892, this is where everyone from John Belushi to Frank Sinatra went for a shvitz. So many infamous New York tough guys were patrons here in fact, that back in the day an alleged job requirement for masseurs was to be hearing impaired (so as to not overhear mob gossip). Bathhouses used to be all over the city in the 19th century, but the 1980s saw many of them close, and this spa is one of the final hold-outs of a bygone era. The crowd today is eclectic, ranging from pot-bellied old-timers to a younger, hipster crowd, which brings us to the grand, Shakespearean-level drama of this place: the never-ending rift between co-owners Boris Tuberman and David Shapiro, which has had the two characters alternating weeks of operation since the 1980s. The reason for the eternal quarrel is unclear, but likely has something to do with David's

Russian and Turkish Baths
© Deacticated

welcoming millennials, smoothie bars and social media, while Boris prefers to keep things old school (and the water temperatures hotter). So decide where to declare your allegiances, and book a "Boris Week" or "David Week" online. After your treatments, you can reward yourself with some borscht, sausages and beer on the rooftop deck modeled after a traditional Russian *Dacha. (268 E 10th St, East Village, NY 10009; +1 212 674-9250; Weekdays 12pm-10pm, weekends 9am-10pm; Russianturkishbaths.com/hours)*

Singing with the Czars of Little Russia

There's a certain point on the boardwalk of Coney Island where you stop hearing English and start hearing Russian. That's when you know you've entered the Little Russia of Brighton Beach. Looking out onto the ocean is **Tatiana**, one of the great Slavic supper clubs of NYC. It's got all the best things about Russia: good vodka, kitsch 80s decor to the max and crazy Russians that know how to party. Watch out for Jacob, the owner that looks like a moody mob boss but turns out to be quite the teddy bear, who loves showing off his dance moves and showering you with vodka shots. Stop in on Thursday evenings for dinner with live singing, courtesy of some rather talented Russians who could give Meat Loaf a run for his money. We also learned that Russian music is really, *really* fun to dance to. And you know what? The food is really good too. Order a portion or two of those *Pelmeni* dumplings and the excellent beef Stroganoff with pan-fried potatoes. If you're up for something a little out of the ordinary, an evening at Tatiana's will be completely memorable. We guarantee it. *Na zdoróvye!*
(3152 Brighton 6th St, Brooklyn, NY 11235; +1 718-891-5151; open everyday for lunch & dinner, Tatianarestaurant.com)

Borscht in a Bread Bowl

Greenpoint is the heart of the New York Polish community, which has managed to co-exist with all the influx of change the area has seen over the years. You'll find Polish shops sprinkled around the area, from pharmacies to food markets, but waiting for you at **Karcszma** is an authentic home-cooked meal from the Polish family you never knew you had. Don't hesitate on the White Borscht, which comes served in a delightful hollowed out bread bowl brought to you by the friendly wait staff wearing traditional dress. Also a must-try: the delicious traditional *Pierogi*, Poland's answer to mini stuffed-crust pizza.
(136 Greenpoint Ave, Brooklyn, NY 11222 Mon-Sat 12pm-11.30pm, Sun 12pm-10pm)

Kleindeutschland (Little Germany)

There were so many German immigrants living in New York in the 1850s, that it was considered the third largest "German" city in the world. Walk down trendy St. Marks in the East Village and above the doorways, you'll find German names carved into the old stonework, traces of an almost vanished New York, once known as *Kleindeutschland*. To recapture a taste of home, beer halls and traditional German saloons soon sprung up on the island, but the German community was decimated when the General Slocum, a pleasure steamboat, caught fire and sunk in the East River in 1904. In what was the worst loss of life in New York City until 9/11, just over a thousand people from the German community perished in the disaster and most of the surviving families moved away soon after. Today, it's still possible, however, to find a taste of *Kleindeutschland* in the city. The traditional beer halls are a welcoming place to kick back and be merry with a big group of friends. And you can't go wrong with cold German beer and the perfect honey mustard pretzel from the old country...

Oktoberfest, NYC

Summertime and Saturdays are well spent at the **Radegast Hall & Biergarten**. This sprawling skylit beer hall in Williamsburg hosts live jazz bands at the weekend, and has an outdoor patio with long picnic tables. Enjoy scrape-the-plate-delicious apple strudel and drink from foaming steins under portraits of mustachioed 19th-century German generals. *(113 N 3rd Street, Brooklyn, NY, 11211; +1 718-963-3973; Mon-Sun 12pm-3am; Radegasthall.com)*

 Ready to strap on your Lederhosen? From Oktoberfest to midsummer to a random night out, if you've got something German to celebrate, **Zum Schneider** rarely disappoints. This East Village Biergarten has its own football team, oom-pah band, and Carol sing-alongs at Christmas time. *(107 Avenue C, East Village, NY, 10009; +1 212-598-1098; Open every day from mid-afternoon until late, open for Sunday brunch; Nyc.zumschneider.com)*

Bavarian Comfort Food

Warm up in winter with a sausage platter and potato pancakes at **Heidelberg Restaurant**, one of the oldest German restaurants in America. It's still family-run and one of the last remnants from when Yorkville was known as "Sauerkraut Boulevard" and the neon signs were still written in German. *(1648 2nd Avenue, New York, NY, 10028; +1 212-628-2332; open all week for lunch & dinner, except Monday evenings only; Heidelberg-nyc.com)*. Over in Brooklyn, the cozy, wood-paneled **Schnitzel Haus** offers generations-old family recipes and the finest pork shank outside of Munich. *(7319, 5th Avenue, Brooklyn, NY, 11209; +1 718 836 5600; schnitzelhausny.com; Tues -Weds 4pm-10pm, Thurs- Sun lunch & dinner)*

▶ Missing Paris in New York

There's a special kind of romance between these two cities, mixed in with a little friendly competition. They kind of wink at one another from across the Atlantic, stealing each other's recipes and habits when one isn't looking. So for Parisians and Parisphiles living in *ze big apple*, we've found some temporary substitutes for the French capital, but of course, for the real thing, we'll always have *Don't be a Tourist in Paris...*

To Pigalle for Brunch

Seemingly plucked from one of the trendier quartiers of Paris and brought to this corner in Greenpoint, Brooklyn, **Sauvage** is a winning mélange of meticulous Art Nouveau detailing and Jean-Luc Godard cool. Camp out at the curving bar with a glass of *Chenin blanc* and a pretty plate of Arugula salad

Sauvage, Brooklyn

(the menu isn't 100% authentic French cuisine but then again, the cool kids of Pigalle aren't exactly loyal to old-fashioned bistro fare these days either). On a sunny day, the light floods in through the curtains and hits the red leather banquettes and café tables in such a way that you won't be able to resist a photo with the caption: "Popped over to Paris for the afternoon."
(905 Lorimer St, Brooklyn, NY 11222; +1 718-486-6816; Mon-Thurs 11am-11pm, Fri 11am-12am, Sat 9am-12am, Sun 9am-11pm; Sauvageny.com)

 Also try Manhattan's French girl hangout, Lucien on pg 158.

A Left Bank *Librairie* under the stars

The French Embassy building in New York is worth visiting in its own right (cue the long-lost Michelangelo sculpture in the foyer), but its bookstore and reading room, **Albertine**, is unlike any other bookshop in the city. Two floors of your favorite French and Francophile reads line the wood-paneled walls, and a sweeping mural of gilded stars covers the ceiling upstairs. They also have a monthly French literature book club (see pg 105) With everything from contemporary French authors to rare 18th-century copies of Molière, Albertine will sweep you off your feet. *(972 5th Ave, Upper East Side, NY 10075; +1 212-650-0070; Tues-Sun 11am-7pm; Check their weekly events at Albertine.com)*

Play Boule!

In the warmer months, take a stroll through Bryant Park during the week in Midtown, and you'll find the strangely familiar sounds of a Provençale village square: that distinct metallic snapping of pétanque balls knocking each other out of the way and the murmur of spectators watching with their hands clasped behind their backs, shuffling their feet in the gravel. **La Boule New Yorkaise** offers daily free lessons from April to October, Monday to Friday 11am-7pm, just look for the instructor with the green badge. At the end of the season, they host a very official US Open Pétanque Tournament. *(Bryant Park, Midtown, 10018; Labouleny.com)*

Where to Find the French Ex-Pats of New York

Whether it's Bastille Day, a big French football match or just one of those days when you've been reading *MessyNessyChic.com* thinking, "Man, I miss Paris", take yourself to Cobble Hill's French-owned **Bar Tabac**. The classic bistro chairs are there, as are the friendly French ex-pats living in Brooklyn. The nicotine-stained walls are a nice touch and antique lace curtains hang from the Parisian café windows with hand-painted lettering that says things like "Vins au Verre" and "Plat du Jour". They serve a perfect omelette, offer live jazz several times a week and just enough French conversation going on around you to make you feel like you're back in Paris. Bastille Day is a big event here and the festivities take up the entire street with live music, food and pétanque tournaments. On a quiet day, there's a foosball table (that's "Babyfoot" to you now) for challenging Frenchies to a World Cup rematch. *(128 Smith St, Brooklyn, NY 11201; +1 718-923-0918; Sun-Tues 11am-1am, Wed, Thurs, Fri 11am-2am, Sat 10am-3am; Bartabacny.com)*

Just like *Grandmère* used to make it

Swap modern-day Manhattan for 1960s Montmartre where the wobbly voices of famous *chanteuses* like Edith Piaf and Frehel are crackling from the speakers, and walls are adorned with antiques of the old French Republics at **Chez Napoléon**. Cozy, comforting and still family-run since Grandmère Marguerite Bruno took over this Hell's Kitchen restaurant in 1982, the bistro's 90-something-year-old chef is no longer cooking in the kitchen every day, but as long as she's still around, you might catch Madame Bruno stopping by at dinnertime to check on her recipes (and her grandchildren). The menu is as classically French and unchanging as the decor. Marguerite's rabbit stew falls off the bone and don't be shy to mop up her sauce with your basket of baguette. *(365 W 50th St, Midtown, NY 10019; +1 212 265-6980; Mon-Sat 4.30pm-9.30pm, closed Sunday; Cheznapoleon.com)*

French Lessons in a West Village Bookshop

Where can you pick up a copy of *Don't be a Tourist in Paris* and brush up on your French at the same time? **Idlewild** is a rare combination of charming travel bookshop and language school – and if we're talking about "not being a tourist" when traveling abroad, these guys are speaking our language. As one of New York's first independent stockists of books by yours truly, you can already tell their library is going to be a lovingly curated place for the curious explorer and intrepid wanderer. In a nod to the golden age of travel, Idlewild is named after the New York International Airport, commonly known as "Idlewild Airport" in the 1950s, before it became the busiest international air passenger gateway into North America, known as JFK.

Lunchtime, evening and afternoon French classes take place right in the bookstore, taught by a native French speaker in a fun and relaxed atmosphere with an emphasis on conversation. Beginners classes will cover practical basics, like ordering in restaurants, before moving on to your social skills and how to chat to good-looking French people at Parisian soirées. But it's not just French classes they offer; sign up for Spanish, Italian and German classes too; practice your grammar, learn useful phrases, and improve overall vocabulary and pronunciation. A seven-week course (90 minutes per class) costs $295 and there's a Cobble Hill location as well as the West Village store. How to surprise your hopeless Francophile loved one for their birthday? With an Idlewild language course gift card of course, and a copy of *Don't be a Tourist in Paris* ... *naturellement.*
(Manhattan store, 170 7th Ave S, West Village, NY 10014; +1 212-414-8888; Mon-Thurs 12pm-8pm, Fri-Sun 12pm-6pm. Cobble Hill location, lessons only, 249 Warren St., Brooklyn, NY 11201; Idlewildbooks.com)

Eclectic/ Encore Props, see pg 66

And if you've done all that, you now have permission to go and be a tourist at the top of the Empire State building – which is open until 2am. The last elevator up is at 1:15am.

Bethesda Terrace, Central Park

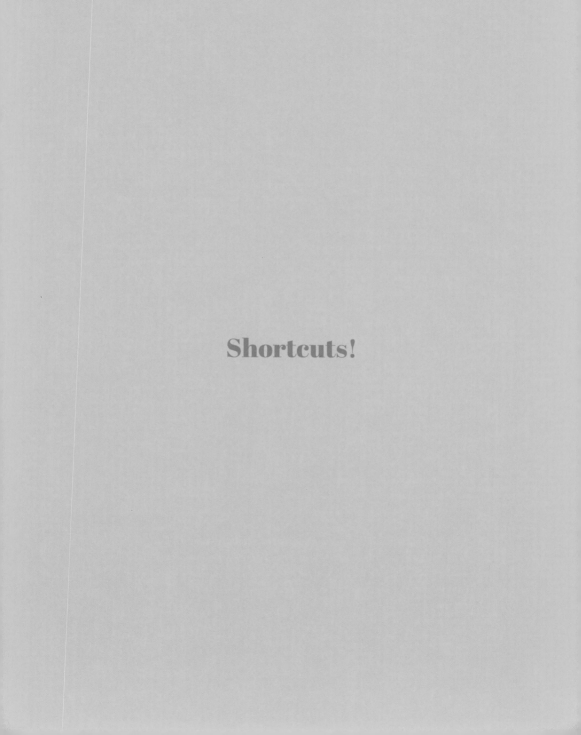

Shortcuts!

Could you just fire off some restaurant suggestions at me?
Sure thing. From cool & casual to 'crazy in love', pick the perfect restaurant for
date night from pg 51-62. See where the cool kids are dining on pg 157-161 or go
undercover with our secret restaurants on pg 184-187. Eating on a tight budget?
Find plenty of choice from pg 32-35, 38.

Without a reservation?
It never hurts to call ahead wherever you're going in New York City, but there
are a few notable gems that don't require reservations, such as, Diner p57,
Frankies 457 Spuntino on p190, Roberta's p157 , Kiki's p158, Sauvage p337, and
you can always swan into one of the old diners of NYC on p77, the historic
saloons on p292, and pretty much anywhere in chapter ten, p317-335.

Help me find the perfect off-beat "brunch" spot!
Escape the city without really trying at Vinegar Hill House pg 189 and weather
permitting, discover our other favourite garden restaurants on pg 188-190.
Cheer up with a gospel brunch in Harlem on pg 88 or choose from our
hangover cures between pg 88-97.

It's raining. What do you recommend I do today?
Take cover at an underrated museum pg 124-130, or kill time snooping through
other people's houses on pg 135. Call it a movie day and enjoy one of NYC's
wonderful independent cinemas on pg 85 and pg 98. Crash an auction on pg 58,
or go digging through the archives at the library on pg 143-149. And regardless
of the season, fake an endless tropical summer in a giant greenhouse on pg 61.

Where do New Yorkers actually go shopping?
Find a his & hers guide to shopping like a local in chapter 6, starting on pg 165

Im' in New York for a 10 hour layover, what should I do?
Discover the secrets of Central Park on pg 272, get a classic New York slice on pg
95, make some new friends at a dive bar, pg 17, and catch a jazz show on pg 217.

Where should I take my friends who are visiting from out of town?
If it's just the girls, pg 239 or just the boys pg 170. Take them to see a live show
in NYC on pg 23-31 or to one of your secret spots on pg 184. Act like you're kids
again on pg 224.

Where should we go for a night on the town?
Find a good night out on page 155, or for a more sophisticated evening, take a
few tips from the jazz-obsessed Dad on page 217. Or why not try a Colombian
party in Jackson Heights on pg 328, something a little more surreal in Little
Russia on pg 334, or sample the burlesque in Bushwick, pg 282. You can always
find a great ambiance with live music at Arthur's Tavern on pg 219.

I'd like to plan a surprise party for my favourite person. Got any suggestions?
Start plotting with our favourite venues on pg 171.

I'm thinking of getting out of town for the day, but I can't go too far...
From charming villages upstate to islands you can reach on the subway, head to
"Escaping the city without really trying" pg 197.

I have a meeting in New York. Where should I suggest we meet?
For a quiet breakfast meeting in the West Village, suggest the Orient Express
on pg 53 and for an impressive business lunch, why not meet at the secret
restaurant in the United Nations pg 184 or the café inside JP Morgan's incredible
library on p146? Hotel lobbies like the ones at the Hoxton Hotel or the Ace Hotel
are always a safe bet too, pg 349-350.

*I'd like to go on an interesting walk through the city. Can you set me on the right
path?*
Take a time traveller's stroll through Brooklyn Heights pg 289-291, Vinegar
Hill p 45 and Ditmas Park pg 295. Pretend you're on vacation in Red Hook pg
201-206, forget your troubles in Queens on pg 302 and go find the little red
lighthouse on the cover of this book! Pg 65.

I'm feeling uninspired. Give me a reason to leave my apartment.
Looking for some drama? Try the criminal courts on pg 72. Stop watching
Netflix and join a post-apocalyptic book club, pg 105.
Bet you've never taken an anamorphic taxidermy class (see pg 278) or gone
digging in New York for colonial treasure like they do on pg 260. Start a
revolution any day of the week at the Interference archive on pg 104 or do
something really naughty on pg 282. Travel around the world without leaving
the city on the International Express, pg 317, or volunteer on the only historic
working farm left in New York City, pg 197. And if you crash a wine & cheese
reception at the Explorer's Club, you might just meet the world's next Indiana
Jones on pg 74.

The Jane Hotel

Where to Stay

Cheap & Cheerful

The Accidental Wes Anderson Hotel

Checking in to the **Jane Hotel** feels very much like checking into Anderson's own *Grand Budapest Hotel*. The staff is dressed in burgundy bell boy uniforms, the concierge stands in front of an antique key rack and the Victorian lobby is a step back in time. The $100-per-night standard cabin rooms resemble the compact living quarters of a ship, designed for a sailor's needs at 25 cents per night circa 1908. You'll need to be organized, but we can personally attest to spending several nights in a cozy 50 square-foot, Wes Anderson-inspired cabin without complaint. Bunk bed rooms are available too, and bathrobes and slippers are provided for making your way down to the clean communal bathrooms at the end of the hall. Upgrade to the spacious Captain's cabin with an ensuite bathroom for an entirely more luxurious experience with a private terrace and giant bathroom. Hip young things flock to its bohemian ballroom on weekends or the rooftop bar and nightclub in the summer, so if you're staying overnight, ask the bellboy to allocate you a room away from the festivities. *(113 Jane St, West Village, New York, NY 10014; +1 212-924-6700; Thejanenyc.com)*

Harlem Renaissance Nights

Step back in time at the **Harlem Flophouse**, a jewel of a guest house in Harlem that is anything but a flophouse today. Built in 1917, this Victorian townhouse saw countless African Americans through the Great Northern Migration after the Civil War, when 1.5 million men and women left the South and Jim Crow oppression, looking for a place to flop down for a breather. This "flophouse" became a place where wanderers, writers, poets, artists and jazz musicians were welcome. Today, the theatrical setting is a popular backdrop for music videos and photo shoots while functioning as a charming B&B where prices run low (rates start at $99), and the hospitality runs high (cuddles with the resident cat, Phoebe). You'll be just a hop and a skip away from Sylvia's gospel brunches (pg 88), the American Legion Post 398 (pg 217) and the world-famous Paris Blues jazz club. *(242 W 123rd St, Harlem, NY 10027; +1 347-632-1960; Harlemflophouse. com)*

A Secret Inn for the Spiritual

How does a Gilded Age 5th Avenue mansion for as little as $100 a night sound? Around Manhattan are a number of specialty lodgings operated by non-profit organizations, churches and the U.S. Military, offering private rooms open to all. **House of the Redeemer** is one such place apart, a retreat house "in the Episcopal tradition," welcoming guests of all faiths to seek relaxation in its historic Upper East Side building, whose interiors are perfectly Baroque. Michelangelo couldn't have kicked it in better fashion. The rooms available are cozy and clean but simple, some with their own bathrooms, but not all, and reduced rates are offered to church groups and non-profits. The house does request that guests seeking accommodation here are doing so for reasons of retreat or business with non-profits, and not simply for the purposes of tourism. There is also no room service or meal service at the House, and guests are asked to respect the quiet hours after 11 pm. If you can hack the Episcopal lifestyle, this Gilded Age mansion that belonged to Cornelius Vanderbilt's great-grand-daughter is a welcoming respite from the city. The library is the crown jewel of House of the Redeemer, constructed in Italy in the 16th century and transplan-ted here in New York at the outbreak of World War I. Contact the house for information about rates and availability. *(7 E 95th St, Upper East Side, NY 10128; Houseoftheredeemer.org)*

Flying the Rainbow Flag

A rainbow-colored, clothing-optional roof terrace? Check. A proud server and supporter of the LGBTQ+ community since 1985? You bet. **The Colonial House Inn**, a beautiful red-brick townhouse in Chelsea has 20 rooms and 2 family suites, with rates starting at $90, including an elaborate continental breakfast. Decorated with bohemian flair, the founder's paintings are hanging all around the house and there's a cozy lounge with a fireplace for reading and working. For Manhattan, the prices can't be beat. *(318 W 22nd St, Chelsea, NY 10011; +1 212-243-9669; Colonialhouseinn.com)*

Hip & Happening

Euro-Cool in Brooklyn

The Hoxton Hotel has thought of everything the modern, design-conscious millennial might need, set inside a former factory that once manufactured all the water towers you see scattered across the New York skyline. Need to borrow a beautiful Dutch bicycle to ride around Williamsburg? No problem. Here on business? Take your meetings in the entrepreneur-friendly lobby, host an intimate event in the beautiful Hoxton apartment or celebrate closing a deal up at the trendy rooftop bar with panoramic views of the city. The cozy rooms with floor-to-ceiling windows start at $159 and all rooms have little perks like the daily breakfast bags, plenty of hidden storage space and a much-appreciated late check out rate of $10 an hour. *(97 Wythe Ave, Brooklyn, NY 11249; +1 718-215-7100; Thehoxton.com)*

Gilded Age Glamour

How did an entire palace, smack in the middle of Manhattan, go untended to for over 70 years? Temple Court, now **The Beekman**, is deeply ingrained in the city's history. Built in 1883, it is the grandfather of all its surrounding modern

high-rises, in fact, it was the first in Manhattan. After years of abandonment, the hotel finally reopened in 2016, unveiling the old-school glamour of the original structure and that breathtaking nine-story atrium and pyramidal skylight. You can imagine Truman Capote and his entire 5th Avenue posse mingling on the plaza level, blowing away cigar smoke and recounting their stories of summers in Europe. The bar is especially buzzing at cocktail hour with a high-powered crowd from the Financial District. Leather couches and velvet upholstery are set alongside dimly-lit lamps, statues, fresh-cut flowers and wooden cabinets of curiosities tracing the history of New York City. A front-desk covered in Persian rugs welcomes guests at the entrance, and the rooms are an elegant time warp. And by good old New York tradition, there is, of course, a penthouse rooftop. Rooms from $230.
(123 Nassau St, Financial District, NY 10038; +1 212-233-2300; Thebeekman.com)

Arty and Inspiring
Hotel-hostel hybrid, the **Freehand Hotel** is endlessly Instagrammable. Fulfill your New York art school fantasy in rooms decked out with works by Bard College students (also for sale), in a building with real historical clout; Keith Haring and W.H. Auden lived here for a time, and during Prohibition, it was used as a bootlegging house. Head to the rooftop bar once you've finished writing your novel, painting your still-life, etc. The 395 rooms start at around $100 for solo stays.
(23 Lexington Ave, Flatiron District, NY 10010; Freehandhotels.com/new-york)

Entrepreneur's Midtown HQ
Bohemian chic is king at the **Ace Hotel** just off Broadway a few blocks down from the Empire State Building. If you're in need of a reliable workspace, the historic building's lobby doubles as a co-working facility by day with long tables, plenty of power sockets, comfy suede sofas and good coffee, frequented by a trendy crowd of freelancers and startup millennials. Expect Pendleton blankets in every room, retro furnishings, Smeg minibars and acoustic guitars beside turntables. The hotel's social calendar is packed with DJ sets, live bands and exhibitions for both travelers and locals to enjoy. Rooms can be pricey but if you can afford to book last minute, you can score a room from $101 per night. You can also bring pets (under 25lb) for $25/night.
(20 West 29th Street; Midtown, 10001; +1 212-679-2222; acehotel.com)

Views from the Water Tower
Start your vacation on top of the world, cocktail in hand, listening to live weekend jazz in a New York water tower with panoramic views of the city and a wraparound balcony that overlooks a rooftop pool. Check in for a cool & casual stay at **The Williamsburg**, which is walking distance from the always-happening

Bedford Avenue, but they also offer guests the use of their Dutch bicycles. The rooms are equipped with luxurious pink bathrobes, hangover kits and sound machines for light sleepers. You can get a perfect avocado toast any time of the day from the Harvey restaurant, and the lobby, with its huge leather booths, doubles as a very welcoming workspace. Rooms with terraces start at $345. (*96 Wythe Avenue, Brooklyn, NY 11249, +1 718 362 8100; Thewilliamsburghotel.com*)

Quirky & Cozy

A Baby Grand Hotel

Once a haunt of Kerouac and the beatniks, now a swanky boutique hotel with an intimate, French-inspired bistro, dining solarium and espresso bar, **The Marlton Hotel** is a Greenwich Village classic. It's the little antique touches, from eclectic brass finishes to the black-and-white checkered baths, that uphold its cred as a true "baby grand hotel" inspired by F.Scott Fitzgerald's *Tender is The Night*. Rates start at $200.
(*5 W 8th St, Greenwich Village, NY 1001; +1 212-321-0100; Marltonhotel.com*)

A Bed for a Booklover

Find a bibliophile's haven in busy Midtown at **The Library Hotel**. Home to thousands of books, each floor of this hotel has its own literary theme. Guests have access to a greenhouse reading library, a rooftop writer's den, poetry garden and every evening, the hotel hosts a wine and cheese reception. Each room is equipped with 50-150 books according to the room's theme, but reading aside, you'll enjoy the hotel's little luxurious gestures such as the Belgian chocolate turndown and the 24-hour reading room offering all the fresh coffee, cookies and fruit you can eat. Try and snag the "Love Room," which has views of the NY Public Library. Rooms start at $211.
(*299 Madison Ave, Midtown, NY 10017; +1 212-983-4500; Libraryhotel.com*)

Art Deco in the Village

The Walker Hotel in Greenwich Village is one of the few independent and family-owned small hotels left in Manhattan. An Art Deco dream inside and out with a touch of the Georgian elegance to the facade, the compact rooms, equipped with bedside rotary telephones, are very luxurious but lacking cartwheel room. Appropriate for its Gatsby-worthy glamour, you're walking distance to the Village's jazz clubs. Prices from $225.
(*52 West 13th Street, Greenwich Village, NY 10011; +1 212-375-1300; Walkerhotel.com*)

A Brooklyn Bronco B&B

Decked out with pot belly fireplaces, exposed brick and thrifty authentic treasures, **Urban Cowboy** is a Brooklyn bed & breakfast townhouse with a Wild West theme. Combining a modern boutique hotel with a country cabin retreat, there are three massive rooms including the annex treehouse. Then through the doors of the open space living area (converted from the old garage), there is the cabin in the backyard that looks like a Presidential Cowboy suite. If you can gather a group of ten of your friends together for a wild night in New York, you can rent the entire house for around $200 a head. Note, there is a hot tub. Make a booking well in advance as this tiny Brooklyn B&B fills up fast.
(111 Powers St, Brooklyn, NY 11211; Urbancowboy.com/brooklyn)

Splurge on Something Special

The Original Brooklyn Palace

You've probably seen a photograph of the incredible rooms at **The Wythe**. Those 13-foot, floor to ceiling windows and the "King Kong skyline views". It was the first luxury hotel to open on the Williamsburg waterfront in 2012 and it remains at the top of the list. Located at the heart of creative Williamsburg, if you can afford to stay here, you absolutely should. They have bunk bed rooms from $285 but it's the Brooklyn King room you want, which averages at around $395 per night.
(80 Wythe Ave, Brooklyn, NY 11249; +1 718-460-8000; Wythehotel.com)

A Bohemian Clubhouse

Pretend you're a high society socialite from the Gilded Age while you're a guest at the **Inn at Irving Place** in the heart of Manhattan. The eight guest rooms of this double townhouse in Gramercy Park are accessible by a grand staircase and furnished with velvet armchairs, Persian carpets and four-poster beds. Recreating all the glamour of Edith Wharton's bygone New York, the boutique hotel is also home to the secret Lady Mendl's Tea Salon (see pg 239) and an intimate bar in the basement with a bamboo garden. Rooms and suites start at $445.
(56 Irving Place, Midtown, NY 10003; +1 212-533-4600; Innatirving.com)

Manhattan's Secret Shoppable Apartment

Sleep in an entirely shoppable home at **The Witness Apartment**, a unique 2,200-square-foot Midtown loft that sheds its skin every 3 months with an enviable new makeover. The furniture and covetable design accents might be hiding the price tags, but the decorating ideas are on the house. Witness Apartment is the creation of Ani Tzenkova, an incredibly impressive and talented young female entrepreneur based in New York. Everything in the loft has been hand-picked by Ani, and the two-bedroom space has all the ingredients of those untouchable dream apartments you see on Pinterest. You can rent it like a secret hotel or borrow it for an event, photo shoot, book club, Mad Hatter's tea party — whatever you imagine. From $650 a night, around $160 per head if you're a group of 4. *(WitnessApt.com)*

Witness Appartment

Short Stay?

Take a Time Travelling Layover

For years, the 1960s TWA terminal at JFK sat empty and abandoned. In 2019, the iconic flight center was restored and reimagined as a first class hotel, bringing back the golden age of air travel. The new **TWA hotel** has over 500 ultra-quiet guest rooms, many with runway views and all with interiors perfected to transport you into a mid-century travel fantasy (there's even a resident museum on the golden era). Wind down in the evening on the 10,000-square-foot rooftop observation deck with pool or choose from its 6 restaurants and 8 bars, one of which is inside a restored 1950s TWA airplane. *(JFK Airport, Jamaica, NY 11430 twahotel.com)*

The "What's Near Me?" Index

Manhattan

Brooklyn

Queens

The Bronx

Further Out...

Rambling Notes of a Traveller

Don't be a Tourist in New York
A book by **Vanessa Grall**

With writers and explorers
MaryFrances Knapp, Luke J Spencer, Scott Walker

A special thanks for the editorial contributions and assistance from
**Angelika Pokovba, Addison Nugent, Adrien Dufayard and
Elizabeth Atassanova**

Art Direction
Vanessa Grall & Alexandre Tavernier

Design and Layout
Alexandre Tavernier & Oksana Kravtsova

Bookstores please contact: **DBTBooks@messynessychic.com**
For general enquiries please contact: **contact@messynessychic.com**

PUBLISHED BY MESSY NESSY CHIC
A DIVISION OF 13 THINGS LTD .
Unit 3, 1st Floor, 6/7 St. Mary at Hill
London, EC3R 8EE
United Kingdom
contact@messynessychic.com

First published 2019

1

British Library Cataloguing in Publication Data.
A catalogue record for this book is available from the British Library.

ISBN: 978-1-9164309-1-4